NEW WAY'S TO A MAN'S HEART

Compiled by the Helpful '8'

Edited by
GILLIAN BURR
Assisted by Marion Cohen with Miki Hildebrand

Illustrated by Jane Finestone

VALLENTINE, MITCHELL

First published in Great Britain by
VALLENTINE, MITCHELL & CO. LTD.
Gainsborough House, Gainsborough Road,
London E11 1RS, England

and in the United States of America by
VALLENTINE, MITCHELL & CO. LTD.
c/o Biblio Distribution Centre
81 Adams Drive, P.O. Box 327, Totowa, N.J. 07511

First Edition 1988
Second Edition 1992

ISBN 0 85303 257 2

Cover photograph by Cameo (071-625 4476)
China and cutlery by courtesy of Chinacraft

Printed in Great Britain by
Hartnolls Limited, Bodmin, Cornwall

Dear Cooks,

We hope you will enjoy using this our fifth book and find it useful when planning both family and party meals. Our first book, *The Way To A Man's Heart*, was published in 1971 and since then most of us have become very much more health conscious, hence this book has more emphasis on healthier eating. Everyone's idea of healthy eating seems to be different, but we have tried to follow the general consensus of opinion and hope that you will be happy with the result.

To help you find your way round the book, on page 4 we have explained how the recipes are coded for 'low cholesterol diets', for Passover and those recipes which are 'naughty but nice' and much too good to leave out.

Our thanks are due to all those who have given us recipes, plus the many people who have helped with the typing, compiling and proof reading, especially Marion Cohen, Miki Hildebrand, Sheila Rosen, Maureen Marks, Ruth Smilg, Jean Simmonds, Rosanna Burr, Lynne Goldwyn, Meriel Joseph, Juliet Moss, Ruth Sotnick, Eve Schwarz and Bondi Zimmerman. The British Heart Foundation and The British Nutrition Foundation were both extremely helpful in the preparation of this book.

Good Health and Bon Appétit to you all!

The Helpful '8' Committee

Symbols: We have placed symbols at the side of some of the recipes so that you can see at a glance whether they are low cholesterol, fattening, or suitable for Passover.

Low Cholesterol

Naughty but nice

Suitable for Passover (P)

These recipes are also listed at the beginning of the index at the back of the book.

Whilst every effort has been made to ensure that the recipes conform to Jewish dietary laws, we have had to leave it to you, the cook, to check on the Kashrut of some individual ingredients, e.g. wine, cheese, wine vinegar, gelatine, etc.

Whilst every effort has been made to ensure that the recipes conform to Jewish dietary laws, we have had to leave it to you, the cook, to check on the Kashrut of some individual ingredients, e.g. wine, cheese, wine vinegar, gelatine, etc.

Contents

MEASURES AND OVEN TEMPERATURE GUIDE

DRY MEASURE

	1 oz	28 grms
	2 oz	56 grms
	3 oz	85 grms
	3½oz	100 grms
(¼ lb)	4 oz	114 grms
	5 oz	142 grms
	6 oz	170 grms
	7 oz	198 grms
(½ lb)	8 oz	225 grms
(¼ kilo)	8¾oz	250 grms
	9 oz	256 grms
	10 oz	283 grms
	11 oz	312 grms
	12 oz	340 grms
	13 oz	368 grms
	14 oz	400 grms
	15 oz	425 grms
(1 lb)	16 oz	450 grms
(½ kilo)	17½oz	500 grms
	1½lbs	700 grms

LIQUID MEASURE

1 tablespoon	1 tablespoon
2 tablespoons	2 tablespoons (1½ DL)
3 tablespoons	3 tablespoons
4 tablespoons	4 tablespoons
5 tablespoons	1 decilitre
6 tablespoons	1¼ decilitres
8 tablespoons (¼ pint)	1½ decilitres
¼ pint – generous	2 decilitres
½ pint – scant	¼ litre (2½ DL)
½ pint	3 decilitres
¾ pint	½ litre – scant
¾ pint – generous	½ litre
1 pint	½ litre – generous
1¼ pints	¾ litre
1½ pints	1 litre – scant
1¾ pints	1 litre
2 pints	1 litre – generous
2½ pints	1¼ litres
3 pints	1½ litres
3½ pints	2 litres
4 pints	2¼ litres
4¼ pints	2½ litres
5 pints	3 litres

OVEN TEMPERATURE GUIDE

Gas No.	Fahrenheit	Centigrade	Description
¼	225	120	
½	250	140	Very Cool
1	275	150	
2	300	160	Cool or Slow
3	325	180	
4	350	185	Moderate
5	375	190	
6	400	200	Moderately Hot
7	425	220	
8	450	230	Hot
9	475	240	Very Hot

Fan ovens cook at a temperature of 20°–30° higher than conventional electric ovens.

2 level tablespoons of flour = 1 oz 1 level tablespoon of sugar = 1 oz
A British pint = 20 fl ozs An American pint = 16 fl ozs
A British cup = 10 fl ozs An American cup = 8 fl ozs

When making American recipes always use American measuring spoons.

Healthier Eating

You have such a healthy life with all your country cooking!

It is a popular theory of our times that diet and health are inextricably linked. The suggestion is that we can improve our health by eating more of certain foods and less of others.

The energy that food gives us is calculated in calories per oz. of food. Daily calorie requirements vary considerably. On the whole, men require more calories than women and a person leading an active life will use up more calories than those of us who lead a more sedentary existence. Obviously the higher the calorie intake the more weight will be gained, but this chapter is not so much to do with slimming as with healthy eating; if you are looking for slimming diets, please see our previous book *Some More Ways To A Man's Heart*, but always check with your doctor before embarking on any diet. You will find a comprehensive calorie counter at the end of this section.

Food is made up of different nutrients. Those nutrients that are necessary for healthy life are:

PROTEINS
CARBOHYDRATES
FATS
VITAMINS
MINERALS
WATER

PROTEINS

All living matter contains protein. Only animal protein contains all the 8 amino acids essential for good health, therefore vegetarians must ensure that they eat a large variety of different sources of protein. Protein is necessary for body growth, repair of bodily tissues and stamina.

Foods high in protein: Fish, meat, brussels sprouts, butter beans, cheese, eggs, wheat, lentils, milk, peanuts, wheatgerm and yeast.

CARBOHYDRATES

Carbohydrates are needed to provide the body with heat and energy and a store of energy for future use. They also provide roughage and stimulate the digestion and they enable the body to burn fats completely.

Foods high in carbohydrate: cereals, pulses, bread, potatoes, jams, cakes, biscuits and all forms of sugar.

Comparative carbohydrate values:
sugar	=	100% carbohydrate
white flour	=	79% carbohydrate
chocolate	=	58% carbohydrate
potatoes	=	21% carbohydrate
carrots	=	6% carbohydrate

Refined sugars (white sugar and golden syrup for example) are considered to be 'empty calories', since they contribute no essential nutrients – only a rapid burst of energy, and any excess is then converted into fat. It is obviously sensible therefore to cut down one's intake of refined sugar. Make certain when buying brown sugar that it is actually unrefined and not just refined white sugar which has been coloured. Unrefined cane sugar is always labelled as such.

FATS

Fats provide heat and energy in a very concentrated form. They provide a store of fuel in the body (around the vital organs and under the skin). They slow down the process of digestion so that the food stays longer in the digestive tract.

There are two main categories of fats:

Animal fats	butter, fish oil, chicken and beef fat and cream.
Vegetable fats	olive oil, corn oil, groundnut oils and most margarines.

Comparative fat values:

olive oil	= 100% fat
butter and margarine	= 85% fat
cheddar cheese	= 35% fat
milk	= 4% fat

Cholesterol is a substance made by the body and is essential for certain bodily functions. It becomes a problem when the body starts to make too much and forms a substance which coats the arteries. This can lead to heart attacks, thrombosis and gall stones. The over production of cholesterol is often attributed to the intake of animal or saturated fats e.g. butter, cream, meat fat, coconut oil and palm oil. Healthier fats include soft margarine which is high in polyunsaturates, corn oil, sunflower oil, soya oil and olive oil. N.B. Tomor is the purest of the margarines.

It is important to realise that the following oils are *not suitable for cooking* as they deteriorate when heated: grape-seed oil, hazelnut oil, walnut oil; olive oil is not suitable for deep frying.

VITAMINS

Vitamins are organic substances essential for life and health, which the body is unable to form for itself. They regulate our metabolism, keeping us functioning at a high performance level. A deficiency in any one vitamin can endanger health. Vitamins cannot be absorbed by the body without the help of minerals (see mineral section).

Vitamin A and Carotene

Helps growth, prevents infection, aids eyesight.	Dried apricots, avocados, carrots, green vegetables, cheese, egg yolk, milk, prunes, mint and parsley, corn on the cob, fish-liver oil.

Vitamin A is not destroyed during cooking.

Vitamin B Complex

Aids appetite, helps growth, revitalizes.

Liver, yeast, beans, wholemeal bread, whole cereals, lentils, peanuts, potatoes, sesame seeds, walnuts, unpolished rice.

Vitamin B is not destroyed at boiling point, but may be destroyed by the high temperatures used in baking and frying.

Vitamin C

Builds up resistance to infection, promotes healthy healing of wounds and fractures.

Rose hips, blackcurrants, oranges, all fresh fruit and vegetables, horseradish.

Vitamin C is easily lost during cooking; it can even be destroyed by bruising and grating.

To preserve Vitamin C during food preparation

Do not soak food in water.
Prepare foods immediately before cooking.
Cook in a covered pan.
Cook in as little water as possible.
Cook for as short a time as possible.
Do not cook vegetables in bicarbonate of soda.
Do not use copper saucepans.
Strain food and serve at once.
Use any cooking water for sauces or soup.

Vitamin D

Essential for teeth and bones

Fish-liver oils, dairy foods and eggs.

Vitamin D is not easily lost during cooking.

Vitamin E

Aids skin healing

Soya beans, wheatgerm, corn, lettuce, watercress

Vitamin K

Essential for normal clotting of blood

Green peas, spinach, watercress.

MINERALS

Minerals are necessary constituents of bones, teeth and body cells. There are six main minerals for body health:

Calcium

For the maintenance of strong bones and teeth, helps blood to clot on wounds and helps muscles to work efficiently.

Egg yolk, fish, cheese, milk, almonds, parsley, spinach, watercress.

Made more accessible to the body through cooking.

Iron

Anti-anaemia factor (helps make haemoglobin). Helps transport oxygen to the tissues.

Liver, egg yolk, pulses, dried fruit, aubergines, watercress.

Made more accessible to the body through cooking.

Iodine

Regulates the thyroid gland

Fish, drinking water, milk, bananas, cheese and cherries.

Sodium

Regulates composition of body fluids.

Salt and all salted foods.

May be lost in cooking (but usually reinstated by extra salt taken at meals).

Potassium

Regulates the working of body cells.

Fresh fruit and vegetables.

May be lost in cooking.

Fluorine

Strengthens teeth

Drinking water

Zinc

Strengthens muscles, helps production of insulin, helps decrease cholesterol levels.

Red meat, wheatgerm, yeast, pumpkin seeds, eggs, mustard.

THE IMPORTANCE OF FIBRE

Fibre is fundamental to a healthy diet; it acts as a natural rationing system as it makes us chew our food. It helps the body cope with the nutrients in a more gradual way by slowing down the digestive system. It helps the intestine move its contents along smoothly and quickly and prevents constipation and all related diseases.

Foods rich in fibre: Oatmeal, brown rice, whole wheat, bran, dried peas and beans, lentils, carrots and apple, most fruit and vegetables, seaweed.

Food Additives

Food additives are a vast and fraught subject, which deserves a book to itself and which indeed has inspired numerous books and pamphlets.

Additives in certain foods are beneficial, in that they ensure that the food does not deteriorate. However, some E.E.C. permitted additives are considered unsafe by various medical authorities. We suggest you check with an authoritative published guide to additives.

In general terms, the categories covered by the E-numbers are roughly as follows:

E100 – E180 are E.E.C. permitted colours.
E200 – E290 are E.E.C. permitted preservatives.
E300 – E321 are E.E.C. permitted anti-oxidants.
E322 – E494 are E.E.C. permitted emulsifiers and stabilizers.
E420 – E421 are E.E.C. permitted sweeteners.
E905 – E907 are E.E.C. permitted mineral hydrocarbons.
E1,400 – E1,442 are E.E.C. permitted modified starches.

The following E-numbers have been designated non-kosher:

E120
E422, E430–436
E470–471, 472a, b, c and e.
E473–478
E481–483
E491–495
E542
E570, E572
E904.

Calorie Counter

FOOD	CALORIES PER OZ	PROTEIN	FAT	CARBO-HYDRATE	AVERAGE HELPING	CALORIES
SAUCES AND SOUPS						
Mayonnaise, homemade	100	high	high	–	1 tablespoon	80
Sauces						
bread	32	low	low	high	1 tablespoon	25
cheese	52	low	high	low	2 tablespoons	104
tartare	100	high	high	low	1 tablespoon	80
tomato	21	–	–	high	1 tablespoon	15
savoury, thick	41	low	high	high	2 tablespoons	70
sweet, thick	47	low	low	high	2 tablespoons	80
Soups – thick, and thin						
with pasta	20	low	low	high	1 medium plate	120
Vinegar	–	–	–	–	–	–

FOOD	CALORIES PER OZ	PROTEIN	FAT	CARBO- HYDRATE	AVERAGE HELPING	CALORIES
DRINKS						
Beers						
Brown Ale, bottled	8	—	—	high	½ pint (3 dcl)	80
Draught Ale, bitter	9	—	—	high	½ pint (3 dcl)	90
Draught, mild	7	—	—	high	½ pint (3 dcl)	70
Pale Ale, bottled	9	—	—	high	½ pint (3 dcl)	90
Stout, bottled	10	—	—	high	½ pint (3 dcl)	100
Stout, extra	11	—	—	high	½ pint (3 dcl)	110
Strong Ale	21	—	—	high	½ pint (3 dcl)	210
Spirits						
Brandy	63	—	—	—	1 small measure	70
Gin	63	—	—	—	1 small measure	70
Whisky	63	—	—	—	1 small measure	70
Cider						
dry	10	—	—	high	½ pint (3 dcl)	100
sweet	12	—	—	high	½ pint (3 dcl)	120
vintage	28	—	—	high	½ pint (3 dcl)	180
Cocoa						
made with milk						
unsweetened	28	high	high	high	1 large cup	150
Cola-type drinks	14	—	—	high	1 glass	80
Coffee						
Black, unsweetened	—	—	—	—	—	
milk and sugar	16	low	low	high	1 large cup	100
Fruit squashes and						
cordials	38	—	—	high	1 glass diluted	50
Juices						
natural, unsweetened						
fruit	15	—	—	high	1 wineglass	70
tomato	7	—	—	high	1 wineglass	30
Lemonade, homemade	13	—	—	high	1 glass	70
Ribena	65	—	—	high	1 tablespoon	40
Tea						
black, unsweetened	—	—	—	—	—	
milk and sugar	10	low	low	high	1 large cup	70
Ovaltine, etc., made with						
milk	28	low	low	high	1 large cup	150
Spirits, all types	63	—	—	high	1 small measure	70
Wines						
Burgundy	20	—	—	high	1 wineglass	100
Beaujolais	19	—	—	high	1 wineglass	95
Champagne	21	—	—	high	1 wineglass	105
Chianti	18	—	—	high	1 wineglass	90
Sauternes	26	—	—	high	1 wineglass	130
Port						
Ruby	43	—	—	high	1 small wineglass	129
Tawny	45	—	—	high	1 small wineglass	135
Sherry						
dry	45	—	—	high	1 small sherry glass	135
sweet	38	—	—	high	1 sherry glass	80

FOOD	CALORIES PER OZ	PROTEIN	FAT	CARBO-HYDRATE	AVERAGE HELPING	CALORIES
FRUITS AND NUTS						
Almonds	170	low	high	low	8 nuts	100
Apples						
eating	10	—	—	high	1 medium	30
cooking, baked						
(no sugar)	9	—	—	high	1 medium sweetened	100
cooking, stewed	20	—	—	high	3 tablespoons	120
Apricots						
fresh	7	—	—	high	3 medium	30
dried, raw	52	—	—	high	6 halves	160
diced, stewed	40	—	—	high	2 tablespoons	200
tinned or stewed	17	—	—	high	3 tablespoons	100
Avocado pears	25	—	high	low	half medium	100
Bananas	22	—	—	high	1 medium	50
Blackberries, tinned or						
stewed	17	—	—	high	3 tablespoons	100
Brazil nuts	183	low	high	low	4 nuts	90
Cherries						
eating	11	—	—	high	12 cherries	30
stewed or tinned	20	—	—	high	3 tablespoons	120
Chestnuts	49	—	—	high	4 chestnuts	30
Cob nuts	113	low	high	low	10 nuts	60
Coconut						
fresh	104	low	high	low	2 tablespoons	200
desiccated	178	low	high	low	1 tablespoon	150
Currants						
black and red, stewed	16	—	—	high	3 tablespoons	80
dried	69	—	—	high	1 tablespoon	70
Damsons, stewed	20	—	—	high	3 tablespoons	120
Dates	61	—	—	high	6 dates	130
Figs						
green	12	—	—	high	2 figs	50
dried, stewed	12	—	—	high	2 tablespoons	150
Fruit salad, tinned or						
stewed	20	—	—	high	3 tablespoons	60
Gooseberries						
dessert	10	—	—	high	6 large	40
stewed or tinned	12	—	—	high	3 tablespoons	80
Grapes						
white	14	—	—	high	12 grapes	28
black	17	—	—	high	12 grapes	34
Grapefruit						
fresh	3	—	—	high	half medium	20
tinned	15	—	—	high	3 tablespoons	60
Greengages						
dessert	13	—	—	high	3 medium	40
stewed or tinned	20	—	—	high	3 tablespoons	120
Lemons	4	—	—	high	1 medium	8
Mandarins, tinned	18	—	—	high	2 tablespoons	100
Melon	4	—	—	high	1 medium slice	30

FOOD	CALORIES PER OZ	PROTEIN	FAT	CARBO-HYDRATE	AVERAGE HELPING	CALORIES
Nectarines	13	–	–	high	1 medium	40
Olives	24	–	high	–	6 olives	30
Oranges	8	–	–	high	1 medium	40
Peaches						
fresh	9	–	–	high	1 medium	40
dried, stewed	45	–	–	high	2 tablespoons	200
stewed or tinned	19	–	–	high	2 large halves	120
Peanuts	171	high	high	low	8 nuts	80
Peanut butter	185	high	high	low	1 dessertspoon	120
Pears						
eating	9	–	–	high	1 medium	50
tinned or stewed	18	–	–	high	3 tablespoons	100
Pineapple						
fresh	13	–	–	high	1 medium slice	50
tinned or stewed	18	–	–	high	3 tablespoons	100
Plums						
dessert	10	–	–	high	3 medium	40
stewed or tinned	15	–	–	high	3 tablespoons	80
Prunes, stewed or tinned	30	–	–	high	2 tablespoons	150
Raisins, dried	70	–	–	high	1 tablespoon	70
Raspberries						
raw	7	–	–	high	3 tablespoons	30
stewed or tinned	28	–	–	high	3 tablespoons	150
Rhubarb, stewed	10	–	–	high	3 tablespoons	50
Strawberries, fresh	7	–	–	high	6 large	20
Sultanas, dried	71	–	–	high	1 tablespoon	70
Tangerines	7	–	–	high	1 medium	28
Walnuts	156	low	high	–	6 walnuts	80

VEGETABLES

The majority of vegetables are of low calorie value (an average helping is seldom more than 20 calories) and should be added freely to any diet. They help to avoid constipation, are a source of vitamin C and give bulk to restricted diets. This 'free' addition to your diet includes the following vegetables (but don't forget that any butter or fat used in cooking them DOES count against your calorie allowance): artichokes – asparagus – aubergines – French or runner beans – broccoli – Brussel sprouts – cabbage of all kinds, including pickled – carrots – cauliflower – celeriac – celery – chicory – cucumber – endive – leeks – lettuce – marrow – mushrooms (but FRIED mushrooms are 62 calories to the ounce, average helping, about 130) – mustard and cress – onions (but FRIED onions are 101 calories to the ounce, average helping about 150) – parsley – peppers – pumpkin – radishes – salsify – seakale – spinach – spring greens – swedes – tomatoes (but FRIED tomatoes are 20 calories to the ounce, average helping about 80) – turnips – watercress.

Only the following vegetables need to be counted against your calorie allowance – and don't forget to add in any butter you may use with them.

FOOD	CALORIES PER OZ	PROTEIN	FAT	CARBO-HYDRATE	AVERAGE HELPING	CALORIES
Artichoke						
globe	5	low	—	low	6 oz	30
Jerusalem	5	low	—	medium	4 oz	20
Asparagus	5	medium	—	low	8 oz	40
Aubergines	5	—	—	medium	4 oz	20
Avocado	54	high	high	low	3 oz	162
Beans						
baked	26	high	—	high	on medium slice toast	180
broad, boiled	12	high	—	high	2 tablespoons	50
butter, boiled	26	high	—	high	2 tablespoons	80
haricot, boiled	25	high	—	high	2 tablespoons	80
red kidney	25	low	—	high	—	—
Beetroot, raw	10	—	—	low	—	—
Brussel sprouts	5	—	—	low	—	—
Cabbage	5	—	—	low	—	—
Carrots	5	—	—	medium	—	—
Cauliflower	5	—	—	low	—	—
Celery	2	—	—	low	—	—
Cucumber	3	—	—	low	—	—
Lentils	27	low	—	high	2 tablespoons	80
Parsnips	16	low	—	high	3 tablespoons	50
Peas						
fresh, boiled	14	low	—	high	3 tablespoons	60
dried, boiled	28	low	—	high	2 tablespoons	80
split, boiled	33	low	—	high	2 tablespoons	90
tinned	24	low	—	high	3 tablespoons	80
Potatoes						
boiled	23	—	—	high	2 small	100
baked inc. skin	24	—	—	high	1 medium	80
chips	68	low	low	high	2 tablespoons	300
mashed	34	—	low	high	1 tablespoon	100
new, boiled	21	—	—	high	3 or 4 small	90
roast	35	—	—	high	2 small	140
sweet, boiled	23	—	—	high	2 small	100

PUDDINGS, PRESERVES AND SWEETS

FOOD	CALORIES PER OZ	PROTEIN	FAT	CARBO-HYDRATE	AVERAGE HELPING	CALORIES
Apple pie	54	—	low	high	2 tablespoons	250
Blancmange, plain	34	low	low	high	2 tablespoons	130
Boiled sweets	93	—	—	high	2 sweets	45
Chocolate						
milk	167	low	high	high	1 small bar	250
plain	155	—	high	high	1 small bar	240
Chocolates, assorted	133	—	low	high	2 chocolates	70
Chutney						
apple	57	—	—	high	1 tablespoon	100
tomato	43	—	—	high	1 tablespoon	80
Custard, baked or boiled	33	low	low	high	2 tablespoons	130
Fruit tart (average)	60	—	—	high	2 tablespoons	300
Honey	82	—	—	high	1 dessertspoon	80
Ice cream (average)	56	low	low	high	1 medium tub	100
Jams, marmalade	74	—	—	high	1 dessertspoon	70

17

FOOD	CALORIES PER OZ	PROTEIN	FAT	CARBO-HYDRATE	AVERAGE HELPING	CALORIES
Jam roll, baked	114	low	low	high	1 medium slice	230
Jelly						
plain	22	–	–	high	2 tablespoons	90
milk	31	low	low	high	2 tablespoons	120
Mincemeat	37	–	–	high	1 tablespoon	70
Pancakes	85	low	low	high	2 small	180
Rice Pudding	42	low	low	high	2 tablespoons	200
Steamed pudding (average)	104	low	low	high	2 tablespoons	300
Sugar, all kinds	112	–	–	high	1 teaspoon	30
Syrup, golden	84	–	–	high	1 dessertspoon	80
Toffee	123	–	low	high	2 toffees	60
Treacle, black	73	–	–	high	1 dessertspoon	70
Trifle	43	low	low	high	2 tablespoons	200

DAIRY PRODUCE AND FATS

FOOD	CALORIES PER OZ	PROTEIN	FAT	CARBO-HYDRATE	AVERAGE HELPING	CALORIES
Butter	226	–	high	–	2 small pats	100
Cheese						
Camembert	88	high	high	–	1 medium piece	100
Cheddar	120	high	high	–	1 medium slice	130
Cream	232	–	high	–	1 dessertspoon	150
Edam	88	high	high	–	1 medium slice	110
Gouda	96	high	high	–	1 medium slice	115
Gruyère	132	high	high	–	1 medium piece	160
Parmesan	118	high	high	–	1 tablespoon grated	100
processed	106	high	high	–	1 portion	110
Wensleydale	115	high	high	–	1 medium piece	130
Cream						
double	132	–	high	–	1 tablespoon	80
single	62	low	high	–	1 tablespoon	40
soured	55					
Eggs						
raw or boiled	46	high	high	–	1 egg	80
fried	68	high	high	–	1 egg	140
omelette or soufflé	57	low	high	–	2 eggs	200
cheese omelette	102	low	high	–	2 eggs	300
poached	45	high	high	–	1 egg	80
poached on toast	130	high	high	high	2 eggs, 1 piece toast	300
scrambled	79	low	high	–	1 tablespoon	250
scrambled on toast	170	low	high	high	1 tablespoon 1 piece toast	350
Margarine	226	–	high	–	2 small pats	100
Milk						
fresh, whole	19	high	high	high	1 pint	380
					usual helping in tea	10
fresh, skimmed	10	high	–	high	1 pint	200
					usual helping in tea	5
condensed and sweetened	100	low	low	high	1 tablespoon	80
Olive oil	264	–	high	–	1 dessertspoon	80

FOOD	CALORIES PER OZ	PROTEIN	FAT	CARBO-HYDRATE	AVERAGE HELPING	CALORIES
Yoghourt	67	high	high	–	¼ pint	150

CEREALS, CAKES, ETC

FOOD	CALORIES PER OZ	PROTEIN	FAT	CARBO-HYDRATE	AVERAGE HELPING	CALORIES
All-Bran, Kellogg's	88	low	low	high	4 tablespoons	90
Barley, pearl, boiled	34	low	–	high	2 tablespoons	120
Biscuits						
cream crackers, water	158	low	low	high	2 biscuits	70
digestive	137	low	low	high	2 biscuits	130
sweet, mixed	158	–	low	high	2 medium	120
Bread						
brown	68	low	–	high	1 medium slice	80
white	69	low	–	high	1 medium slice	80
either toasted	85	low	–	high	1 medium slice	80
or toast and butter	140	low	high	high	1 round	120
Cake (general average, not iced)	130	low	low	high	1 medium slice	280
fruit cake (Dundee type)	110	low	low	high	1 slice	300
sponge	88	low	low	high	1 medium slice	180
Cornflakes	104	low	low	high	6 tablespoons	100
Doughnuts	101	–	low	high	1 medium	250
Flour	99	low	–	high	1 tablespoon	75
Jam tarts	112	–	low	high	2 medium	300
Macaroni, boiled	32	low	–	high	2 tablespoons	130
Oatmeal porridge	13	low	low	high	3 tablespoons	80
Rice, boiled	35	–	–	high	2 tablespoons	130
Ryvita, and other crispbreads	110	–	–	high	2 pieces	50
Sandwiches, average, savoury	–	–	varies	–	1 round	300
Shortbread	148	low	low	high	1 piece	120
Yorkshire Pudding	62	low	low	high	1 slice	70

POULTRY

FOOD	CALORIES PER OZ	PROTEIN	FAT	CARBO-HYDRATE	AVERAGE HELPING	CALORIES
Chicken						
boiled	38	high	low	–	4 slices	200
roast	29	high	low	–	4 slices	150
Duck, roast	48	high	high	–	4 slices	250
Goose, roast	53	high	high	–	4 slices	270
Turkey, roast	34	high	low	–	4 slices	170

FISH

FOOD	CALORIES PER OZ	PROTEIN	FAT	CARBO-HYDRATE	AVERAGE HELPING	CALORIES
Bass, steamed	19	high	low	–	1 medium steak	110
Bloaters, grilled	54	high	high	–	2 medium	250
Cod						
steamed	19	high	–	–	1 medium steak	110
fried	36	high	low	–	1 medium steak	180
grilled	39	high	low	–	1 medium steak	200
roe, fried	59	high	high	–	2 slices	180
Fishcakes	61	high	high	low	2 medium	250
Fish pie	58	low	high	low	3 tablespoons	300
Flounder						

FOOD	CALORIES PER OZ	PROTEIN	FAT	CARBO-HYDRATE	AVERAGE HELPING	CALORIES
steamed	15	high	low	–	1 medium piece	100
fried	42	high	high	low	1 medium piece	200
Haddock						
fresh, steamed	21	high	–	–	1 medium fillet	84
fresh, fried	46	high	low	–	1 medium fillet	200
smoked, steamed	18	high	–	–	1 medium fillet	110
Hake						
steamed	24	high	–	–	1 medium piece	150
fried	59	high	high	low	1 medium piece	330
Halibut, steamed	28	high	–	–	1 steak	150
Herring						
baked	50	high	high	–	1 medium fish	250
fried	59	high	high	low	1 medium fish	300
roe, fried	74	high	high	low	2 tablespoons	220
Kedgeree	43	high	low	low	3 tablespoons	200
Kipper, grilled	31	high	low	–	medium pair	200
Lemon sole						
steamed	18	high	–	–	1 medium	100
fried	49	high	low	low	1 medium	250
Mackerel, fried	39	high	low	–	1 medium	200
Mullet, grey or red, steamed	24	high	–	–	1 steak	150
Pilchards, tinned	63	high	high	–	2 large	200
Plaice						
steamed	14	high	–	–	1 medium	100
fried	40	high	high	low	1 medium	200
Salmon						
fresh, steamed	46	high	high	–	1 medium steak	180
tinned	39	high	low	–	2 tablespoons	140
Sardines	84	high	high	–	3 medium	170
Sole						
steamed	14	high	–	–	1 medium	90
fried	68	high	high	low	1 medium	320
Sprats						
fresh, fried	111	low	high	–	3–4 medium	400
smoked, grilled	81	high	high	–	3–4 medium	320
Trout, steamed	25	high	–	–	1 medium	150
Whiting						
steamed	17	high	–	–	1 medium fillet	100
fried	49	high	low	low	1 medium fillet	250
Whitebait, fried	152	low	high	low	3 heaped tablespoons	300

NOTE: Weight includes bones, where normally served, and includes an allowance for egg and breadcrumbs coating for frying.

Starters

What do you mean, 'All ten of them'?

HINTS

Tomato cups: Look attractive served with different fillings either for cocktails or on a bed of lettuce as a starter. Select large firm tomatoes and cut a slice from the side opposite the stalk end. Scoop out the pulp with a teaspoon and use the pulp from the cut slices. Blend the pulp with finely chopped cucumber, 1 tablespoon chopped chives and seasoning. Spoon the mixture into the tomato cases and cover with a good layer of grated cheese. Bake in a moderate oven for 10–12 minutes and garnish with parsley.

Courgette cups: Cut unpeeled courgettes into $1\frac{1}{2}''$ (3.5 cm) sections and scoop out the insides to form a cup-like shell. Blanch in salted water for 2 minutes and plunge immediately into cold water. Drain and fill with cheese and herb pâté. Bake in moderate oven for 10 minutes until bubbling and golden.

ARTICHOKE DELIGHT   Essie Harris

Serves 4   Preparation 15 mins.   Cook 40 mins.   Marinate 2 hours

4 artichokes
1 red apple
1 green apple
4 oz chopped nuts (hazel or Barcelona
  only) (115 gm)
3 oz sultanas or raisins (85 gm)

Small sprigs of watercress
Small cauliflower in florets
½ pint vinaigrette dressing (280 ml)
Very small cubes of cooked chicken
Small hard boiled egg, chopped

This is a very filling starter, ideal when soup is not being served. Boil artichokes in the usual way and open very wide. Take off 'furry' top of heart and leave clean for filling. Dice the apples small, leaving coloured skins on. Marinate these with all the ingredients except watercress for 2 hours. Add to artichokes before serving and top with sprig of watercress and a curl of lemon slice.

Microwave Instructions
Wrap artichokes in cling film and microwave on full power for 10–11 minutes. Then make rest of recipe as above.

 FEUILLETES D'ARTICHAUTS   Anne Moss

Serves 6   Preparation 30 mins.   Cook 15 mins.   Advance   Freezable

14 oz tin artichoke hearts (400 gm)
1 clove garlic
2 level tbls pine kernels
2 tbls parsley, chopped
2 egg yolks
Salt and pepper
1 lb packet vegetarian puff
  pastry (450 gm)

GLAZE: 1 egg

SAUCE
¼ pint plain yoghurt (145 ml)
1 clove garlic
1 tsp pesto sauce
2 oz chopped walnuts (55 gm)
Sesame seeds

GARNISH: lemon or lime twists
              6 small pâté tins

Drain artichokes and set aside 3 for decoration. Place artichokes, garlic, pine kernels, egg yolk, salt, pepper and parsley in magimix and roughly chop. Roll out pastry to 12 round shapes 3½" (9 cm) diameter and line pâté tins. Place a spoonful of mixture on each and cover with other round of pastry. Seal well by painting a rim of egg on first round of pastry and pushing top well down. Glaze top of pastry with egg yolk and sprinkle with sesame seeds and bake for 15 minutes in preheated oven Gas No. 6, 400°F, 200°C.

Sauce: Blend all ingredients in liquidiser or food processor until fairly smooth. Serve feuilletés warm with spoonful of sauce and decorate with half an artichoke heart and twist of lime or lemon.

AUBERGINE CAVIAR Gillian Burr

Serves 4   Preparation 25 mins.   Refrigerate 2 hours   Advance

3 small aubergines, or 1 large
Slice of crustless white bread
1 clove garlic, crushed
4 tbls olive oil
Lemon juice to taste

1 tbls parsley, chopped
$\frac{1}{2}$ tsp dried marjoram
Salt and black pepper
1 shallot, finely chopped

Set oven to Gas No.5, 375°F, 190°C. Brush the aubergines with oil and bake until soft or grill until the skins are crinkled and the insides soft. Peel and cut the flesh into a bowl. Soak the bread in water and squeeze dry. Place aubergine in blender with garlic, shallot and bread, herbs, salt and pepper and liquidise until smooth. Gradually beat in the olive oil and when the mixture is stiff stir in the lemon juice and check the seasoning. Chill for 2 hours before serving.

 AVOCADO SALAD Maureen Marks

Serves 4   Preparation 15–20 mins.

$\frac{1}{2}$lb any smoked fish (225gm)
2 slices white bread
8 radicchio leaves
12 frisé leaves
Oil for shallow frying

2 tbls lemon juice
1 egg, beaten
2 tbls sesame seeds
8 tbls French dressing
2 avocados
$\frac{1}{2}$ bunch watercress

Cut fish in $\frac{1}{2}''$ (13mm) pieces. Cut bread into $\frac{3}{4}''$ (19mm) squares, dip in beaten eggs and then in sesame seeds. Fry in shallow oil until golden brown. Drain and cool. Break lettuce leaves in small pieces and arrange on 4 plates. Add watercress sprigs. Slice avocados thickly and toss in the lemon juice until completely coated. Add to salads. Scatter pieces of fish and croûtons over salads and pour over the French dressing.

23

CARROT SOUFFLE Gloria Greenberg

Serves 4   Preparation 15 mins.   Cook 35 mins.

8 oz cooked carrots (225 gm)   Little grated lemon rind
2 oz butter (55 gm)   Cayenne pepper
2 oz plain flour (55 gm) $\frac{1}{4}$ tsp nutmeg, grated
3 tbls carrot stock   4 eggs
$\frac{1}{2}$ pt milk (280 ml)   Little parsley, chopped

Mash, sieve or liquidise the carrots to a smooth purée. Melt the butter in a saucepan and stir in the flour. Gradually add the carrot stock and milk and simmer to make a creamy sauce, stirring continuously. Flavour with lemon rind, cayenne pepper and nutmeg. Add the carrot purée and blend with the sauce. Separate the eggs, adding the yolks to the carrot mixture. Whisk the egg whites until they are stiff but not too dry. Using a metal spoon, lightly fold the whites into the sauce. Butter a 2 pint (1.25 litre) soufflé dish, sprinkle with chopped parsley, then put in the carrot mixture. Bake for 35 minutes in the centre of a moderately hot oven Gas No.6, 400°F, 200°C. Serve as soon as the soufflé is cooked.

CHEESE PUFFBALLS Marion Cohen

Serves 4–6   Preparation 15 mins.   Standing time 30 mins.   Cook 5–10 mins.

3 eggs, separated   2 oz plain flour (55 gm)
8 oz cheddar cheese, grated (225 gm)   1 tsp baking powder
2 tbls pale ale   30 stuffed green olives
Salt and pepper
                                         TO SERVE: Tartare sauce

Put egg yolks in a bowl and mix with the cheese, ale, seasoning, sifted flour and baking powder. Beat egg whites until stiff and fold into cheese batter. Allow to stand for 30 minutes. Form into 30 balls, with floured fingers, putting an olive in the centre of each ball. Deep fry in oil until golden and puffed out. Drain and serve with tartare sauce.

SPICY CHEESE
AND CARROT PATE Marion Cohen

Serves 4   Preparation 10 mins.   Cook 15 mins.   Refrigerate 2 hours   Advance

8 oz carrots, chopped (225 gm)   1 clove garlic, crushed
1 small onion, chopped   1 tbls oil
4 oz Leicester cheese, grated (115 gm)   1 tsp sugar
                                         Salt and black pepper

Sauté the carrots and onions and garlic in the oil until softened. Barely cover the mixture with water and simmer until tender. Liquidise until nearly smooth using a little of the cooking liquid. Add the cheese and season to taste with the sugar, salt and pepper.

Variation: flavour with 1 tsp mustard, curry powder or cumin.

CHEESE AND CUCUMBER
MOUSSE
Gloria Goldring

Serves 8   Preparation 30 mins.   Refrigerate 2 hours   Advance

1 large cucumber
Salt
8 oz curd cheese (225 gm)
1 tsp onion juice
¼ pt boiling water (140 ml)

½ oz gelatine (15 gm)
3 tbls cold water
2 tbls white wine vinegar
1 tbls caster sugar
Pinch mace
¼ pt double cream (140 ml) or Greek yoghurt

Dice unpeeled cucumber very finely, sprinkle with salt and leave pressed for 30 minutes. Beat cheese with onion juice, salt and pepper. Soak gelatine in cold water for a few minutes, pour on boiling water, stir until dissolved. Stir in cheese mixture and leave until cold. Drain cucumber and mix with vinegar, sugar, mace. Fold cucumber mixture and lightly whipped cream or yoghurt into cheese mix. Turn into lightly oiled mould and chill until set.

 ## CHEESE AND HERB PATE
Lynne Goldwyn

Serves 6–8   Preparation 10 mins.   Advance

5 oz butter (145 gm)
1 lb cream cheese (450 gm)
1 clove garlic, crushed with a little salt

1 tbls chervil, parsley and
  chives, finely chopped
1 lb loaf tin (450 gm)

Grease tin and line with greaseproof paper. Slowly melt butter in a saucepan. Place the other ingredients in a bowl and mix thoroughly or use a food processor. Check that herbs are evenly blended. Leave butter to cool, then fold into cheese mixture and transfer to the tin. Put in fridge to set. It will keep for up to 10 days in fridge.

400–500 calories per serving

 ## CUCUMBER DE MOULIN
Marilyn de Keyser

Serves 4   Preparation 15 mins.   Refrigerate 2–3 hours

2 large cucumbers
1 lb 2 oz carton Fromage Frais (500 gm)
2–3 tbls chives, chopped

2–3 tbls salt (depending on size of
  cucumber
Pepper

GARNISH: paprika and parsley

Peel cucumbers. Cut in half. With a teaspoon scoop out seeds, then finely slice cucumber halves. Place in bowl and sprinkle with salt. Refrigerate for 2½ hours. Rinse cucumber and drain in colander and press down to squeeze out excess water. Then pat dry with paper towel. Add chives to Fromage Frais together with seasoning. Pour over cucumber. Sprinkle a little paprika and parsley over it. Delicious served with cold salmon.

HUNGARIAN EGGS WITH LECSO   Ruth Smilg

Serves 4   Preparation 15 mins.   Cook 10 mins.

4 eggs, beaten
2 medium onions, chopped
1 large green pepper, chopped
Parsley, chopped

½lb ripe tomatoes, peeled and
  chopped (225gm)
Salt, pepper, paprika
Oil

Fry onions in a little oil, when brown add peppers and after a few minutes the tomatoes. Season. Prepare eggs as for scrambling and when lecso mixture is soft and well cooked pour over eggs and stir in lightly. Serve immediately with a sprinkling of chopped parsley and toast.

 **COQUILLES DE POISSON
CORDON BLEU**   Anne Moss

Serves 6   Preparation 30 mins.   Cook 50 mins.

1¼lb white fish (cod or
  halibut) (570gm)
3 large ripe tomatoes, skinned and
  quartered

SAUCE

½pt thick mayonnaise (280ml)
1 clove garlic, crushed
1 tsp tomato purée
Salt and pepper

COURT BOUILLON

2 pts water (1.14 litres)
2 tbls vinegar
1 carrot
1 onion
6 peppercorns
Bouquet garni

*(Simmer
together for
8 minutes)*

6 ramekins

GARNISH: red pepper

Place fish in a pan, cover with court bouillon and poach gently for 30–40 minutes. Allow to cool in the liquid. When cold, drain, skin and bone the fish and divide carefully into large flakes. De-seed the tomatoes and reserve any juice for the sauce. Add the garlic to the mayonnaise together with the tomato purée and seasonings and a little of the reserved tomato juice. Put a layer of the tomato pieces at the bottom of the ramekins, spoon the flaked fish on top and coat with the mayonnaise. Garnish with rings of red pepper.

FISH TERRINE
WITH TOMATO COULIS
Anita Shore

Serves 6   **Preparation 20 mins.**   **Cook 45 mins.**   **Advance**

8 oz fresh haddock, skinned (225 gm)
4 eggs
½ cup lemon juice
4 fl oz sunflower oil (115 ml)
4 oz fromage frais (115 gm)
2 oz smoked salmon (55 gm)
Chopped dill and parsley
1 lb loaf tin (450 gm)

TOMATO COULIS

1 small onion chopped
1½ lb very ripe tomatoes, skinned and
   chopped (675 gm)
½ oz butter (15 gm)
1 tbls olive oil
1 tsp salt
1 tsp sugar
1 tsp parsley, chopped
1 clove garlic, crushed
½ tsp dried basil

Put the haddock, eggs, lemon juice, sunflower oil and fromage frais into the food processor and blend until smooth. Place half the mixture into a greaseproof paper lined loaf tin; then lay small slices of smoked salmon on top. To the other half of the mixture add the dill and parsley and mix well, then place on top of the smoked salmon. Bake in a bain-marie for 45 minutes at Gas No. 3, 340°F, 175°C. When cool turn onto a serving dish.

Coulis: heat fat in a shallow pan and sauté onion until it glistens. Add the tomatoes and simmer for 15 minutes with all the other ingredients. Blend in food processor or blender, then sieve. Test for seasoning. Serve slices of terrine surrounded by the tomato coulis.

HAZELNUT PATE
CROUTONS SALAD
Bondi Zimmerman

Serves 6   **Preparation 15 mins.**   **Cook 15 mins.**

SALAD

Curly endive
Radicchio
18 fresh asparagus tips
2 raw carrots, cut into very fine matchsticks
Vinaigrette

CROUTONS

6 slices brown bread
6 oz smoked trout pâté (170 gm)
4 dsp hazelnuts, roasted, peeled,
   chopped
Hazelnut oil

To make the croûtons, cut 4 heart shapes out of each slice of bread. Heat the hazelnut oil and fry the croûtons until golden brown. Drain on absorbent paper. Mix the pâté with the hazelnuts and keep chilled. Before serving, spread the pâté on each croûton.

Wash and dry the salad leaves and arrange them on 6 small plates. Boil the asparagus in salted water for 10 minutes and drain. Arrange the warm asparagus over the salad and pour over some good vinaigrette. Arrange the croûtons on the salad and sprinkle with the carrots.

HIGH SPEED HUMMOUS   Renata Knobil

Serves **4**   Preparation **5 mins.**   Advance

15 oz tin chickpeas (430 gm)   **2 tbls olive oil**
Juice of 1 lemon   **3 tbls sesame paste**
Paprika or cayenne pepper   **Salt**

Drain the chickpeas and place with all the other ingredients in a food processor or liquidiser and blend until smooth.

 # TERRINE MOUSSELINE OF HADDOCK AND TOMATO
Helen Meller

Serves **6–8**   Preparation **30 mins.**   Cook **8–15 mins.**   Advance essential

10 oz haddock fillets cut into halves or   **1 tbls fresh basil or tarragon,**
quarters (285 gm)   **chopped**
$\frac{1}{4}$ pt water (140 ml)   **A little oil for greasing**
1 clove garlic, finely chopped   **Salt and black pepper**
3 tsp gelatine
2 pt mould or loaf tin (1.1 litres)   **TO GARNISH: whole basil or tarragon**
14 oz tin tomatoes (400 gm)   **leaves**
Juice $\frac{1}{2}$ lemon
2 eggs, separated

Cook haddock in a covered pan with a little water and 1–3 tsp salt. Simmer gently for 8–15 minutes (depending on whether the fish is fresh or frozen) until just cooked and opaque. Strain the liquid through a sieve into another saucepan and put the drained fish on a plate to one side. Add the chopped garlic to the liquid in the saucepan and sprinkle in the gelatine. Dissolve the gelatine, stirring over a low heat.

Chop the canned tomatoes and add them with their juice and the lemon juice to the pan. Stir the egg yolks into the tomato mixture and season with salt and black pepper. Add the chopped basil or tarragon and pour into a mixing bowl. Flake the cooked fish into the mixture, discarding any skin. Stir gently and leave until cold and on the verge of setting.

Oil a mould or loaf tin. Whisk egg whites until they form soft peaks and fold into the fish and tomato mixture. Pour into mould and chill in the fridge until well set. Turn on to a serving dish (you might have to loosen the edges gently with a knife). Chill again until ready to serve. Garnish with fresh basil or tarragon leaves.

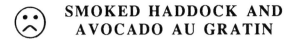

SMOKED HADDOCK AND AVOCADO AU GRATIN
Gloria James

Serves 4–6   Preparation 10 mins.   Cook 10–15 mins.

8oz smoked haddock (225gm)
1oz butter (30gm)
1oz flour (30gm)
½ pt creamy milk (use top of the milk
  or add a little cream) (280ml)

Pepper and mace
1 bay leaf
1–2 avocados (depending on size)
6–8 tbls gruyère or mature cheddar
  cheese, grated

Place the skinned fish in a saucepan with the bay leaf and the milk, bring gently to simmer and draw to the side of the stove; cover and leave for 5–10 minutes (the fish will then be cooked). Melt the butter in another saucepan, add the flour and cook for 2–3 minutes over a moderate heat. Draw off the stove, wait for the sizzling to cease (make sure it does, because you are adding hot liquid), and add the strained milk from the fish. Whisk with a wire whisk and bring to the boil. Simmer for 1–2 minutes, fold in the flaked fish and season with pepper and mace, adding salt only if necessary. Spoon into individual ramekins, top with slices of peeled avocado, sprinkle heavily with cheese and grill until brown and bubbling.

SMOKED HADDOCK PATE
Bobbie Benscher

Serves 6   Preparation 20 mins.   Cook 10 mins.   Advance   Freezable

1lb smoked haddock fillets (450gm)
3 hard boiled eggs, finely chopped
2–3oz butter (55–85gm)
¼pt double cream (140ml)

¼pt single cream (140ml)
Salt and freshly ground black pepper

TO SERVE: French bread or toast

Soak fish for 10 minutes in cold water, then drain. Line grill pan with foil, lay on the haddock fillets and dot with butter. Grill on both sides under a medium heat for about 10 minutes or until flesh flakes easily. Remove the skin and any bones from the haddock and put in an electric blender with its juices and the butter. Reduce to a purée and turn into a bowl. Whisk the two creams together and fold in the fish purée and hard boiled eggs. Season well and turn into a 1 pt (600ml) foil dish. Smooth the top.
To freeze: Cool, cover and label, then freeze.
To serve: Thaw overnight in the refrigerator and serve with hot French bread or toast.

DANISH HERRING
Vivienne Prevezer

Serves 6–8   Preparation 10 mins.   Advance

6–8 salt herrings (if too salty soak in
   cold water for 30 mins to remove
   excess)
1 cup apple, chopped
1 cup onion, chopped
½ cup oil

¾ cup sugar
½ tsp mustard
1 cup brown vinegar
1 cup tomato purée

Cut the herring into bite-size pieces. Mix the rest of the ingredients together and add to the herring.

 ## LEEK AND CHEESE PARCELS
Maureen Marks

Serves 6   Preparation 45 mins.   Cook 30 mins.

4 medium leeks cut into ½"
   pieces (1 cm)
½ tsp dried thyme
1 oz unsalted butter (30 gm)
9 oz chopped onions (255 gm)

1 garlic clove, finely chopped
2 tbls single cream
5 oz Gruyère or Swiss cheese,
   grated (140 gm)
12 sheets filo pastry

In a large frying pan heat oil and half the butter over medium heat. Add leeks, onion, garlic, thyme, salt and pepper. Cook, stirring often, for 12 minutes.

Stir in cream and continue cooking until the liquid is absorbed. Transfer mixture into a bowl and let it cool slightly. Stir in the cheese and refrigerate for 30 minutes. Preheat oven Gas No.7, 425°F, 220°C. Lay out 2 sheets of pastry, one on top of the other, mound about ⅙ of the leek mixture 3" (7½ cm) from the lower right corner of the dough. Fold up the dough to form a compact parcel. Make 6 parcels and put them seam sides down on a lightly buttered baking sheet. Melt remaining butter and brush the parcels with it. Bake until golden – about 30 minutes.

Serve hot with a dollop of soured cream mixed with chives or parsley or fresh tomato sauce.

  ## RED MELON STARTER
Faith Garfield

Serves 8   Preparation 10 mins.   Refrigerate 1 hour   Advance

1 red watermelon
6 spring onions, chopped

French dressing

Either cut the melon into bite-size pieces or use a melon baller to make into balls. Toss in the dressing together with the spring onions and chill for 1 hour. For variety, use a selection of 3 different types of melon.

MUSHROOMS
IN GARLIC BREADCRUMBS

Jane Jaffe

Serves 2   **Preparation 5 mins.**   **Cook 5 mins.**   Microwave

½lb mushrooms, peeled and sliced
   (225gm)
1 tbls lemon juice

3 tbls breadcrumbs
4 cloves garlic, crushed
4oz butter (115gm)

Fry mushrooms in 1oz (30gm) butter and when slightly soft, add lemon juice. Cook on low light for 3 minutes. In another pan, melt remaining butter. Add breadcrumbs and garlic and cook for 2 minutes. Add mushroom mixture. Stir and serve.

Microwave instructions

Prepare exactly as above, in two separate dishes. Microwave each on high for 2 minutes, mix together and serve.

 MUSHROOMS A LA GRECQUE   Marion Cohen

Serves 2–4   **Preparation 5 mins.**   **Cook 15 mins.**   Advance

½lb small button mushrooms (225gm)
Juice of ½ lemon
3 tbls olive oil
3 tbls water
Bayleaf

2 tomatoes, skinned and chopped
4 peppercorns, crushed
10 coriander seeds
Thyme
Salt

Put all the ingredients, except mushrooms and lemon juice, into a pan and bring to the boil. Let it simmer for about 3 minutes, then add the mushrooms and lemon juice. Cook gently for about 5 minutes. Remove the mushrooms to a serving dish and boil the remaining liquid for another 5 minutes or so, until somewhat reduced. Pour over the mushrooms. Serve cold or just tepid.

Microwave instructions

Place all ingredients, except mushrooms and lemon juice, in a suitable dish, cover with cling film and microwave on full power for 2 minutes. Then add lemon juice and mushrooms and cook on power level 6 for 3 minutes. Remove mushrooms and heat liquid on full power for 1 minute, pour over mushrooms.

MUSHROOM AND OLIVE PATE Olive Paté

Serves 6–8   **Preparation 10 mins.**   **Cook 25 mins.**   **Advance preferable**

8 oz flat mushrooms, sliced (225 gm)
12 black olives, stoned
2 tbls olive oil
1 medium onion, chopped
1 clove garlic, chopped

1 tbls lemon juice
1 tbls capers
Salt and freshly ground black pepper

GARNISH: 1 tbls fresh parsley,
chopped

Heat oil in pan and sauté the onion and garlic until translucent. Add the mushrooms and cook together for 20 minutes approximately, stirring occasionally.

Add all the remaining ingredients, except parsley and thoroughly mix together. Allow to cool slightly then blend or process briefly so that the pâté is not too smooth. Spoon the mixture into individual ramekins, garnish with parsley and serve with hot toast.

N.B. This starter improves if made 24 hours in advance.

HOT MUSHROOM SOUFFLES Maureen Marks

Serves 6   **Preparation 10 mins.**   **Cook 25 mins.**

5 level tbls Parmesan cheese, grated
8 oz button mushrooms, finely
  chopped (225 gm)
3 oz onion, finely chopped (85 gm)
1 level tbls granular mustard

2 oz butter (55 gm)
3 level tbls plain flour
$\frac{1}{4}$ pt milk (140 ml)
3 separated eggs plus 1 extra white
6 x $\frac{1}{4}$ pt ramekins (140 ml)

Lightly butter ramekins and dust with 2 level tablespoons Parmesan. Melt butter in a large heavy-based saucepan. Add onion and mushrooms and cook over high heat stirring occasionally until moisture has evaporated and vegetables are lightly browned. Remove from heat, stir in flour, milk, mustard and seasoning and blend well. Return to heat, bring to boil stirring all the time and cook for 2 minutes. Cool slightly and off heat, beat in yolks, one at a time, followed by the remaining cheese. Whisk whites stiffly and fold gently into mixture. Spoon into dishes and stand them on a baking tray and cook at Gas No.5, 375°F, 190°C for 18 minutes or until just set.

SAVOURY STUFFED ONIONS

Gloria Levy

Serves 4   **Preparation 10 mins.**   **Cook 1¼ hours**

4 medium onions
Salt and pepper
1 tsp chopped sage or ¼ tsp dried
  sage
2 eggs

2 oz soft breadcrumbs (55 gm)
1 oz margarine (30 gm)
½ pt cheese sauce (280 ml)
  (See Sauce section, p.157)

GARNISH: parsley

Cover the peeled onions with salted water and boil steadily for 30 minutes. By this time they will not be cooked but it will be possible to remove the centre cores. Keep the onion stock. Chop the onion cores finely, add remaining ingredients (except margarine and cheese sauce) and pile this stuffing back into the centres. Put the onions into a greased casserole. Pour over 7 fl oz (200 ml) onion stock and put a small piece of margarine on each onion. Bake for 45 minutes covered in a moderately hot oven Gas No.5, 375°F, 190°C. Lift out of the stock and coat with cheese sauce. Garnish with parsley and serve hot.

 # MINTED PEARS

Lisa Rose

Serves 4–6   **Preparation 15 mins.**   **Advance**

4–6 ripe pears
3 tbls fresh mint, chopped
2 tbls fresh parsley, chopped
1 tsp fresh tarragon, chopped or
  ½ tsp dried tarragon

1 tsp Dijon mustard
2 tbls lemon juice
5 tbls olive oil
Salt and pepper

Place the salt, pepper and mustard in a bowl, add the lemon juice and stir well to dissolve the salt. Gradually beat in the oil to produce an emulsified vinaigrette and stir in the finely chopped herbs (if using dried tarragon, steep in a few drops of boiling water for five minutes).

In a food processor chop all the herbs finely, then add the seasoning, mustard, lemon juice and oil. Peel, core and slice the pears into the dressing, leave for an hour or so to marinate and chill, turning once or twice, then put in individual bowls or glasses and spoon over the dressing. Serve with crisp cheese staws.

PALM HEART SALAD
Yaffa Wagner

Serves 4   Preparation 10 mins.

Variety of different coloured lettuce leaves
14oz tin palm hearts (400gm)
$\frac{1}{2}$ apple, sliced

Blue cheese
Walnuts
French dressing

Lay the mixed leaves in a mound on each plate. Crumble cheese on top of mounds. Place palm hearts and apple up the sides of the mounds in alternate lines. Decorate with walnuts and dress with salad dressing.

SIMPLE SALAD STARTER
Sandra Seifert

Serves 4   Preparation 15 mins.

Mixed lettuce leaves
16 baby tomatoes
8 fresh asparagus spears, cooked
4oz smoked salmon, cut into strips (125gm)

Croûtons
Vinaigrette dressing
Chopped chives

Divide lettuce leaves, tomatoes and smoked salmon strips onto four separate plates. Just before serving throw a handful of croûtons over the top, pour on the vinaigrette and decorate with the chopped chives. A couple of fresh asparagus spears on the side of each plate gives this dish an extra special finish.

SALMON MOUSSE
June Melzak

Serves 8   Preparation 15 mins.   Setting time 2 hours

2 tbls gelatine
1 tsp dry mustard
2 tbls sugar
5 tbls lemon juice
$\frac{1}{4}$ tsp paprika
$\frac{3}{4}$ cup milk

1 cup mayonnaise
15oz tin salmon (420gm)
2 egg whites
$\frac{1}{4}$ cup cold water
1 tsp salt
1 dsp oil

Soften the gelatine in the cold water. Mix salt, mustard, paprika, sugar and milk. Heat this gently. Then add lemon juice gradually until it curdles. Add oil and gelatine in water. Chill this mixture until it begins to thicken. Stiffly beat egg whites. Add the salmon and mayonnaise to the chilled mixture and beat well. Then add the egg whites. Oil a mould and pour in mixture.

SALMON TARTARE   Gloria Goldring

Serves 4   **Preparation 5 mins.**   **Advance**   **Freezable**

9 oz tail of fresh salmon (250 gm)
6 oz smoked salmon pieces (175 gm)
2 tbls shallots, finely chopped
Juice of ½ lemon

Ground pepper
Several pinches of paprika
1½ tbls parsley, chopped

Remove skin and bone from the fish, leaving approx. 5 oz (150 gm). Mince finely both fresh salmon and smoked salmon pieces. Stir in remaining ingredients. Serve on lettuce or chicory leaves.

  ## SMOKED SALMON AND
AVOCADO TERRINE   Gillian Burr

Serves 6–8   **Preparation 15 mins.**   **Refrigerate 5 hours**   **Advance**

¼ lb smoked salmon (225 gm)
¼ lb soft butter (115 gm)
½ pt double cream (280 ml)
White pepper
2 lb loaf tin (950 gm)

3 avocado pears, peeled and sliced
2 tbls spring onions, chopped
Juice of 1 lemon

GARNISH: lemon slices and cucumber

Oil and line the loaf tin with greaseproof paper. Cream butter, then add the salmon, onion, some pepper, lemon juice and a little salt if required. Blend until smooth. Add the cream and incorporate.

Cover the bottom of the tin with a third of the salmon mixture and then lay some sliced avocado on top. Continue in this way until you have three layers of the salmon mixture and two of the avocado. Refrigerate. Turn on to a serving dish and decorate with cucumber slices.

SMOKED SALMON AND
CUCUMBER SALAD   Jo Luck

Serves 4   **Preparation 10 mins**

6 oz smoked salmon (170 gm)
1 cucumber
Juice of ½ lemon

3 tbls Fromage Frais

GARNISH: mustard and cress

Make a ring of cucumber slices on 4 plates. Cut the remaining cucumber and smoked salmon into strips and mix together with the lemon juice and Fromage Frais. Lay this mixture carefully in the middle of the plates and garnish with the cress.

SMOKED SALMON TIMBALES

Serves 4   Preparation 10 mins.   Refrigerate 4 hours   Advance

Oil for greasing
6 oz smoked salmon, thinly
    sliced (170 gm)
6 oz taramasalata (170 gm)
5 fl oz whipped cream (140 ml)

Juice of ½ lemon
Freshly ground black pepper

GARNISH: 4 twists lemon
            4 slices of lemon

Oil 4 ramekin dishes. Line them with smoked salmon. Mix together the taramasalata with cream, lemon juice and black pepper. Divide the mixture between the ramekins and seal with the remaining smoked salmon. Chill for 4 hours.

Turn the timbales on to slices of lemon in the centre of each plate and decorate the top of the timbales with a twist of lemon. Keep chilled until needed.

 ## SEAFOOD STUFFED CROISSANTS   Avril Kleeman

Serves 8   Preparation 10 mins.   Cook 10 mins.

1 onion, chopped
4 oz mushrooms, sliced (115 gm)
1 clove garlic, peeled and crushed
Salt and ground pepper
½ pt single cream (280 ml)

12 oz fillets of haddock or similar
    white fish, cubed (340 gm)
1 croissant per person
Butter
Chopped dill or parsley

Heat croissants through and split. Melt butter, soften onion in the butter. Add the mushrooms and sauté for 2–3 minutes then add the garlic. Add the cream and allow to bubble for one minute. Then add the cubes of fish and cook for 2–3 minutes. Spoon the fish and sauce over the croissant half, put the other half on top, sprinkle with the herbs and serve immediately.

 ## SHAK SHUKA I   Naomi Pope

Serves 8–10   Preparation 20 mins   Cook 25 mins.

2 ladles corn oil
4 tbls tomato purée
1 tbls paprika
1 garlic, crushed – to taste
12 eggs, left whole

1 large tin of tomatoes, liquidised
Chopped green peppers (optional)
Salt
1 glass water

Using large saucepan, heat the oil and add all the ingredients, except eggs. Add one glass of water, let sauce thicken – about 10 minutes. Then break the eggs into the mixture, one at a time. Let them simmer for a few minutes, until they harden. Serve with French bread.

This sauce is very good for spaghetti, minus the paprika.

SHAK SHUKA II
Yaffa Wagner

Serves 4   Preparation 10 mins.   Cook 45 mins.   Advance

1 lb tin tomatoes (450 gm)
1 lb courgettes, diced (450 gm)
1 lb aubergines, diced (450 gm)
1 lb green or red peppers,
    diced (450 g)
2 large onions, sliced

4 eggs, left whole
Salt and pepper
Oil
Tabasco
Cumin powder

Fry sliced onion until transparent. Add diced vegetables and seasoning. Cook until soft (about 40 minutes). Place in greased ovenproof dish. Make holes large enough to drop the eggs in whole. Cook in oven Gas No.5, 375°F, 190°C – until just set.

Can be microwaved.

SPINACH PARMESAN PIE
Sheila Fox

Serves 6   Preparation 15 mins.   Cook 35–40 mins.   Advance   Freezable

4 spring onions, chopped
4 tbls butter/margarine
$\frac{1}{4}$ lb mushrooms, chopped (115 gm)
8 oz frozen spinach, thawed and
    drained (225 gm)
1 clove garlic, crushed
$\frac{1}{2}$ tsp tarragon

3 tbls parsley
4 eggs
$\frac{1}{2}$ cup milk
1 tsp salt
$\frac{1}{2}$ tsp pepper
$\frac{1}{2}$ cup parmesan cheese, grated

Sauté onions and mushrooms in butter for 5 minutes. Stir in spinach, garlic, tarragon and parsley. Simmer, constantly stirring until liquid evaporates. Beat eggs with milk, salt and pepper and add cheese. Combine with sautéed vegetables and pour into a lightly buttered flan dish. Bake in Gas No.2, 300°F, 160°C for 35 minutes or until a knife inserted in centre comes out clean. Cut in wedges and serve.

Microwave instructions
In a suitable flan dish sauté onions in the butter on full power for 2 minutes, stir in spinich, garlic, tarragon and parsley and simmer on power level 6 until liquid evaporates stirring after each minute. Beat the eggs as above with the milk, salt, pepper, add the cheese and add the puréed vegetables. Pour into lightly buttered flan dish. Bake on full power for 3 minutes and then power level 7 for 5 minutes.

TAHINA STARTER Gillian Burr

Serves 4–6   Preparation 10 mins.   Advance

2 cloves of garlic, crushed
¼ pt tahina paste (140ml)
2 tbls parsley, chopped
Water
Juice of 1½–2 lemons

Salt
1 tsp olive oil

GARNISH: A little chopped parsley

TO SERVE: Pitta bread

Place the garlic in a mixing bowl, add the juice of ½ lemon and beat in the tahina with a wooden spoon. Gradually add the juice of 1 lemon stirring all the time. Add 2 tbls cold water slowly beating the mixture until it forms a thick cream, add as much water as you need to achieve this. Stir in the chopped parsley and season with salt. Serve with some extra chopped parsley on top and trickle over a little olive oil. Serve with warm pitta bread.

TAPENADE Helen Meller

Serves 4–6   Preparation 15 mins.   Advance

4oz black olives (115gm)
10–12 tinned anchovy fillets, drained
3 tbls capers
8 tbls olive oil

2 tbls brandy
1 tbl lemon juice (optional)
Pepper (optional)

Stone the olives and put into blender with anchovies and capers. Blend and slowly add the olive oil. Add brandy. Taste to see if you would like to add lemon juice and pepper. Serve with toast, hard boiled eggs or use just as you would a dip. Will keep in a fridge in covered jars.

MOROCCAN TCHOUKTCHOUKA Peduth Emanuel

Serves 6–8   Preparation 45 mins.   Cook 45 mins.   Advance   Freezable

4 green peppers
24oz tin tomatoes, drained and
   chopped (675gm)
1 tsp garlic powder

2 tsp sugar
½ cup vegetable oil
Salt to taste

Grill peppers until skin turns black, remove skin and discard seeds. Cut up in small pieces and put in a saucepan with tomatoes. Add sugar, garlic and salt to taste. Cook on a high light for 30 minutes, stirring very often. Add oil and cook for a further 10–15 minutes. The longer you cook it the better it tastes.

POMMES D'AMOUR
Sybil Sinclair

Serves 4   Preparation 15 mins.   Cook 15 mins

8 tomatoes, skinned and quartered
1 tsp caster sugar
Salt and pepper

1½oz Parmesan cheese, grated (40gm)
⅛ pt double cream (70ml)

GARNISH: parsley

Butter 4 individual ovenproof cocottes. Place 8 quarters of tomatoes in each dish. Sprinkle with sugar, pepper and cheese and add enough cream to cover. Bake in a fairly hot oven – Gas No.7, 425°F, 220°C. Decorate with parsley and serve immediately.

HUNGARIAN HOT STUFFED TOMATOES
Ruth Smilg

Serves 6   Preparation 30 mins.   Cook 15–20 mins.

6 firm medium tomatoes
½lb mushrooms, chopped (225gm)
2oz onions, chopped (55gm)
Margarine
Salt and pepper
Parsley

2 eggs
4oz breadcrumbs (115gm)
Grated cheese

TO SERVE: boiled rice and tomato sauce

Cut the tops off the tomatoes, scoop out insides. Fry onions until golden brown in the margarine, add mushrooms and fry well. Season with salt and pepper, add a little chopped parsley. Stir in the breadcrumbs, then the beaten eggs and cook until the mixture is solid.

Cool, form into balls and stuff the tomatoes. Place into a greased ovenproof dish, sprinkle with grated cheese and bake in a moderate oven for about 15–20 minutes. Serve on a bed of boiled rice with a tomato sauce.

SPICY STUFFED TOMATOES
Alexandra Martyn

Serves 4   Preparation 15 mins.

4 beef tomatoes
2 avocados
1 onion, finely chopped
½ chilli, finely chopped

3 drops Tabasco sauce
Salt
Pepper
Lemon juice

Cut the lids off the tomatoes and scoop out the flesh. Reserve. Peel and mash the avocados and sprinkle with lemon juice. Add onion and chilli to mashed avocado. Season with salt, pepper and Tabasco. Combine flesh of tomatoes with avocado mixture. Return mixture to tomato shells. Place lid back on each tomato and keep refrigerated until ready to serve.

39

VEGETABLE TARTLETS AND
MINT HOLLANDAISE SAUCE   Rosanna Burr

Serves 6   Preparation 15 mins.   Cook 15 mins   Advance: vegetables

14oz shortcrust pastry (400gm)

MINT HOLLANDAISE SAUCE

4 egg yolks
6oz boiling melted butter (170gm)
1 dsp lemon juice
Fresh mint (or fresh tarragon for a
   tarragon hollandaise)
Salt and pepper

VEGETABLES

Baby carrots, cut into tiny strips
Young haricots verts, cut into similar
   lengths
Little cauliflower florets

GARNISH: fresh mint/tarragon

Roll out the pastry on a floured board. Make 12 tartlets and bake blind until crisp. Cook each of the vegetables separately in salted boiling water. They must be crunchy. Keep them warm.

Hollandaise: Mix the eggs with the lemon juice, mint leaves, salt and pepper in a food processor and pour in the boiling butter with the machine running until the sauce is thick. Fill each warm tartlet with warm vegetables and pour over a little sauce. Serve the rest of the sauce around the tartlets. Decorate with some fresh mint.

VEGETABLE TERRINE
WITH TOMATO COULIS   Lisa Rose

Serves 6   Preparation 20 mins.   Cook 50 mins.   Refrigerate   Advance

4oz baby mangetouts (115gm)
4oz haricots verts (115gm)
4oz petit pois (115gm)
5 eggs
3oz cream cheese (85gm)
3oz Gruyère, grated (85gm)
Salt, pepper, nutmeg
1 tbls parsley, chopped

TOMATO COULIS

1lb fresh or tinned tomatoes (450gm)
Chopped herbs (thyme and oregano)
Salt and pepper
2oz butter (55gm)
9″ (23cm) terrine tin
Butter to grease terrine tin
Bakewell paper to line tin

Set oven at Gas No. 4, 350°F, 180°C. Grease and line the terrine tin. Clean and trim the vegetables and blanch them all separately in salted boiling water for a few minutes. Take out the vegetables and drain them on a clean towel. Beat the eggs with the seasoning and nutmeg, incorporate the cream cheese, Gruyère and parsley. Gradually layer the egg mixture with the vegetables in the Terrine tin until it is full. Cook in the bain marie for 40–50 minutes and leave to cool. Chill in the refrigerator, turn out the terrine and continue to keep it chilled.

Tomato Coulis: cook the tomatoes in the butter with the herbs and seasoning until soft, sieve or purée the tomatoes until smooth and then chill until needed.

To assemble: pour the sauce onto each plate. Cut 6 slices of terrine and place them in the centre of the sauce and decorate.

40

Soups

HINTS

Instead of adding cream to soup, thin a little Fromage Blanc with skimmed milk and swirl this over the top. Add a blob of yoghurt to garnish vegetable soups before serving.

Chicken soup with a difference: Purée the soup with the vegetables still in it.

Thick lentil soup served with wholewheat bread makes a meal in itself. A healthy lentil soup may be varied by the addition of a spoonful of curry powder and served with circles of lemon.

If you are very health conscious, don't fry the vegetables before adding stock.

You'll love it –
I'm doing Consommé
Tomate Farci – and
a Bombe Framboise!

41

(P) ALMOND AND FENNEL SOUP   Jane Jaffe

Serves 4   Preparation 10 mins.   Cook 30 mins.   Advance essential   Freezable
Refrigerate without cream

1 large head of fennel
1½ pts vegetable stock (0.85 litre)
Salt and pepper to taste

4oz whole blanched almonds (115gm)
½ pt single cream (225ml)

GARNISH: sour cream and toasted
flaked almonds

Wash fennel, cut into small pieces and cook with almonds in stock until tender. Purée. Chill for several hours. Before serving stir in single cream. Serve hot or cold.

ARTICHOKE SOUP   Joan Lipkin-Edwards

Serves 4–6   Preparation 25 mins.   Cook 20 mins.   Advance

¼lb butter or low fat
    margarine (115gm)
1½lbs Jerusalem artichokes, sliced
    thickly (675gm)
1 sweet potato, sliced thickly
    (optional)
3 onions, chopped

½ – 1 pt milk (280ml–560ml)
Vegetable stock cube
Salt and pepper
Ground nutmeg (optional)

GARNISH: chopped chives or
    parsley or fresh coriander leaves

Melt butter. Add artichokes, sweet potato and onion and cook gently. When softened add stock cube and enough boiling water to cover. Add milk. Do not bring to boil. Liquidise thoroughly, reheat and serve in soup plates in preference to bowls. Decorate.

(♥) JERUSALEM ARTICHOKE SOUP   Gillian Carmel

Serves 4   Preparation 10 mins.   Cook 45 mins.   Advance   Freezable

1lb Jerusalem artichokes, roughly
    chopped (450gm)
3 medium onions, roughly chopped
1 small carrot, sliced
1 tbls oil

1½ pts parev chicken stock (850ml)
Salt and pepper to taste

GARNISH: 2 tbls parsley, chopped

Sauté the vegetables in the oil, stirring frequently, until they begin to soften, about 10–15 minutes. Cover with stock and cook gently until vegetables are really soft, about 20 minutes. Purée. Add seasoning and when serving add the chopped parsley.

ASPARAGUS AND ORANGE BROTH   David Burr

Serves 4   Preparation 10 mins.   Cook 20–30 mins.

8 oz fresh asparagus, scraped and cut   2 pts vegetable stock (1.1 litres)
   into chunks (225 gm)   ½ cucumber
2 small oranges

Put the stock in a saucepan, bring to the boil, add the asparagus pieces. Cook for 20 minutes, stirring frequently, each time pressing the asparagus against the sides of the pan. Wash the cucumber; setting aside 4 slices and chopping the rest into pieces 1″ (2.5 cm) thick. Cut the oranges in half and squeeze the juice from 3 of the halves. Slice the remaining half into 4 and put one orange slice and one cucumber slice into each soup bowl. Remove the soup from the heat, add the orange juice and cucumber pieces and serve right away.

AVGOLEMONO   Marian Warshaw

Serves 4   Preparation 5 mins.   Cook 30 mins   Advance

2 pts chicken stock (1.1 litres)   2 oz long grain rice (55 gm)
3 fl oz lemon juice (85 ml)   2 eggs
Salt   Freshly ground black pepper

Place rice in saucepan, add stock and bring to boil over a medium heat. Stir once and cover. Lower heat and simmer for 20 minutes.

In a bowl beat the lemon juice and eggs together, then add a few spoons of the hot stock and mix well. Add this mixture to the saucepan and stir whilst reheating gently. DO NOT ALLOW THE SOUP TO BOIL OR IT WILL CURDLE. Adjust seasoning and serve immediately.

AVOCADO
AND APPLE SOUP   Michael Zimmerman

Serves 4   Preparation 10 mins.   Cook 10 mins.

2 ripe avocados   1 small dsp apple, chopped
½ pt parev chicken stock (280 ml)   5 fl oz cream (140 ml)
½ pt apple juice (280 ml)   2 tbls parsley, chopped
2 tbls lemon juice   Salt and pepper to taste

Blend all the ingredients except cream and parsley until smooth. Pour into saucepan and simmer for 10 minutes. Stir in cream and parsley just before serving.

Total calories per portion 340

BEANSPROUT SOUP   Jill Summers

Serves 4   Preparation 15 mins.   Cook 40 mins.   Advance   Freezable

10oz beansprouts (280gm)
½ lettuce, shredded
2 onions, chopped
Salt and pepper to taste

1 tbls olive oil
1 pt strong vegetable/chicken
  stock (570ml)

GARNISH: chopped parsley or chives

Heat the oil in a saucepan on a low heat; add the onions, lettuce and beansprouts, and season to taste. Cover the pan and leave the vegetables to sweat for 15 minutes. Add the stock and simmer for a further 20 minutes. Liquidise. Reheat gently when required. Garnish.

Microwave instructions

Put oil and vegetables into a large bowl and microwave on high for 3 minutes, stirring once. Add the liquid, cover with clingfilm and microwave on high for 6 minutes, stirring once or twice. Liquidise.

BROCCOLI SOUP   Jennifer Davis

Serves 4–6   Preparation 5 mins.   Cook 30 mins.   Advance   Freezable

1lb thin stemmed broccoli (450gm)
2oz butter (55gm)
Salt and pepper

1 large onion, thinly sliced
2½ pts water (1.4 litres)

Sweat the onion gently in the butter in a covered saucepan until soft but not coloured. Add broccoli cut up and cook until wilted. Add water and bring to boil. Cover and simmer gently until vegetables are soft. Liquidise, then return to saucepan. Season to taste, heat and serve. This is a very simple soup, but has a good rich taste without the addition of stock or cream.

BRUSSELS SOUP   Pam Goodman

Serves 4   Preparation 20 mins.   Cook 20 mins.   Advance   Freezable before *

1lb sprouts (450gm)
1oz butter or margarine (30gm)
½oz flour (15gm)
1½ pts parev chicken stock (850ml)

1 egg yolk
¼ pt single cream (140ml)
Salt and pepper
Grated nutmeg

Prepare sprouts in usual way and cook in boiling salted water until just tender. Drain thoroughly. Melt butter in heavy saucepan and toss sprouts over gentle heat, sprinkle in flour and gradually blend in hot stock stirring continuously. Cook gently until sprouts are quite soft. Liquidise. * Beat egg with cream and blend into the soup. Season with salt, pepper and nutmeg.

The egg yolk and cream may be omitted or replaced with low fat yoghurt if a less rich soup is required.

CARROT AND CASHEW NUT SOUP   Gillian Burr

Serves 6   Preparation 10 mins.   Cook 35 mins.   Advance   Freezable

1 lb carrots (450 gm)
1 large cooking apple, chopped
2 oz butter or margarine (55 gm)
Salt and pepper to taste

1 large onion, chopped
1 small potato, chopped
2 pts vegetable stock (1.1 litres)
2 oz broken cashew nuts (55 gm)

Chop the apple and vegetables. Melt the butter in a saucepan and sweat the vegetables in it for 5 minutes stirring occasionally. Add the rest of the ingredients except for the nuts, bring to the boil and simmer for approx. 30 minutes until the vegetables are tender, adding the nuts after 20 minutes. Allow the soup to cool a little and then semi-liquidise.

    ## CARROT AND LEEK SOUP   Eileen Brecker

Serves 8–10   Preparation 10 mins.   Cook 20 mins.   Advance   Freezable

1½ large carrots
4 large leeks, white parts only
1 medium potato
1 clove garlic, crushed
1 medium onion

5 oz tin tomato purée (140 gm)
14 oz peeled tomatoes (400 gm)
3 chicken stock cubes
3 pts boiling water (1.70 litres)
Salt and black pepper

GARNISH: chives or parsley

Wash and scrape carrots and cut in half. Peel onion and potato and cut into medium sized pieces. Wash the leeks and cut into pieces. Dissolve chicken cubes in water, add all ingredients and simmer for 20 minutes. Cool. Liquidise. Season to taste and reheat when required and garnish. Soup tastes better the following day.

CAULIFLOWER SOUP   Miki Hildebrand

Serves 8–10   Preparation 15 mins.   Cook 45 mins.   Advance   Freezable

1 lb raw cauliflower, chopped (450 gm)
1 large potato, peeled and chopped
8 oz onion, chopped (225 gm)
8 oz leek, chopped (225 gm)
8 oz celery, chopped (225 gm)
1 bouquet garni

4 oz butter (115 gm)
2 oz flour (55 gm)
2 pts vegetable stock (1.14 lt)
2 pts skimmed milk (1.14 lt)
Salt and black pepper to taste

GARNISH: croûtons

Melt butter in a large saucepan, add vegetables, cover with lid and sweat until vegetables are fairly soft, about 10 minutes. Stir in flour and cook for another 5 minutes. Add bouquet garni, stock and milk and simmer covered for 30 minutes, stirring occasionally. Liquidise and season to taste. Serve garnished with croûtons.

HARLEQUIN CHEESE SOUP Anna Cohen

Serves 4–6 Preparation 10 mins. Advance

1 lb cottage cheese (450 gm)
1 pt low fat yoghurt (560 ml)
1–2 tomatoes, skinned and diced
1 small red pepper, finely chopped

2 tbls parsley, chopped
2 tbls chives, chopped
1 small leek or 2–3 spring onions,
 finely chopped
Salt and pepper to taste

Either rub the cheese through a sieve or put into a liquidiser or food processor. Add the yoghurt and beat or liquidise until smooth. Add salt and pepper. Pour all the vegetable ingredients into the soup and chill.

Variations: A little finely grated lemon rind and juice may be added if desired. If you prefer this soup hot, put into the top of a double saucepan or over a basin of boiling water, then heat gently.

Low calorie

CHESTNUT AND SHERRY SOUP Gillian Burr

Serves 8 Preparation 10 mins. Cook 15 mins. Advance

15 oz chestnut purée,
 unsweetened (425 gm)
1 large onion, finely chopped
2 oz butter (55 gm)
Medium sweet sherry to taste
Salt, pepper and nutmeg

$1\frac{3}{4}$ pt strong parev chicken
 stock (1 litre)
$\frac{1}{2}$ pt single cream (280 ml)

GARNISH: 8 slices of lemon
 8 sprigs of parsley

Sauté the onions in the butter over medium heat until transparent but do not brown them. Stir in the chestnut purée, a spoonful at a time. Gradually add the stock, sherry and seasoning, simmer gently for 10–15 minutes. Liquidise the soup until smooth, stir in the cream and reheat the soup. Serve decorated with the slices of lemon and parsley.

CORN CHOWDER

Gillian Burr

Serves 4–6   Preparation 10 mins.   Cook 35 mins.   Advance   Freezable

1 oz butter or margarine (30 gm)
1 medium onion, finely chopped
1 green pepper, white pith removed, chopped
1 tbls flour
2 medium potatoes, chopped and parboiled
1 lb canned sweetcorn, drained (450 gm)

8 fl oz light vegetable stock (225 ml)
10 fl oz milk (280 ml)
4 oz mushrooms, wiped clean and sliced (115 gm)
$\frac{1}{2}$ tsp white pepper
1 tsp salt
8 fl oz double cream (225 ml)

In a small frying pan, melt the butter or margarine over a moderate heat. When the foam subsides, add the onion and green pepper. Cook, stirring occasionally, for 5 minutes, or until the onion is soft and translucent but not brown. Remove the frying pan from the heat. With a wooden spoon, stir in the flour and make a smooth paste. Set the pan aside. Place the potatoes, sweetcorn, stock and milk in a large saucepan over moderate heat, bring the mixture to the boil, stirring occasionally. Pour a little of the liquid into the onion, green pepper and flour mixture. Stir to form a smooth, thick liquid and stir this into the potato mixture. Add the mushrooms. Cover the saucepan, reduce the heat to very low and simmer the chowder for 15–20 minutes. Season with the salt and pepper and add the cream, stirring to blend it thoroughly into the mixture. Heat for a further 2 minutes over very low heat. Serve immediately.

 ## COURGETTE SOUP

Peduth Emanuel

Serves 8–10   Preparation 10 mins.   Advance   Freezable

2 medium onions, sliced
2 lb courgettes, sliced (900 gm)
1 tbls flour
1 tbls parsley

2 tbls oil or margarine
3 tbls parev chicken stock powder
Salt and pepper to taste

GARNISH: croûtons

Boil the courgettes in 4 pts (2.3 lt) of water until soft, then stir in the stock powder. Sauté the onions in the fat until brown, stir in the flour and parsley, add courgettes and water and cook until soft. Liquidise, season to taste and serve with croûtons.

Ⓟ☺ COURGETTE AND LETTUCE SOUP   Penny Leibu

Serves 6   Preparation 10 mins.   Cook 30 mins.   Advance   Freezable

2 lb courgettes, sliced (900 gm)
1½ pt chicken stock (850 ml)
2 tbls corn oil

2 round lettuces, shredded
Salt
Freshly ground black pepper

Sauté courgettes in oil until soft, add lettuce with chicken stock. Season to taste.
Bring to boil and simmer for 20 minutes. Liquidise. Serve hot.

CUCUMBER AND SORREL SOUP   Ruth Starr

Serves 4–6   Preparation 10 mins.   Cook 40 mins.   Advance   Freezable

1 large cucumber, peeled and diced
1 small onion, finely chopped
8 oz peeled and cubed potatoes (225 gm)
1 tsp fresh or ½ tsp dried tarragon or dill
1½ pt light parev chicken stock (850 ml)

1 tsp white vinegar
¼ pt cream (150 ml)
A good handful of sorrel, finely
   shredded
A little cream
Salt and pepper

Place the cucumber (retaining some for garnish), onion and potatoes in a pan with the
tarragon, stock and vinegar, season lightly and simmer for 20–30 minutes until the
potato is cooked. Purée until very smooth in the liquidiser or food processor and
sieve. Put the cream and sorrel in a non-aluminium saucepan (sorrel reacts with
aluminium) and simmer for a few minutes until the sorrel is tender but still in strips.
Stir the sorrel and cream into the soup, correct the seasoning and serve hot (or chill to
serve cold) with a swirl of cream and a sprinkling of tiny cucumber pieces.

GAZPACHO   Marion Warshaw

Serves 4   Preparation 20 mins.   Refrigerate 3 hours   Advance

½ lb ripe tomatoes, skinned, deseeded
   and chopped (225 gm)
1 large spanish onion, chopped
1 clove of garlic, crushed
1 large green/red pepper, deseeded
   and chopped

2 oz fresh white breadcrumbs soaked
   in 1 tbls wine vinegar
2 tbls olive oil
Salt and freshly ground black pepper

GARNISH: croûtons, diced green
   pepper, cucumber, tomatoes and
   spring onions

Liquidise all vegetables with soaked breadcrumbs. Pour into large bowl and beat in
the olive oil and enough water to make the soup fairly runny. Season to taste. Chill for
3 hours and serve with the accompaniments listed above.

QUICK GAZPACHO   Jean Simmonds

Serves 4–6   Preparation 15 mins.   Advance   Refrigerate

14oz tin of tomatoes (400gm)
19oz tin tomato juice (535gm)
3 tbls olive oil
3 tbls wine vinegar
1 clove garlic, crushed

½ green pepper, finely chopped
½ cucumber, finely chopped
1 onion, finely chopped
Salt and pepper to taste

GARNISH: croûtons and diced vegetables

Liquidise tomatoes and add olive oil, vinegar and garlic. Place half the cucumber pepper and onion in blender for a few seconds. Add tomato juice. Season to taste. Refrigerate for one hour. Optional: ½ pt (284ml) double cream added just before serving. Serve garnished with diced vegetables and croûtons.

LEEK, COURGETTE AND WATERCRESS SOUP   Gillian Burr

Serves 8   Preparation 20 mins.   Cook 35 mins.   Advance   Freezable

2 medium leeks, chopped (white parts only
4 medium courgettes, thickly sliced
1 tbls unsalted margarine

1 bunch watercress
1 tbls olive oil
5½ cups light chicken stock
Salt and freshly ground black pepper

GARNISH: watercress

Place the courgettes in a sieve and sprinkle with salt. Leave for 15 minutes. Remove and discard bottom half of watercress stems, wash and spin dry. Reserve a few of the stems for garnish. Heat oil and margarine in a saucepan and then sauté the leeks until they are transparent. Add the courgettes and sauté for a few more minutes. Add 5 cups chicken stock and bring to the boil, reduce the heat and continue cooking covered until the courgettes are soft approx. 10 minutes. Add watercress and again let the soup come to the boil before reducing heat. Cook until the watercress has wilted with the saucepan uncovered. Allow to cool a little and then purée. Pour the purée through a sieve into a bowl, using a large wooden spoon to push through most of the solids. Return to heat and adjust consistency with the remaining stock. Season. Serve this soup piping hot, garnished with the reserved watercress leaves.

LEEK AND POTATO SOUP   Beatrice Lipman

Serves 6   Preparation 15–20 mins.   Cook 20 mins.   Advance   Freezable

2 large leeks, finely chopped
1 lb potatoes, roughly
    chopped (450gm)

1½oz butter or margarine (45gm)
2 pts chicken stock 1.14 litres)
Salt and black pepper

Cook leeks in 1oz (30gm) butter in a large pan until soft but not coloured. Add potatoes and stock. Season lightly with the salt and pepper. Bring to boil and simmer until potatoes are quite tender. Remove soup from heat and allow to cool slightly. Sieve or liquidise. Before serving, reheat the puréed soup, adjust seasoning and stir in remaining butter.

 # LENTIL SOUP   Sylvia Owide

Serves 6   Preparation 15 mins.   Cook 30–45 mins.   Advance   Freezable

4oz red lentils (115gm)
1 large Spanish onion, sliced
1 lb carrots, finely sliced (450gm)
1 tbls vegetable oil

2 pts chicken or vegetable
    stock (1.14 litres)
Salt and pepper
Milk (optional)

In a blender, grind the lentils to a pulp. In a large saucepan heat the oil and sweat the onion in it until translucent. Add carrots and lentils with the stock. Stir. Bring to boil stirring occasionally, season to taste and simmer for 30–40 minutes until carrots are quite soft. Cool a little and then liquidise. When reheating soup a little milk may be added for extra creaminess.

MUSHROOM SOUP   Marion Cohen

Serves 6   Preparation 15 mins.   Cook 30–40 mins.   Advance   Freezable

2 large sprigs parsley, finely
    chopped
2 onions, chopped
2½oz butter or margarine (70gm)
1½oz flour (42gm)
2½ pt parev chicken stock (1.25
    litres)

¾lb firm button mushrooms, finely
    sliced (340gm)
1 tsp lemon juice
Salt and pepper to taste.

OPTIONAL: 2 egg yolks
    ¼ pt single cream (140ml)

Melt half the butter and cook onions until soft. Stir in flour and gradually add the stock until it thickens. Add chopped mushroom stalks to the soup. Meanwhile sauté the sliced mushroom caps in remaining butter and lemon juice and add to the soup. Season and add parsley. Beat egg yolks and cream together and add to the soup stirring constantly before serving but do not boil.

PARSNIP SOUP   Laura Phillips

Serves 4–6   Preparation 15 mins.   Cook 20 mins.   Advance preferable
                                                            Freezable (without yoghurt)

1 medium onion, chopped   Milk
2oz butter (55gm)   Salt
1lb parsnips, peeled and   Pinch white pepper
   chopped (450gm)   Pinch ground ginger
Water

                                     GARNISH: freshly chopped parsley
                                              Greek yoghurt

Place butter in large soup pan, melt over gentle heat. Add onion. Sweat until soft, not brown (about 10 minutes). Add parsnips, stir well. Cover with water and simmer for approx 20 minutes, until parsnips are very soft. Blend in liquidiser or force through a sieve. Return to pan, season to taste. Add milk to thin, if required. Serve with a dessertspoon of plain Greek yoghurt and a pinch of parsley for each bowl. A sprinkling of grated cheese can also be added to each bowl if desired.

PARSNIP AND CURRY
SOUP   Madeleine Cope-Thompson

Serves 6   Preparation 10 mins.   Cook 30 mins.

2 medium parsnips, sliced   A little oil
1 medium onion, chopped   2 tbls flour
2oz butter or margarine (55gm)   Salt and pepper to taste
1 tsp curry powder   Cream (optional)
2 pt chicken or vegetable stock (1.14 litres)

Melt fat and oil together and fry parsnips and onions for 10 minutes. Add the curry powder and flour and stir in thoroughly. Add the stock slowly, stirring constantly and bring to the boil. Season to taste and simmer for 30 minutes. Liquidise when cool. Reheat to serve, adding 3 tbsp of cream if desired.

 PASTA FAGIOLI SOUP   Maria Leoni

Serves 4   Preparation 10 mins.   Cook 40–45 mins.   Advance (without pasta)

14oz tin cannelini beans in salt $\frac{1}{2}$lb small pasta (225gm)
   water (400gm) $\frac{1}{2}$ clove garlic, crushed
8$\frac{1}{2}$oz crushed tomatoes (230gm)   Salt and pepper
1 dsp tomato purée   1 pt boiling water (560ml)
1 small onion, chopped finely

Sauté onions in oil, add tomatoes, purée and garlic and simmer for 10 minutes. Add water, season and simmer for 30 minutes. Cook pasta separately as per packet instructions. When partially cooked, drain the pasta and add it to the soup with remaining liquid. Add drained and rinsed beans and reheat.

CREME ST. GERMAIN   Gillian Burr

Serves 4–6 Preparation 5 mins. Cook 25 mins. Advance Freezable without cream

1½ oz butter (42gm)
1 small onion, chopped
6 iceberg lettuce leaves, shredded
1 lb fresh or frozen peas (450gm)
1 pt boiling water (570ml)

1 tsp sugar
2 tsp cornflour
Salt and pepper
¼ pt double cream (140ml)

GARNISH: a few frosted mint leaves or finely chopped mint

Melt butter in pan and soften onion in it. Stir in lettuce and peas for 2–3 minutes until lettuce has collapsed. Add water (and sugar only if using fresh peas) and bring to boil. Cover the pan and simmer for 12 minutes until peas are tender (frozen peas will probably take less time). Blend the contents of the pan and sieve it. Return the soup to the saucepan and add cornflour mixed with a little water and cook stirring occasionally until the soup has thickened. Adjust seasoning. Remove soup from heat and allow to cool a little. Then add cream. Decorate with mint leaves. Serve hot or cold.

PEAR VICHYSSOISE   Marion Cohen

Serves 6   Preparation 10 mins   Cook 20 mins.   Advance

3 ripe juicy pears, peeled and diced
  into a little lemon juice
2 leeks (white part only), chopped
1 pt parev chicken stock (560ml)

1 pt single cream (560ml)
½ small onion, finely chopped
Salt, pepper and nutmeg
2 oz butter (55gm)

GARNISH: chopped chives

Gently sauté the onion in the butter with the leeks. Do not brown them. Pour over the stock and simmer for 20 minutes. Cool the soup and liquidise the stock with the pears and cream. Season according to taste and chill until ready to serve. Decorate with chopped chives.

GREEN PEPPER SOUP   Gloria Goldring

Serves 6–8   Preparation 20 mins.   Cook 30 mins.   Advance   Freezable

4 large green peppers, deseeded and
  quartered
1 large onion, chopped
1 oz butter (30gm)
1 pt chicken or vegetable
  stock (570ml)

WHITE SAUCE
1 pt milk (570ml)
1 oz beurre manié (30gm)
Salt, pepper and nutmeg to taste
Juice of ½ lemon

Reserve one piece of pepper. Sauté the rest of peppers in butter with the onion in a covered pan until soft without browning. Blend in liquidiser with a little stock until puréed. Return to pan with rest of stock. Bring gently to boil and simmer for 10 minutes. In a separate pan heat milk to boiling point and whisk in beurre manié. Season well, leave to simmer gently until thickened. Whisk in the pepper purée. Before serving, chop reserved piece of pepper and add to soup with lemon juice.

QUICK PISTOU SOUP

I wish I knew!

Serves 6–8 **Preparation 25 mins.** **Cook 30 mins.**

3 tbls olive oil
1 large Spanish onion, chopped
3 leeks, sliced
3 celery stalks, chopped
3 carrots, sliced
2 medium potatoes, cubed
1 small cabbage, sliced
8 oz French beans, topped and
   tailed (225 gm)
2½ pt water (1.4 litres)

8 oz tomatoes, finely chopped (225 gm)
10 oz tin white cannelini beans (400 gm)
12 oz courgettes, thickly sliced (340 gm)

PISTOU

4 large cloves garlic
12 or more basil leaves, fresh if possible
3 tbls grated parmesan
½ cup olive oil

Liquidise all Pistou ingredients together. Sweat vegetables in order. After the French beans add water and when the vegetables are nearly soft add the courgettes, tomatoes and tinned beans. Cook for 10 minutes then add the Pistou. Serve extra cheese with soup if required.

This is a peasant dish and vegetables may be varied to suit those available.

SPINACH SOUP

Jacqueline Barnett

Serves 4 Preparation 30 mins. Cook 25 mins. Advance Freezable without milk

1 oz butter or margarine (30 gm)
1 small onion, chopped
1 tbls cornflour
¾ pt parev chicken stock (425 ml)

8 oz chopped frozen spinach (225 gm)
4 fl oz milk (115 ml)
Salt and pepper to taste

GARNISH: 4 tbls single cream (optional)

Melt the butter and add the onion. Cook until golden but not brown. Stir in the cornflour and cook for 1 minute, constantly stirring. Gradually stir in the stock, salt and pepper to taste and frozen spinach and simmer with the lid on until the spinach has melted. Purée. Add milk. Gently reheat. Do not allow to boil.

CREAM OF SPINACH
AND COURGETTE SOUP   Nanette Stolerman

Serves 4–6   Preparation 20 mins.   Cook 30 mins.   Advance   Freezable

1 medium onion, chopped
2 large courgettes, chopped
2 medium potatoes, chopped
4oz spinach, chopped (115gm)
1 dsp oil

A few sprigs of parsley
2 pt vegetable stock (1.14 litres)
Salt and pepper to taste

GARNISH: a swirl of cream

Heat oil in a saucepan and sauté onion and courgette until the onion is transparent. Add potatoes and spinach, parsley and stock. Bring to the boil, reduce heat, cover and simmer for 20 minutes. Blend when cool. Reheat gently, season and garnish with cream.

   TOMATO SOUP   Jean Simmonds

Serves 6–8   Preparation 15 mins.   Cook 30 mins.   Advance   Freezable

2lb fresh tomatoes, peeled and
    chopped (900gm)
1 onion, chopped
1 leek, sliced
1 dsp sugar

1 dsp corn oil
2 pt vegetable stock (1.14 litres)
Seasoning to taste

GARNISH: parsley, oregano or basil
    (optional)

Sauté onion in oil. Do not allow to dry out. Add stock, tomatoes and sliced leek. Season. Simmer for 30 minutes, liquidise for 1 minute and strain if desired. Reheat before serving. Sprinkle with herbs.

TOMATO AND PRUNE SOUP   Miki Hildebrand

Serves 4–6   Preparation 10 mins.   Cook 30 mins.   Advance preferable   Freezable

2 onions, chopped
2lb ripe tomatoes, quartered (900gm)
1 tbls olive oil
12 prunes, ready to eat
2 tsp sea salt

1 tsp brown sugar
1 tbls tomato purée
1½ pt parev beef stock (850ml)
3 tbls brown rice
Black pepper

Heat oil in saucepan. Add onions and soften but do not brown. Add tomatoes, cover with lid and sweat for 5 minutes. Now add prunes, salt and pepper, stock, purée and sugar. Bring to boil and simmer for 20 minutes. Meanwhile cook rice in separate pan. Remove prunes from soup and liquidise. Return them to soup. Check seasoning and add a little rice to each bowl before serving. This soup tastes better if made the day before.

VEGETABLE SOUP I
Anita Rapp

Serves 6–8   Preparation 5 mins.   Cook 20 mins.   Advance   Freezable

1 lb courgettes (450 gm)
1 medium onion, chopped
12 oz frozen peas (340 gm)
1½ pt water (850 ml)
1 tbls parev chicken stock

1 oz butter or margarine (30 gm)
2 tbls dried milk
1 tsp dried tarragon or basil
Salt and pepper to taste

Sweat onion and vegetables in the butter, add the water and stock powder and cook until soft. Add the herbs and dried milk and liquidise.

VEGETABLE SOUP II
Cherry Faulkner

Serves 6–8   Preparation 15 mins.   Cook 1¾ hours   Advance   Freezable

1 medium swede, chopped
1 medium turnip, chopped
4 carrots, chopped
4 leeks, sliced
4 courgettes, sliced

2 pts water or stock (1.14 litres)
14 oz tin tomatoes (400 gm)
Parsley
3 tbls pearl barley
1 oz butter (30 gm)
Salt and pepper to taste

GARNISH: chopped parsley

Sweat the vegetables in the butter for about 15 minutes. Add the rest of the ingredients and bring to the boil. Season to taste and cook for about 1½ hours. Blend in liquidiser to desired consistency. Garnish with some chopped parsley.

WALNUT SOUP
Barbara Jane Scott

Serves 4 Preparation 15 mins. Cook 30 mins. Advance (before cream) Freezable

2 oz walnuts, shelled (55 gm)
1 medium onion, finely chopped
2 sticks celery, finely chopped
2 tbls vegetable oil
1 oz walnut butter or nut fat (30 gm)
1 oz flour (30 gm)
1¼ pt milk and water (750 ml)

1 level tsp curry powder
1 level tsp salt
½ level tsp pepper
1 egg yolk
2 tbls cold milk

GARNISH: chopped chives or paprika, cubes of fried bread

Blanch walnuts for 1 minute in boiling water and remove as much brown skin as possible. Mince, liquidise or process them. Gently fry onion and celery in oil and fat until pale yellow. Add flour, hot milk and water. Stir and cook until thick. Add walnuts, curry powder, salt and pepper. Simmer covered, for 5 to 10 minutes. Pour into a soup tureen or casserole. Mix cream, yolk and cold milk together and pour into the hot soup. Garnish with chives or paprika. Serve with cubes of fried bread.

Fish

Take three glasses wine and lay on shallow tray before poaching?

HINTS

Some cultures believe fish to have magical properties and certain Middle Eastern Jews believe fish to be a sign of fertility.

White fish is very low in fats and very high in protein.

A Polish way to make Gefilte fish: add a drop of Kiddush wine with the ground almonds.

BRILL BRILL

Sara Raiher

Serves 4 **Preparation 10 mins.** **Cook 10–15 mins.** Microwave

1 brill, filleted into 4 pieces
Fresh breadcrumbs
2 oz butter, melted (55 gm)
2 tbls dry vermouth
1 tbls cream (optional)

Milk
Parsley
Juice of ½ lemon
2 shallots, chopped finely

Dip fillets in milk and then in breadcrumbs to coat. Grease an ovenproof dish with melted butter. Add the lemon juice, chopped parsley and shallots then place fillets on top. Dribble the vermouth around the edges of the dish. Sprinkle the melted butter on top. Cook on Gas No.7, 425°F, 220°C.

When cooked place fish on a warm plate. Pour the remaining liquor into a saucepan and whisk in a little more butter and cream. Pour over fish.

Microwave instructions

Prepare fish etc. as above. Microwave on full power for 7 minutes and leave in warm dish. Make sauce as above.

COD AND ORANGE SALAD

Simone Ross

Serves 4 **Preparation 15 mins.** **Cook 10 mins.**

4 cod cutlets
1 oz butter (30 gm)
1 oz breadcrumbs (30 gm)
1 tbls oil
Salt and pepper

1 oz cheese, grated (30 gm)
3 small oranges
1 tsp lemon juice

GARNISH: 1 bunch of watercress

Wipe the fish and season well. Dot with half the butter and grill for 5 minutes. Mix the breadcrumbs and the cheese together. Turn the cutlets and cover with the cheese mixture; dot with the remaining butter and grill for another 5 minutes. Meanwhile peel the oranges, cut them into thin slices and turn them in the oil and lemon juice. Arrange cutlets on a platter, drain the orange slices and place them on top of the fish. Garnish with the watercress.

Microwave instructions

Place the cutlets in a microwave dish and dot with a little butter, cook on full power for 3 minutes, turn over and coat with the cheese mixture as above. Cook for a further 3 minutes on full power. Follow the instructions above to finish the dish.

COD PROVENÇAL
Bobbie Tarn

Serves 4–5   Preparation 10 mins.   Marinate 10 mins.   Cook 35 mins.

$1\frac{1}{2}$ lbs cod, skinned and filleted (675 gm)
1 medium onion, chopped
1 clove garlic, crushed
1 bay leaf
3 tbls white wine
1 tsp sugar
Salt

14 oz tin crushed tomatoes (400 gm)
Oregano
10 grinds black pepper
1 oz butter (30 gm)
1 tsp oil

GARNISH: chopped parsley

Put fish into a shallow dish and pour the wine over, leave to marinate for 10 minutes. Cook the onion in the butter and oil in a covered pan until soft and golden. Add the crushed garlic and the wine drained from the fish. Allow the mixture to bubble for 2 minutes, then add the tomatoes, bay leaf, oregano, sugar, salt and pepper. Simmer for 5 minutes until slightly thickened, adding a little tomato purée if too pale in colour. Arrange the fish in a buttered ovenproof dish, pour on the hot sauce and cook on Gas No. 6, 400°F, 200°C for about 20–30 minutes. Just before serving sprinkle with chopped parsley.

BRAZILIAN COLD FISH
Angela Harding

Serves 6   Preparation 10 mins.   Cook 15 mins.   Marinate 24 hours

$2\frac{1}{4}$ lb filleted white fish
   (hake or cod etc.) (1 kg)
6 medium sized onions, sliced
4 tbls almonds or cashew nuts

GARNISH: parsley and black olives

MARINADE
$\frac{1}{2}$ cup white vinegar
1 cup salad oil
2 bay leaves
4 tbls sugar
2–3 cloves garlic, crushed
Paprika
Cayenne pepper
Salt and freshly ground black pepper

Steam fish in salted water. Remove and place in a dish. Blend together all marinade ingredients. Blanch the sliced onions. Pour the marinade over the fish and scatter the onions on top. Leave to marinate for 24 hours. Before serving roast the almonds or cashews and sprinkle these on top of the fish. Garnish with black olives and parsley.

CURRIED FISH

Ghita Tarn

Serves 4 **Preparation 10 mins.** **Cook 10–15 mins.**

8 fillets of sole
1 lb cooked long grain rice (450 gm)
14 oz tin pineapple chunks (400 gm)
2 oz sultanas (55 gm)

SAUCE
¾ cup vinegar
¾ cup water
2 bay leaves
10 peppercorns
2 tbls tomato sauce
2 tbls brown sugar
2 tbls mango chutney
2 dsp curry powder

Poach the fillets of sole in seasoned, simmering water for about 10 minutes. Boil all the sauce ingredients, together with the pineapple chunks and the sultanas, for about 10 minutes. Drain the fish and put on a warmed serving dish. Pour the sauce over and serve with the boiled rice.

FISH IN GINGER
AND SPRING ONION

Erika Crocker

Serves 4 **Preparation 10 mins.** **Cook 15–20 mins.**

2 lb fillet of white fish, bass, sole,
    lemon sole (900 gm)
Piece fresh ginger, finely chopped
Bunch spring onions, finely chopped

2 tbls soya sauce
6 tbls white wine
¼ lb mushrooms, sliced
    (optional) (115 gm)
1–2 oz butter (30–55 gm)

Lay fish fillets on buttered dish. Sprinkle the ginger and spring onions (and mushrooms if used) under and on top of fish. Pour soya sauce and wine over, and put a few knobs of butter on top. Bake on Gas No. 4, 350°F, 180°C, for 15–20 minutes. Serve with rice and mangetout or petit pois.

FISH HOT POT
Marian Goodisman

Serves 3–4   Preparation 10 mins.   Cook 25 mins.   Advance

1 tbls margarine
2 small onions, finely chopped
2 or 3 stalks celery, finely chopped
3 young carrots, finely chopped
1 lb cod fillets (450 gm)
Salt and pepper
1 bayleaf

10 black peppercorns
4 oz mushrooms, finely sliced (115 gm)
3 tbls milk
1 dsp parsley, chopped
½ lb frozen French beans (225 gm)
1 tbls water

Melt margarine in non-stick frying pan and fry onions, celery and carrots for 5–7
minutes until soft. Cut fish into 4 pieces and add to vegetables. Turn so that both sides
are coated with vegetables. Sprinkle with salt and pepper then add mushrooms and
enough hot water to cover the bottom of the pan. Add bayleaf and peppercorns.
Cover and simmer for 5 minutes. Turn fish and cook for another 5 minutes or until fish
looks creamy, and can be easily flaked with a fork. Add the milk and French beans,
cover and cook until they are tender, then stir in the parsley. Taste and re-season if
necessary. Serve hot with boiled or jacket potatoes.

 # ONE-PAN FISH SUPPER
Jo Luck

Serves 4   Preparation 15 mins.   Cook 15–20 mins.

4 cutlets of hake, haddock or cod
4 large old potatoes, thickly sliced
4 onions, thinly sliced
Salt and ground pepper

2 tbls parsley, chopped
Large knob of butter
Little water

In a large saucepan put layers of potato slices and onion. Lay the fish cutlets on top
and cover with the water and seasonings. Cover tightly with the lid and cook for 15–20
minutes. Using a slotted slice or spoon, remove the fish and vegetables to a warm
serving dish. Add the butter and parsley to the fish stock, heat until boiling again and
pour over the fish.

OVEN-BAKED FISH WITH
BUTTER AND MUSTARD SAUCE   Jennifer Davis

Serves 4   **Preparation 15 mins.**   **Cook 20 mins.**

3 shallots, finely chopped
$\frac{1}{4}$ pt dry white wine (140 ml)
$\frac{1}{4}$ pt water (140 ml)
1$\frac{1}{2}$ lb haddock or whiting fillets,
   skinned (675 gm)
Salt and pepper

3 tbls parsley, chopped
1–2 tbls Dijon mustard
4 oz cold butter (115 gm)
Few drops lemon juice

Set the oven at Gas No.6, 400°F, 200°C. Butter a shallow baking dish and put in shallots, wine and water. Rinse and dry the fillets (fold in half if necessary i.e. tail pieces of haddock or whiting, skin side inwards) and lay on top of shallots. Season with salt and pepper, sprinkle with parsley, cover with greaseproof paper and bake for 8–10 minutes or until flesh is no longer translucent. Drain the cooking liquid into a saucepan. Arrange fish on a platter, cover and keep warm. Boil cooking liquid for 5 minutes or until reduced by half. Remove from heat and whisk in mustard. Then, with pan sometimes over low heat sometimes off the fire, whisk in butter in small pieces so that it thickens sauce without melting and becoming oily. Add a few drops of lemon juice and taste for seasoning. Drain off any liquid that has escaped from fish. Coat with sauce and serve immediately.

  # BAKED FISH WITH PEPPERS   Faith Garfield

Serves 2   **Preparation 5 mins.**   **Cook 25 mins.**

1 lb haddock or cod fillet (450 gm)
$\frac{1}{4}$ red pepper, sliced lengthways
$\frac{1}{2}$ green pepper, sliced lengthways

4 spring onions, sliced lengthways
2–3 tomatoes, skinned and cubed
Freshly ground black pepper

Place fish in an ovenproof dish and spread the peppers and onions over the fish together with the tomatoes. Season to taste with black pepper and cover the dish with greased foil. Bake on Gas No.5, 375°F, 190°C.

Microwave instructions
Place the ingredients in a microwave dish, cover with clingfilm and cook on full power for 10 minutes.

FISH SALAD Jackie Slesenger

Serves 6–8   Preparation 10 mins.   Cook 15 mins.   Refrigerate

2 lb cod, skinned (middle cut) (900 gm)
3–4 pickled cucumbers, finely
  chopped
1 Spanish onion, finely chopped
3–4 tbls mayonnaise
1 tbls yoghurt (Greek or natural)

Salt and black pepper
Parsley
1 tbls oil
1 tbls vinegar

GARNISH: pickled cucumber and
       parsley

Steam fish with 1 tsp salt and sprig of parsley until it begins to flake. Drain well and remove all bones. Leave to cool. Flake into small bite-size pieces and mix gently with the cucumbers and onion. Add the oil and vinegar then season with salt and freshly ground black pepper. Bind all together with mayonnaise and yoghurt. The mixture should look like a heavy mousse. Arrange on a fish-shaped plate and decorate with extra slices of cucumber and parsley. Chill well before serving. Serve with salads or baked potatoes as a main course or with brown bread as a starter.

 FISH STEW CATALAN Audrey Jacobs

Serves 6   Preparation 10 mins.   Cook 30 mins.   Advance preferable

6 slices cod or haddock
½ pt tomato juice (285 ml)
14 oz tin tomatoes, chopped (400 gm)
2 garlic cloves, crushed
1 large onion, chopped
1 stick celery, chopped
1 tbls tomato purée
Juice of 1 lemon

2 sweeteners
2 tbls parsley, chopped
1 bay leaf
Salt
Freshly ground black pepper
Fish seasoning to taste

Place tomatoes, tomato juice, onion, celery, garlic, sweeteners, lemon juice, seasonings and bay leaf in saucepan. Bring to boil then simmer gently. Season fish lightly, add to saucepan, cover with the sauce. Place lid on pan and cook on top of stove or transfer to oven Gas No.4, 350°F, 180°C, and bake for about 20 minutes or until fish is tender. Remove from pan and top with parsley. Serve with any desired vegetables. The flavour improves if cooked a day in advance.

BAKED FISH WITH VEGETABLES Penny Leibu

Serves 4   Preparation 10 mins.   Cook 25–30 mins.   Advance   Freezable

1¼lb skinned and boned white fish
  fillet (haddock or cod etc.) (565gm)
Pepper to taste
12oz leeks, sliced (340gm)

12oz mushrooms, sliced (340gm)
½ pt parev chicken stock (285ml)
14oz tin chopped tomatoes (400gm)

OPTIONAL: 1 tsp dried tarragon or
  chervil

Spread half the vegetables on the base of an ovenproof casserole. Cover with the fish and top with remaining vegetables. Sprinkle with herbs if desired. Pour over chicken stock and add pepper to taste. Cover with foil and bake in Gas No.5, 375°F, 190°C for 25–30 minutes or until vegetables are tender and fish flakes easily with fork.

HADDOCK MONTE CARLO   Hazel Kaye

Serves 4   Preparation 25 mins.   Cook 10 mins.

1 large smoked haddock
2oz butter (55gm)
1 small onion, chopped
1 clove garlic, crushed
10oz tomatoes skinned, seeded and
  chopped (285gm)
3–4 fresh basil leaves, chopped

2 tbls thick cream
Fresh ground black pepper
Salt to taste
Milk

GARNISH: fresh basil leaves

Sweat onion until soft, add garlic, tomatoes and basil and cook gently, uncovered for about 10 minutes. Cook smoked haddock in milk until soft. Remove from liquid, flake fish onto oval gratin dish. Retain milk. Add cream and half a cup of the milk to the tomato sauce, reduce for a few minutes then pour over fish. Leave in a warm oven Gas No.2, 300°F, 150°C for about 10 minutes. Serve with fresh pasta, or creamed potatoes.

SWEDISH HALIBUT SALAD   Gill Fenner

Serves 6   Preparation 20 mins.   Cook 10 mins.   Advance

2lb cold poached halibut (900gm)
4 sharp eating apples
2 tbls butter
2 tbls cider
¼ pt sour cream (140ml)
Salt and pepper

2 tbls horseradish, grated
1 tbls prepared mustard
2 tbls lemon juice

GARNISH: 2 hard boiled eggs and
          fresh watercress

Flake halibut. Peel, core and slice apples thinly. Combine butter with cider in pan and sauté apple until soft. Put apple with pan juices through sieve, add sour cream, horseradish, mustard and lemon juice. Beat the mixture until foamy – add more cider if necessary. Toss the flaked fish in this dressing. Season. Place in glass bowl and decorate with chopped eggs and watercress.

63

HALIBUT CASSEROLE   Jean Simmonds

Serves 6–8   Preparation 30 mins.   Cook 25 mins.   Advance

1½lb halibut in 1" (2 cm)
  slices (675gm)
½lb mushrooms, sliced (225gm)
2oz butter or margarine (55gm)
Juice of one lemon

10fl oz sour cream (285ml)
2 tbls tomato ketchup
3 tbls cheese, finely grated
6–8 tomatoes, sliced
Ovenproof dish 2" (5 cm) deep

Wash and salt fish, drain for 10 minutes. Generously butter bottom and sides of dish. Lay fish slices in one layer in dish. Sprinkle each slice with salt and pepper, add small knob of butter on top. Sauté mushrooms until tender, add lemon juice. Arrange slices of tomato and mushrooms around dish, pack in tightly. Meanwhile add cream to bowl with pinch of salt and pepper, add tomato ketchup and add mixture to the fish. Top with grated cheese, cover with foil and cook in oven Gas No.4, 350°F, 180°C, for 20 minutes. Remove foil and place under hot grill for 2–3 minutes until golden brown.

HRAIMI – HOT SPICY FISH   Dinny Charkham

Serves 4–6   Preparation 10 mins.   Cook 35 mins.   Freezable

2lb fish (cutlets of salmon, haddock,
  cod etc.) (900gm)
3 tbls tomato purée
1 tbls garlic paste (see next column)
3 tbls oil
Juice of ½ lemon
1 tsp cumin

GARLIC PASTE
6 cloves garlic, crushed
1 tsp salt
2 tbls hot red paprika powder
1 tbls oil
Lemon juice to moisten

TO SERVE: French bread

Blend garlic paste ingredients until smooth, then in a deep saucepan heat the oil, garlic paste and tomato purée stirring constantly. When amalgamated, add half a cup of water and stir again. Add a full cup of water and when it comes to the boil, place the fish carefully in it. Add the salt, and cook for about 20–30 minutes, depending on which fish you use. Then add the cumin and lastly the lemon juice and cook for another 5 minutes. Serve hot with crispy French bread.

 FRESH FRIED MACKEREL   Charlotte Davis

Serves 2   Preparation 10 mins.   Cook 10 mins.   Advance

2 fresh mackerel fillets
1 egg
Oil for frying

Medium matzo meal to coat
Salt and pepper

Wash fish and dry well. Season with salt and pepper. Dip fish into beaten egg and cover in matzo meal. Deep fry in very hot oil.

MEDITERRANEAN RED MULLET Maureen Marks

Serves 4   Preparation 15 mins.   Cook 25 mins.

4 medium sized red mullet, scaled and
   cleaned
1 tsp olive oil
1 onion, chopped
1 clove garlic, crushed
1 lb tomatoes, chopped (450 gm)

2 tsp oregano
1 bay leaf
$\frac{1}{4}$ pt red wine (142 ml)

GARNISH: chopped parsley and
     oregano

Place mullet in ovenproof dish brushed with oil. Add onion, garlic, tomatoes, bay leaf, salt and pepper. Pour over wine and oregano. Cover with foil and bake on Gas No.6, 400°F, 200°C, for 25 minutes. Remove fish, place in dish and keep warm. Place vegetables and liquid in pan and simmer for 5 minutes. Press through a sieve to give a thick sauce. Pour over fish and garnish. Serve immediately.

 ## RED MULLET TART   David Cohen

Serves 4–6   Preparation 15 mins.   Cook 40 mins.

8 oz shortcrust pastry (225 gm)
2 small red mullet, skinned and
   filleted
8 black olives, stoned and halved
Olive oil
9″ flan tin (23 cm)

FILLING

1 tbls olive oil
1 onion, chopped
1 lb tomatoes, peeled, seeded and
   chopped (450 gm)
1 red pepper, seeded and chopped
$\frac{1}{2}$ tsp sugar
$1\frac{1}{2}$ tbls Pernod
Salt and pepper

Line the flan tin with pastry; prick the base, line with tin foil and bake blind on Gas No.5, 375°F, 190°C, for 15 minutes. Remove foil and bake for another 5–10 minutes to dry out.

Filling: Cook the onion and red pepper in olive oil until soft but not browned. Add all remaining filling ingredients plus 4 tablespoons of water and simmer until sauce is thick. Liquidise, and adjust the seasoning. Cut the fish into thick strips; spread the tomato and pepper purée onto the base of the tart then cover with strips of fish, arranged like the spokes of a wheel, pressing them into the purée. Dot olives in the gaps. Brush the fish and olives with a little olive oil and bake on Gas No.5, 375°F, 190°C, for 10–15 minutes until mullet is cooked through and tart is hot. Serve hot or warm.

PASTAFISHIO
Stella Abrahams

Serves 4   Preparation 20 mins.   Cook 15 mins.   Advance   Freezable

14 oz ratatouille (400 gm)
8 oz calabrese (225 gm)
8 oz pasta (225 gm)
¾ lb white fish fillets, skinned eg. cod
    or haddock (340 gm)

1 oz plain flour (30 gm)
1 oz margarine (30 gm)
½ pt milk (skimmed) (280 ml)
Salt and pepper
4 oz grated cheese (115 gm)

Trim and divide calabrese into small pieces. Cook in boiling salted water for 5 minutes. Poach the fish in a little of the milk with salt and pepper and flake. Reserve any liquid. (This can be done in a microwave oven according to instructions.) Cook pasta in boiling salted water until al dente. Make a white sauce by melting the margarine, add the flour and cook for 1 minute stirring all the time. Continue stirring and slowly add the milk and the reserved liquid from the fish. Butter the serving dish and spread ratatouille in the bottom, add pasta and arrange calabrese and fish. Top with white sauce and then the grated cheese. Bake in oven Gas No.6, 400°F, 200°C for 15 minutes.

PLAICE AND SPINACH PARCELS
Leala Cohen

Serves 4   Preparation 1 hour   Cook 30–40 mins.

8 small fillets of plaice
8 oz button mushrooms,
    sliced (225 gm)
4 large spinach leaves
Lemon juice

¼ tsp mace
Salt and pepper

TOPPING

Brown breadcrumbs
1 oz grated parmesan cheese (30 gm)
2 oz melted butter (55 gm)

Marinate the fish fillets in lemon juice, mace and seasoning for at least 1 hour. Then sandwich two fillets of fish together with a quarter of the mushrooms. Wrap up in a spinach leaf. Continue in the same way with the rest of the fish. Place the parcels in a shallow ovenproof dish and top with the breadcrumbs and cheese mixture. Pour over the melted butter. Cover with foil and bake for 30–40 minutes, at Gas No.3, 325°F, 160°C.

POISSON CECILE
Jessica Mendelssohn

Serves 6   **Preparation 10 mins.**   **Cook 20 mins.**   **Refrigerate**

2¼lb haddock or cod, skinned
  and filleted (1kg)
2oz butter or margarine (55gm)

GARNISH: chopped parsley and/or
  chives

SAUCE
8 tbls mayonnaise
2 tsp lemon juice
Dash Worcester sauce
Dash tabasco
Dash tomato ketchup or purée
Salt and pepper
1 clove garlic, crushed

Put fish in baking dish, season and dot with butter. Cover with foil and bake for 20 minutes Gas No.2, 300°F, 150°C. Cool slightly then flake fish into large pieces. Mix all sauce ingredients together and cover the fish. Serve chilled, garnished with chopped parsley or chives.

SALMON IN CHAMPAGNE
Michelle Oster

Serves 10 **Preparation 20 mins.**   **Cook 50 mins.**   **Advance**

6½lb whole salmon (3kg)
6 shallots, chopped
1 bottle champagne or white wine
1lb button mushrooms, sliced (450gm)
6 whole button mushrooms

Salt and pepper
Lemon juice
¾ pt double cream (455ml)

Season cavity of salmon with black pepper. Butter base of roasting/baking tin and place salmon on top. Pour over bottle of champagne or white wine. Sprinkle with black pepper and a little salt. Cover top of salmon with shallots and mushrooms. Bake uncovered for 45 minutes at Gas No.7, 425°F, 220°C. Meanwhile take 6 whole mushrooms and poach in lemon juice for 5 minutes. Reserve. When the salmon is ready remove the shallots and mushrooms and reserve. Lift out salmon, skin and place on warm serving dish and leave in warm place. Strain cooking liquid into saucepan and reduce rapidly by half. Add cream and reduce liquid again. Liquidise sliced mushrooms and shallots and stir into cream sauce. Simmer gently stirring constantly for 2–3 minutes. Just before serving stir in briskly 2–3 small knobs of butter and pour over the salmon. Decorate with the whole mushrooms. This can be prepared in advance until the point where the butter is stirred in.

HOT SALMON MOUSSE
IN PASTRY
Maureen Marks

Serves 6   Preparation 30 mins.   Cook 30 mins.   Refrigerate

1lb salmon, skinned and
  filleted (450gm)
3 egg whites
1 pt double cream (560ml)
$\frac{1}{2}$ tsp ground mace
Salt and pepper

1lb puff pastry (450gm)
Lemon juice to taste

SAUCE

Yoghurt and cucumber sauce
  (see page 159)

Liquidise salmon with salt, pepper, lemon juice and mace. Chill. Blend in whites of eggs and chill again. Add double cream, liquidise and chill again. Leave in fridge until required. Roll out pastry to round cake shape and put mousse on half of it. Cover with the other half. Seal edges well and brush pastry with egg yolk. Bake at Gas No.5, 375°F, 180°C. Serve cut into wedges with cucumber and yoghurt sauce.

FRESH SALMON QUICHE
Maureen Marks

Serves 4   Preparation 10 mins.   Cook 40 mins.   Freezable

4oz shortcrust pastry (115gm)
8oz cooked salmon, flaked (225gm)
$\frac{1}{2}$oz butter (15gm)
1 small onion, finely chopped

3 eggs
$\frac{1}{2}$ pt single cream (280ml)
2oz gruyère cheese, grated (55gm)
8" quiche dish (20 cm)

Line the quiche dish with pastry. Bake blind for 10 minutes at Gas No.6, 400°F, 200°C. Flake the salmon and put in cooled pastry case. Melt butter and add onion. Cover and fry gently for a few minutes until tender, but not browned. Drain onion and sprinkle over salmon. Mix eggs, cream and seasoning and pour over salmon and onion. Sprinkle cheese over the top and bake on Gas No.4, 350°F, 180°C, for 30 minutes or until filling is set and browned.

POACHED SALMON
WITH SORREL SAUCE
Rosanna Burr

Serves 6   Preparation 15 mins.   Cook 50 mins.

4 lb sea trout (salmon trout) or salmon (1.8 kg)

CHIFFONNADE OF SORREL

Handful sorrel leaves
½ oz butter (15 gm)

GARNISH: small bunch of parsley or watercress

SORREL SAUCE

5 oz unsalted butter (140 gm)
¼ pt double cream (140 ml)
Squeeze of lemon juice
Salt and pepper

Poach the salmon in gently simmering salt water for 18 minutes. Take the pan off the stove and leave for 30 minutes before removing fish from the water. Skin the salmon, dish up on a large plate and decorate with a bunch of fresh parsley or watercress.

Chiffonnade of Sorrel: Take a handful of sorrel leaves, wash, shake, remove the tough midribs and shred finely. Melt the butter in a small saucepan (not aluminium) and add the sorrel. Cover and cook gently until the sorrel is soft but still in strips and the moisture has gone.

Sorrel Sauce: Chop the butter and heat gently to melt (it must not separate), add the cream and heat, but not to boiling. Take off the stove and beat in a good squeeze of lemon juice (this thickens and binds it), a teaspoon or so of sorrel chiffonnade and seasoning. Serve hot.

SALMON WITH SORREL
AND WATERCRESS BUTTER
Helen Rose

Serves 8   Preparation 10 mins.   Cook 20 mins approx.   Butter advance

Melted butter
8 salmon steaks

SORREL AND WATERCRESS BUTTER

8 oz unsalted butter, softened (225 gm)
Handful fresh sorrel, stalks removed
1 bunch watercress, stalks removed
1 handful fresh parsley, stalks removed
A few fresh tarragon leaves
Salt and pepper

To cook the salmon brush with melted butter or a herb marinade and cook in foil until the flesh is firm in a moderate oven.

To make butter: Combine all the ingredients together in a magimix. Spoon the butter onto some foil in a long sausage shape, wrap up and chill. Cut into pats and freeze if you wish. Serve one pat per person, placed on the salmon steak immediately after cooking.

SOLE AVOCADO PARCELS
Bobbie Tarn

Serves 4   **Preparation 20 mins.**   **Cook 20 mins.**

4 lemon sole fillets, skinned
1 avocado, peeled and quartered
1 bunch spring onions, finely chopped
4 tsp lemon juice
4 tbls white wine
$\frac{1}{4}$ pt fish stock (140ml)
2 tbls flour

2oz butter (55gm)
2 tbls double cream
1 tbls parsley, chopped
Salt and pepper

GARNISH: extra avocado slices, lemon twists, parsley sprigs.

Cut each fillet in half lengthways to give 8 fillets. Arrange slices of avocado over the tail end of each fillet, sprinkle lightly with salt and pepper, onion and 2 tsp of lemon juice. Fold over the uncovered half of each fillet to cover the filling and to form neat parcels.*** Melt half the butter in a shallow ovenproof dish and arrange the fish parcels in it. Pour over 2 tbls of wine and the remaining lemon juice. Cover the dish and bake Gas No.4, 350°F, 185°C, for 15–20 minutes. Remove the fish to a serving dish and keep warm. Measure the liquor left in the ovenproof dish together with the fish stock to make up to 8 fl. oz. (225ml), adding water if necessary.

Sauce: melt 1oz (30gm) butter and stir in the flour, then slowly blend in the fish stock mixture and heat, stirring constantly, until it thickens. Whisk the cream and remaining wine into the sauce. Adjust the seasoning; spoon the sauce over the fish, and garnish.

Microwave instructions

Prepare recipe as above until ***. Melt butter in a shallow dish on high for 15 seconds. Arrange fish on top, with wider portions at the outside of the dish. Pour over 2 tbls of wine with the remaining juice. Cover dish with pricked clingfilm and microwave on medium power for 4 minutes. Remove fish onto a serving dish (not flat). Mix the liquid from the shallow dish with the fish stock and make up to 8 floz (225ml) with water if necessary. Melt half the butter in a bowl on high and then stir in the flour; whisk in the fish stock mixture. Microwave, uncovered, on high for 2 minutes, whisking the sauce after 1 minute and at the end of cooking to ensure a smooth mixture. Whisk in the cream and remaining wine and microwave for 30 seconds on medium power. Spoon sauce over fish and microwave for 4 minutes until heated through. Garnish.

SOLE PASTRY PARCELS
Maureen Marks

Serves 6 Preparation 20 mins.   Cook 30 mins.   Freezable

13oz puff pastry (370gm)
6 or 12 sole fillets, skinned – see below
2oz butter (55gm)
6oz spinach leaves (170gm)
Salt and pepper
Nutmeg

SAUCE

4oz smoked roe (115gm)
Approx. 2 tsp lemon juice
1 tbls onion, grated
$\frac{1}{4}$ pt whipping cream (140ml)

Either use a double fillet of 6–8oz to make one large parcel, or 2 x 3–4oz fillets to make 2 small parcels per serving. Sprinkle fillets with salt, pepper and nutmeg. Dot with a little butter. Blanch spinach in boiling, salted water for about 1 minute. Drain very well on kitchen paper. Wrap a leaf round each rolled up fillet of fish. Roll out pastry and cut into squares to fit the fish. Form into parcels round the fish, making the seal (brushed with beaten egg) on the underside. Place on a greased baking tray and decorate parcels with pastry trimmings and brush with beaten egg. Cook in pre-heated oven Gas No.7, 425°F, 220°C, for 30 minutes until golden and cooked through.

Sauce: Skin roe and place in food processor with onion and lemon juice. Scrape down, mix again and slowly add cream and seasonings until a delicate pink pouring sauce forms. Serve at room temperature.

SOLE WITH TARRAGON
CREAM SAUCE
Kate Bennett

Serves 4   Preparation 15 mins.   Cook 20 mins.

4 large sole fillets
4 fl oz single cream (115ml)
$1\frac{1}{2}$ tsp dried tarragon

8 fl oz medium dry white wine (225ml)
1oz flour (30gm)
1oz butter (30gm)

Cut the fillets of sole in half lengthwise then roll the fillets up and place them in a buttered dish. Season with salt and pepper and pour over the wine plus $\frac{1}{2}$ tsp of tarragon. Cover the dish with foil and bake in oven Gas No.4, 350°F, 180°C, for 10–15 minutes until fish is cooked through. While the fish is cooking make a roux with the butter and flour, then gradually add the cream stirring constantly to prevent lumps forming, then set aside. Pour off the wine in which the fish has cooked, into another pan. Keep the fish covered and warm in the oven, let the wine simmer and reduce by half. Then add it slowly to the cream mixture, stirring over a very low flame. Cook for 3–4 minutes. Add remaining tarragon, stir and pour over fish. Serve immediately.

BAKED TROUT
AND FENNEL SAUCE

Marion Cohen

Serves 4–6 Preparation 10 mins. Cook 15–20 mins.

4–6 trout
Little butter
Bunch fresh fennel
Salt and pepper

SAUCE

6 tbls double cream
2–3 tbls fresh fennel, chopped
6 tbls yoghurt
$\frac{1}{4}$ tsp arrowroot or potato flour
1–2oz butter (30–55gm)
Few drops lemon juice
Salt and pepper

Butter a shallow ovenproof dish and lay in the prepared trout, each stuffed with some fennel. Season with salt and pepper, cover with well-buttered greaseproof paper and tinfoil and bake in a moderately hot oven Gas No.5, 375°F, 190°C, for 15 minutes or until done (the flesh feels firm and will just flake).

Sauce: Heat the cream with the chopped fennel until well flavoured, combine the yoghurt and arrowroot and stir in. Bring to a simmer slowly, stirring all the time. Simmer for 1–2 minutes until thickened, draw off the stove and whisk in the butter in little pieces, season and add a squeeze of lemon juice if necessary. Keep well covered if not serving at once.

satisfaction . . .

72

Meatless Main Courses

Walter – I think we'll call it Instant Smash!

HINTS

If you forget to soak dried vegetables (peas, lentils, beans etc.) which need 8 hours, the process can be speeded up by using boiling water. Soak for 1–2 hours.

Wholewheat pasta has a mild, nutty flavour and a high fibre content.

Basic pancakes can be filled with all sorts of savoury fillings such as cooked vegetables in cheese sauce, vegetable purées and even lentil curry.

For Cheese fondue: pieces of raw vegetables can be substituted for bread.

For non-dairy soufflés, use a thin vegetable purée instead of milk.

Soufflés are an excellent way to combine the protein value of eggs with other ingredients in a savoury or sweet dish.

Quiches and pies can be considered 'healthy' if you use wholewheat flour and polyunsaturated fats for the pastry, and replace any cream in the filling with fromage blanc.

Beans and Pulses

BROAD BEAN
AND ARTICHOKE CASSEROLE   Gloria Cohen

Serves 4–6   Preparation 15–20 mins.   Cook 50 mins.   Advance

1 lb frozen broad beans (450 gm)
1–1½ lb peeled Jerusalem artichokes
   (450–675 gm)
1 oz butter or margarine (30 gm)
1 oz flour (30 gm)
1 clove garlic, chopped

1 lemon
3 oz dry white breadcrumbs (85 gm)
3 oz gruyère or cheddar cheese,
   grated (optional) (85 gm)
½ oz butter (15 gm)
Salt and pepper

Cut any large artichokes in pieces. Combine in pan with the broad beans and garlic and cover with about 1 pt (600 ml) boiling water. Add salt and the juice of half the lemon. Boil for about 7–10 minutes until the artichokes are just tender and the beans are cooked. Drain off the cooking liquid retaining $\frac{3}{4}$ pint (450 ml). Return this liquid to the beans and artichokes. Cream the butter and flour together and add in little pieces to thicken the sauce. Stir until melted, simmer for 1–2 minutes and correct the seasoning and lemon. Turn onto a buttered gratin dish and cover with breadcrumbs, the cheese if you wish, and little dabs of butter. Brown under the grill and serve. This will keep warm, or re-heat in a moderate oven Gas No.4, 350°F, 180°C for 30–40 minutes.

SPICED BEAN
AND VEGETABLE CASSEROLE   Marion Cohen

Serves 8   Preparation 20 mins.   Cook 1½–2 hours   Advance   Freezable

4oz haricot beans, soaked overnight (115gm)
¼ pt olive oil (140ml)
4 cloves garlic, crushed
½ tsp each whole cumin, cardamom,
   coriander, mustard and fenugreek seeds
1 tsp turmeric
Salt and pepper

2 heads celery, chopped
1lb carrots, trimmed and sliced
   (450gm)
4 baby turnips, quartered
1lb leeks, chopped (450gm)
1 small cauliflower, broken into
   florets
½ pt red wine (280ml)

Drain beans; put into saucepan and cover with fresh water; bring to boil, reduce heat and simmer, covered, for 1 hour. Remove from heat and reserve. Heat oil in large flameproof casserole and add garlic and spices. Cook, stirring for 1 minute then add carrots, celery and turnips. Cook for a further minute, then add half the beans and liquid. Bring to boil, reduce heat and simmer for 15 minutes. Blend remaining beans to smooth purée; add to casserole with all remaining ingredients. Stir and cook for 10 minutes.

RED KIDNEY BEAN CURRY   Sandy Prevezer

Serves 4–6   Soak 8 hours   Preparation 10 mins.   Cook 20 mins.   Advance

12oz red kidney beans (340gm)
* 2 green chillies
* 1″ fresh ginger (2.5cm)
2 floz oil (56ml)
2 onions, chopped
14oz tin tomatoes, chopped (400gm)
(* ground to a paste)

¾ pt water (425ml)
Salt
Pinch of chilli powder (optional)

GARNISH: fresh coriander leaves

Soak kidney beans for 8 hours then cook covered in water until tender. Heat oil in a shallow pan, add onions, fry for 3 minutes. Add ginger and chilli paste with chilli powder if desired and fry for 1 minute on a low heat. Add cooked beans with their liquid. Add tomatoes and salt and cook for another 15 minutes. Serve hot.

FUL MESDAMES
Jane Cohen-Setton

| Serves 6 | Soak 8 hours | Cook 4 hours | Advance |

1½lb British field beans (700gm)
6 eggs
2–3 Spanish onions

3 lemons
6 dsp olive oil
Salt and pepper

Soak beans overnight (at least 8 hours). Rinse thoroughly and boil gently in fresh water for at least 4 hours. After 3 hours add the eggs (in their shells). Keep topping up with water to ensure beans do not dry out. When beans are soft, serve in some of their juice in soup plates. Add salt, pepper, oil and lemon juice and mash roughly with fork. Shell eggs and slice over the top together with thinly sliced Spanish onion. Serve with pitta bread.

LENTIL FRITTERS
Naomi Greenwood

| Serves 6 | Preparation 5 mins. | Cook 40 mins. | Advance |

8oz lentils (225gm)
2oz cheese, grated (55gm)
1 onion, chopped
1 egg, beaten
2 tbls flour

Salt and pepper
1 tbls turmeric
½ tsp cayenne
Oil for shallow frying

Cook lentils, onions and seasoning with enough water to cover, until lentils are very soft. Add spices, cheese and egg. Mix in flour. Beat well. Drop tablespoons of mixture into hot oil. Fry 5–6 minutes until crisp and golden. Drain. Serve hot or cold. Makes 12.

NOODLE AND LENTIL HOTPOT
David Burr

| Serves 8 | Preparation 10 mins. | Cook 50 mins. | Advance |

14oz lentils (400gm)
3 pt water (1.7 litres)
1 tsp salt
3fl oz olive oil (85ml)
2 onions, chopped

3 cloves garlic, crushed
3oz egg noodles (85gm)
Freshly ground black pepper

TO SERVE: wholemeal pitta cut into wedges

Wash and drain the lentils. Put them into a large pan with the boiling water, bring to the boil and add the salt. Reduce the heat and simmer covered until the lentils are almost soft. Heat the oil in a frying pan and sauté the onions and garlic until translucent. Add the onion mixture to the lentils, together with the noodles and pepper, stir thoroughly and simmer until the noodles are just tender enough to eat, about 15 minutes. If the hotpot seems too thick, add a little boiling water. Serve with wedges of pitta bread.

LENTIL ROAST

Simone Ross

Serves 4 Soak 6 hours Preparation 20 mins. Cook 40 mins. Advance Freezable

8oz red lentils (225gm)
1 bay leaf
4oz cheese, grated (115gm)
2 eggs, lightly beaten
2 tomatoes, skinned and chopped
Salt and black pepper

1 onion, finely chopped
1 tbls parsley, finely chopped
2oz fresh breadcrumbs (55gm)
$\frac{1}{2}$ tsp fresh herbs, chopped or $\frac{1}{4}$ tsp
  dried herbs

Soak lentils for 6 hours in cold water. Drain and simmer in fresh water with the bay leaf until just cooked. Mix the cheese, tomatoes, eggs, onion and parsley in a large bowl. Add the drained lentils and breadcrumbs, mix and season. Place in a greased loaf tin and bake on Gas No.3, 325°F, 160°C until firm to the touch. Serve hot or cold.

SPICY VEGETABLE RISSOLES

Sandy Prevezer

Serves 4–6   **Preparation 5 mins.**   **Cook 5–10 mins.**

8oz brown lentils, cooked and
  mashed (225gm)
2 carrots, grated
1 large onion, chopped
3 sticks celery, chopped
2 eggs
Matzo meal (medium)

Salt
$\frac{1}{4}$ tsp each of grated cumin,
  coriander, chilli, ginger, fenugreek
or
1 tsp curry powder
Oil for frying

Mix vegetables and lentils with one of the eggs in a large bowl. Add the seasoning and enough matzo meal to make a suitable consistency for making oval shapes. Dip in beaten egg and matzo meal and fry until brown and crunchy. Can be eaten hot or cold.

Practice run!

Pasta and Rice

I asked you for long grain rice!

PAPPARDELLE
AL SUGO DI NOCI
(Egg noodles with walnut sauce)

Helen Meller

Serves 4 **Preparation 8 mins.** **Cook 12 mins.**

4 oz walnut pieces (115 gm)
3 oz butter/margarine (85 gm)
2 tbls olive oil
4 oz freshly grated parmesan or
   mature cheddar cheese (115 gm)

1 clove garlic
12 oz pappardelle (340 gm) (or any
   other egg noodle)
Salt and freshly ground pepper

Spread walnuts on a baking sheet and put into preheated oven Gas No.4, 350°F, 180°C for 8 minutes. Rub walnuts with a clean cloth to remove most of the skins. Place them with butter, garlic and oil in a blender and mix to a fairly smooth paste. Put mixture in a bowl and stir in half the cheese. Season to taste. Cook the pasta 'al dente' and stir 6 tablespoons of the cooking water into walnut sauce. Drain pasta, pour on walnut sauce and toss together. Serve with remaining cheese.

FETUCCINE WITH ONIONS
Cecily Mendelssohn

Serves 4   Preparation 5 mins.   Cook 30 mins.

3 tbls olive/sunflower oil
3 large onions, thinly sliced
12oz noodles (or macaroni) (340gm)
2 tbls tomato purée
5 floz parev chicken/vegetable
  stock (140ml)

Knob of butter
1 clove garlic, crushed
Salt and pepper

GARNISH: chopped parsley
2oz parmesan, freshly grated (55gm)

Heat oil in a saucepan and cook the onions very slowly until golden and tender (up to 20 minutes). Dissolve the tomato purée in the stock and add to the onions with garlic and seasonings. Meanwhile, cook pasta in a separate pan and when 'al dente', drain and transfer to a heated bowl. Pour tomato and onion sauce over it and sprinkle with parsley. Serve immediately with parmesan.

 ## PASTA WITH JULIENNE OF VEGETABLES
Erika Crocker

Serves 4   Preparation 20 mins.   Cook 10 mins.

1 cup spicy tomato sauce
12oz very fine pasta (340gm)
1 tsp mixed herbs
1 tbls parsley, chopped
Salt and pepper to taste

* 3 carrots
* 3 courgettes
* 2 spring onions
* 1 green or red pepper

(* cut into julienne strips)

Add vegetables to sauce, together with herbs, parsley, salt and pepper. Cook for 5 minutes. At the same time cook pasta in a separate saucepan. When cooked, drain well and place in serving dish then pour sauce over pasta and serve.

RIGATONI ALLA PORRO
Cecily Mendelssohn

Serves 4   Preparation 5 mins.   Cook 20 mins.

1lb leeks, thinly sliced (450gm)
2oz butter/margarine (55gm)
½ pt parev chicken/vegetable
  stock (280ml)
12oz tubular pasta (340gm)

1 clove garlic, crushed
2oz fresh parmesan (55gm)
Salt and pepper
3 floz single cream to taste (85ml)

Melt the butter in a heavy saucepan and stir in leeks until thoroughly coated. Add enough stock to cover the leeks and simmer until tender and the leeks have absorbed most of the stock. Meanwhile, cook the pasta until 'al dente'. Drain and put in a warm serving bowl. Reheat the leeks with some cream and garlic and seasoning and pour this over the pasta. Add half the cheese and toss together. Serve at once with rest of the cheese in a separate bowl.

SPINACH LASAGNE
Madeleine Cope-Thompson

Serves 8   Preparation 15 mins.   Cook 1 hour 15 mins.   Freezable

1 lb cottage cheese (450 gm)
2 cups mozzarella, shredded
10 oz pkt frozen spinach (285 gm)
6 oz tomato sauce (170 gm)
8 oz lasagne (no precooking) (225 gm)

1 baking dish 13″ x 9″ x 2″
   (32.5 x 23 x 5 cm)

1 egg
$\frac{3}{4}$ tsp oregano
Dash black pepper
1 cup water
1 tsp salt

Thaw and drain spinach. In large bowl mix cottage cheese, 1 cup mozzarella, egg, spinach, salt, oregano and pepper. In greased baking dish layer a half cup sauce, third of lasagne and half cheese mixture. Repeat and top with remaining lasagne, then pour over sauce. Sprinkle top with mozzarella. Pour water around edges, cover tightly with foil. Bake and let stand for 15 minutes before serving.

SPINACH AND MUSHROOM LASAGNE
Sarah Bennett

Serves 4   Preparation 15 mins.   Cook 35–40 mins.

8 strips of lasagne
$1\frac{3}{4}$ lb spinach (800 gm)
1 tsp butter or margarine
1 tsp dried marjoram
12 oz ricotta or mixture of curd and
   cream cheese (340 gm)
Salt and freshly ground black pepper

SAUCE

10 oz mushrooms, finely
   chopped (280 gm)
1 oz butter (30 gm)
$\frac{1}{4}$ pt vegetable stock (140 ml)
1 tsp soy sauce
6 oz cheddar cheese, grated (170 gm)

3 pt rectangular dish (1.7 lt)

Preheat oven to Gas No.6, 400°F, 200°C. Prepare spinach by washing in several changes of water. Cook gently in heavy saucepan without adding any water for 6–8 minutes. When cooked, strain off excess water, chop finely and return to saucepan and season well. Put pan on gentle heat and add butter and marjoram. Stir, then take pan off heat. When spinach cools, mix in ricotta cheese and season well.

Sauce: Cook mushrooms in butter, then reduce the heat and cook for 10 minutes in covered pan so plenty of juice is created. Add stock and simmer for another 5 minutes. Purée for a few seconds in a liquidiser or put through a sieve or mouli. Add soy sauce and season to taste. Lightly oil the dish. Spoon in spinach filling, cover with 2 or 3 pieces of lasagne, then coat with mushroom sauce. Repeat layers ending with mushroom sauce. Sprinkle with cheddar cheese and bake for 35–40 minutes until cheese is bubbling. Serve immediately.

SPINACH TAGLIATELLI
AND MUSHROOMS
Sheila Kustow

Serves 4–6   Preparation 10 mins.   Cook 35 mins.   Advance   Freezable

8 oz fresh spinach tagliatelli (225 gm)
5½ oz pkt Boursin garlic cream
   cheese (155 gm)
1 large onion, chopped

12 oz mushrooms, sliced (340 gm)
Salt and pepper to taste
GARNISH: parsley, chopped

Boil noodles in salted water with a drop of oil until 'al dente', then drain. Meanwhile, fry onion until lightly brown, add mushrooms and sweat for a short time. Remove from heat. Place cream cheese in a saucepan and add hot noodles. Cover and leave to sweat for 5 minutes. Stir in mushrooms and onions. Transfer to a large pyrex dish. Cover with foil and cook for 30 minutes. Garnish with parsley.

FISH LASAGNE
Naomi R. Pope

Serves 6–8   Preparation 40 mins.   Cook 30 mins.   Advance   Freezable

1 lb pkt. green lasagne (450 gm)
2 x 7 oz tins tuna (198 gm)
1 oz anchovies (30 gm)
Bay leaf
1 tbls oil

SAUCE

4 oz margarine or butter (115 gm)
4 oz flour (115 gm)
1½ pt vegetable stock (850 ml)
5 oz tomato purée (140 ml)
1½ pt milk (850 ml)
2 oz parmesan cheese (55 gm)

Cook half the lasagne at a time in boiling water for 6 minutes with the oil. Plunge into cold water and drain. Drain and flake tuna. Mix together 2 oz margarine and 2 oz flour. Add stock, tin of tomato purée, half a tin anchovies, parsley and pepper and fold in flaked tuna.

Béchamel Sauce: Melt rest of margarine, stir in remaining flour then stir in milk and bay leaf until cooked.

Place in oval or rectangular dish 1 layer of tuna sauce, 1 layer lasagne, 1 layer Béchamel and repeat. On top, sprinkle parmesan cheese. Cook on Gas No.5, 375°F, 190°C for 30 minutes.

TUNA AND PASTA
Stella Abrahams

Serves 2   Preparation 5 mins.   Cook 10 mins.   Advance   Freezable

7 oz tin tuna, drained (200 gm)
8 oz pasta tubes, spirals, or shells, etc. (225 gm)

10½ oz condensed mushroom soup (290 gm)
Freshly ground black pepper
2 oz cheese, grated (55 gm)

Cook pasta until 'al dente' and drain. Add the drained tuna and mushroom soup and heat gently. Turn into individual dishes and top with grated cheese and black pepper. Place under grill until cheese has melted.

PENNE CON TONNO ED ACCIUGHE
Helen Meller
(Pasta tubes with Tuna and Anchovies)

Serves 2–3   Preparation 15 mins.   Cook 10 mins.

12 oz penne or other tubular pasta (340 gm)
4 tbls olive oil
2 oz butter (55 gm)
7 oz tin of tuna, drained (200 gm)

1¾ oz tin anchovy fillets (50 gm)
Salt and freshly ground black pepper

GARNISH: 2 tbls parsley, freshly chopped

Cook the pasta in boiling water to which has been added 2 tsp salt and a drop of olive oil (this will prevent the pasta becoming sticky). Heat oil and butter in a saucepan and add the tuna and anchovies. Mash together with a fork and cook until well heated. Taste for seasoning. Use plenty of black pepper (salt may not be needed). Drain the pasta. Mix in the sauce and sprinkle with parsley.

CAULIFLOWER PILAU
Sue Curran

Serves 4   Preparation 5 minutes   Cook 10 minutes

3 cups precooked brown rice
2 tbls oil
8 oz cauliflower florets (225 gm)
1 onion, chopped
5 cloves garlic, finely chopped

GARNISH: finely sliced onion and tomatoes

½ tsp cinnamon
1 tsp ginger
½ tsp paprika
2 tsp sea salt
1 tsp cumin
½ tsp garam masala
1 cup yoghurt

Sprinkle cauliflower with salt and pepper and fry in oil until golden. Remove from pan and fry onion and garlic. Add spices and rice and stir fry for 5 minutes. Stir in yoghurt. Cook another few minutes. Garnish with finely sliced onion and tomatoes. Serve hot with brown rice.

VEGETABLE LASAGNE   Angela Wilson

Serves 6–8   Preparation 20 mins.   Cook 20 mins.   Advance   Freezable

3 medium potatoes, sliced
3 carrots, in thin strips
2–3 leeks, sliced
3 small heads of cauliflower in small
   florets
12 oz green lasagne (340 gm)

WHITE SAUCE
3 oz butter/margarine (85 gm)
4 tbls flour
¾ pt milk (455 ml)
Salt and pepper
Few shakes of nutmeg
Parmesan cheese

Boil vegetables until cooked, but not 'mushy'. Cook pasta as necessary.

Sauce: melt butter, add flour and mix until smooth. Add milk stirring continually until thickened. Add salt, pepper and nutmeg to taste.

Spread a thin layer of vegetables into ovenproof dish. Add a thin layer of white sauce followed by a layer of pasta. Repeat layers finishing with white sauce. Sprinkle with parmesan cheese. Cook until golden brown for 15–20 minutes on Gas No.6, 400°F, 200°C.

RISOTTO WITH MUSHROOMS
AND PINE-KERNELS   Gillian Burr

Serves 4–6   Preparation 30 mins.   Cook 20 mins.

2 oz butter (55 gm)
1 onion, finely chopped
4 oz button mushrooms,
   diced (115 gm)
¾ lb long grain rice (350 gm)
1 pt hot parev chicken stock (560 ml)
2–3 slices dried cèpe mushrooms

1 bay leaf
½ tsp fresh or lemon thyme, finely
   chopped
1 oz pine-kernels browned in butter
   or substitute with flaked browned
   almonds (30 gm)
Dot of butter
Salt and pepper

Soak the cepe mushrooms for 30 minutes or more in a little of the hot stock. Melt the butter in a casserole and gently fry the onion and mushrooms until all the moisture has evaporated. Add the unwashed rice, stir over moderate heat for 2–3 minutes until the rice first glistens then goes whitish; this seals in the starch so that the rice does not become sticky. Add the hot stock, chopped up cèpe mushrooms and their liquid. Season and add the bay leaf and thyme. Bring to the boil and cook in a moderate oven Gas No.4, 350°F, 180°C for 15–18 minutes. Test the rice, which should be 'al dente', but do not stir. All the liquid should have been absorbed. Toss the pine-kernels in some butter to brown and scatter over the risotto on serving. This risotto will keep warm quite happily.

KASHMIRI PILAU Marion Cohen

Serves 6   Preparation 15 mins.   Cook 30 mins.

1½ cups rice
10oz vegetables, cubed (280gm)
1″ piece of ginger, finely
  chopped (2.5cm)
1″ piece cinnamon, broken up (2.5cm)
1 tbls soft brown sugar
20 almonds, blanched and chopped
¾ tsp saffron, pounded in a little
  warm milk

1 tsp salt
Juice of 1½ lemons
2 tbls ghee (or oil)
8 peppercorns
6 cloves
3 green cardamoms
Rose water
2 tsp coriander seeds

Put vegetables in saucepan with two cups of boiling water. Add ginger, coriander, cinnamon and salt and cook until tender. Add sugar and the juice of 1 lemon. Meanwhile, boil rice with remaining lemon juice until half cooked. Heat ghee and fry cloves, peppercorns and cardamoms. Add rice, vegetables with their stock, almonds and saffron milk. Mix well and cook gently until all liquid is absorbed. Sprinkle with rose water before serving.

TANGY RICE WITH OLIVES   Theodore Matoff

Serves 6   Preparation 15 mins.   Cook 30 mins.

8oz cooked rice (225gm)
6oz stuffed olives, chopped (170gm)
4 anchovy fillets, chopped
1 tbls capers, chopped
1oz parsley, chopped (30gm)
3 tbls onion, chopped
Salt and pepper

8½oz tin tomatoes, chopped (235gm)
or two large tomatoes, peeled and
  chopped
2oz parmesan cheese, grated (55gm)
½ tsp dried thyme or 1 tsp fresh,
  chopped
½ tsp dried basil or 1 tsp fresh,
  chopped

Butter a good sized casserole and put in all the ingredients except the cheese. Stir well, top with the cheese and bake for 30 minutes in moderate oven. Gas No.4, 350°F, 180°C.

SAFFRON RISOTTO
Carole Margo

Serves 4 **Preparation 35 mins.** **Cook 25 mins.**

RISOTTO
½ tsp saffron
2 tbls hot milk
2 tbls vegetable oil
8 oz basmati or risotto rice, well
 washed (225 gm)
3 oz fried cashews (85 gm)
2 whole cardamom seeds, crushed
12 fl oz water (350 ml)

8 oz peas (225 gm)
Salt

EGG PANCAKES
1 egg, beaten
2 tbls milk
A little oil for greasing
Salt and pepper

Risotto: Soak the saffron in the hot milk. Heat the oil in a pan and stir the rice in it for a few minutes. Add the nuts and the crushed cardamom seeds, then pour in the water and add the peas with salt to taste. Mix once, then cover and cook slowly until the liquid is absorbed, about 20 minutes. Add the saffron in its milk and stir until well mixed and the rice grains cooked through. Whilst the rice is cooking prepare the pancakes:

Pancakes: Beat the egg with a little milk and season with salt and pepper. In a large pan heat a tiny amount of oil, pour in the egg and make a paper-thin omelette with it. When it is cool, roll it up, cut it into strips and decorate the risotto with these egg whirls.

'Tell Charlie he owes me a fiver and he can start eating his hat!'

85

Eggs, Cheese and Savoury Tarts

AUBERGINE AND FETA CIGARS Danielle Gross

Makes 54   **Preparation 45 mins.**   **Cook 30 mins. Gas No.7, 425°F, 220°C**
Advance   Freezable

14oz packet of filo pastry (400gm)
Oil

FILLING
2 large aubergines

6oz feta cheese, diced (170gm)
1 small clove of garlic, crushed
2 tbsp oil
Pepper

Grill the aubergines for 20 minutes on each side. Spoon the flesh out and drain excess liquid. Sauté garlic in the oil. Add the aubergine diced. When the moisture has evaporated, add the diced feta cheese until it melts and forms a thick paste. Add pepper to taste. Cut your filo pastry in rectangles 6″ x 4″ (15cm x 10cm) and leave them in oil. Take one rectangle at a time to make your cigars following the diagram:

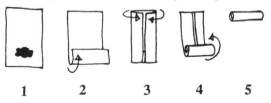

1   2   3   4   5

1. Put a little bit of paste on your pastry. 2. Fold the small side over the paste.
3. Then the sides. 4. Then roll it over until your have no more pastry. Cook.

AUBERGINE PIE
Avril Kleeman

Serves 4　　　**Preparation 2 hours**　　　**Cook 30 mins.**　　　**Advance**

2 large aubergines, thickly sliced
3 hard boiled eggs, chopped
6 large tomatoes, thickly sliced
2oz cheese, grated (55gm)

4oz breadcrumbs (115gm)
1 onion, chopped
Fresh basil or marjoram
Oil for frying

Sprinkle aubergines with salt and leave for 1–2 hours. Drain and dry aubergines. Fry onion slowly until soft. Fry the aubergines until browned on both sides. Add the tomatoes. Line an ovenproof dish with half the aubergines. Top with the onions and the tomatoes. Sprinkle the egg on top and then the herbs. Place the rest of the aubergines on top. Cover with the breadcrumbs and cheese. Cook on Gas No.6, 400°F, 200°C for 30 minutes. Serve hot or cold.

MELANZANE ALLA PARMIGIANA
Joanne Bloom

Serves 4 Preparation 1 hour 35 mins. Cook 45 mins. Advance Sauce freezable

2–3 long aubergines
2 mozzarella cheeses
Parmesan cheese, enough to cover top
Oregano and basil
Salt and pepper

SAUCE

1lb tin tomatoes, peeled (450gm)
2 tbls olive oil
$1\frac{1}{2}$ tbls butter
$\frac{1}{2}$ onion, chopped
Fresh basil, chopped

Cut the aubergine lengthways and cover in salt for an hour. Fry the onion in the butter until golden brown and then add the tin of tomatoes and salt and mix thoroughly crushing the tomatoes. Add the basil leaves and let it simmer slowly until fairly thick. In a rectangular ovenproof dish place a layer of aubergine, having washed off all the salt and excess liquid, then a layer of sauce and then a layer of mozzarella. Repeat as many times as possible. Cover the top with grated parmesan and oregano and place in the oven on Gas No.3, 325°F, 180°C for 45 minutes, or until golden brown.

AUSTRIAN CABBAGE STRUDEL   Ruth Smilg

Serves 12   Preparation 1 hour   Cook 1 hour   Freezable

PASTRY

8 oz plain flour (225 gm)
A little salt
1 tsp oil
1 whole egg
1 tsp vinegar
4 tbls lukewarm water

FILLING

2½–3 lb white cabbage, finely chopped
    (1.2–1.3 k)
6 oz margarine (170 gm)
1 medium onion, chopped
Salt, pepper, paprika, sugar
A little broth (chicken or vegetable) or water
1 tsp flour

Pastry: Knead all ingredients except oil together on a floured board or in a basin until a smooth dough is obtained, brush over a little oil, cover and leave for at least 30 minutes in a warm draught free place.

Prepare filling: Remove thick stems from cabbage, wash and chop finely. Put in a bowl, sprinkle with salt and leave for 15 minutes. Squeeze out the water. Fry the chopped onion in the margarine with 1 tsp sugar until golden brown, add the cabbage, season with pepper and paprika, mix well, add the broth or water and cook slowly until soft. Sprinkle on a little flour, stir well and add salt to taste. Allow the mixture to cool completely, then fill the strudel pastry. Sprinkle flour over a tablecloth, roll the dough once lengthwise and then, palms uppermost, pull the pastry out from underneath in all directions until it is paper thin and covers the cloth. Cut off the thick edge surround. Place the cabbage filling in a thick strip about a third of the way along the pastry. Flap over the short end, grip the tablecloth with both hands and roll up the strudel. Place carefully onto a greased baking tray, brush with a little melted margarine and bake for ¾–1 hour in a medium hot oven.

This basic strudel pastry can also be used for apple strudel and with other fillings such as cheese, potatoes, nuts, cherries. Filo pastry may be substituted.

CHEESE FONDUE

Edward Greenbury
(by courtesy of friends who tried it)

Serves 4   **Preparation 15–20 mins.**

1 clove garlic
⅓ pt dry white wine (185 ml)
1 sqeeze of lemon juice
6 oz Gruyere cheese, cut into thin
   strips (170 gm)
6 oz Emmenthal cheese, cut into
   strips (170 gm)

2 level tsp cornflour
1 liqueur glass Kirsch
Pepper
Grated nutmeg

To serve: French bread

Rub the inside of a flameproof dish with the garlic. Place the wine and lemon juice in the dish and warm over a gentle heat. Add the cheeses and continue to heat gently stirring well until the cheeses have melted and begin to cook. Blend the cornflour and seasonings to a smooth cream with the Kirsch and add to cheese mixture. Continue cooking for a further 2–3 minutes. When the mixture is of a thick and creamy consistency it is ready to serve. Keep warm on fondue base. Cut French bread into bite sized pieces and using a long pronged fork dip into fondue and coat well.

CHEESE AND MUSHROOM CHARLOTTE

Gloria Stone

Serves 4–6   **Preparation 15 mins.**   **Cook 45 mins.**

3 eggs
1 tsp made mustard
1 pt milk (560 ml)
5 slices buttered bread

6 oz cheese, grated (170 gm)
4 oz button mushrooms, thinly
   sliced (115 gm)
1 oz butter or margarine (30 gm)
Salt and pepper

Melt the butter in a pan and toss the mushrooms in it for 2–3 minutes. In a bowl, beat the eggs and add the mustard, seasonings and milk. Cut the buttered bread into small squares. Put a layer of the bread at the bottom of an ovenproof dish, and most of the cheese. Add the mushrooms to the egg mixture and pour it over the bread. Top with the remaining cheese and bake at Gas No.5, 375°F, 190°C until golden brown and puffy. Serve hot or cold.

CELERY CHEESE PIE
Lynne Goldwyn

Serves 4   Preparation 10 mins.   Cook 40 mins.

1 head celery, chopped
Salt and pepper
1 oz margarine (30 gm)
1 oz flour (30 gm)
$\frac{1}{4}$ pt milk (140 ml)

6 oz cheese, grated (170 gm)
2 tbls tomato purée
1 egg
1 lb potatoes, mashed (450 gm)
2 tomatoes, peeled and sliced

Cook the celery in boiling salted water until just tender, about 15 minutes. Strain and save $\frac{1}{4}$ pt (140 ml) stock. Place the celery in an ovenproof dish. Make a white sauce with the margarine, flour, milk and celery stock. Season well, stir in most of the cheese and tomato purée and lastly the beaten egg. DO NOT ALLOW TO BOIL. Pour the sauce over the celery. Top with mashed potato, then the rest of the cheese and tomatoes. Cook for approx. 20–25 minutes towards the top of a moderately hot oven, Gas No.5, 375°F, 190°C. Serve hot with a green salad.

SWISS CHEESE PIE
Avril Kleeman

Serves 4   Preparation 30 mins.   Cook 35–40 mins.   Advance   Freezable

12 oz shortcrust pastry (340 gm)
6 oz cheddar cheese, grated (170 gm)
2 eggs

Salt and pepper
$\frac{1}{4}$ pt milk (140 ml)
Rounded tsp flour

Line 8″ (20 cm) flan case with pastry. Mix the cheese and flour. Season with salt and pepper. Lightly mix eggs and milk and add to the cheese mixture. Pour into the flan case. Check that the cheese is evenly distributed. Cook in middle of oven Gas No.5, 375°F, 190°C.

NO COOK COTTAGE CHEESE RISSOLES
Maralyn Frazer

Serves 4–6   Preparation 10 mins.   Refrigerate 1 hour   Advance

4 oz mixed nuts, roughly ground (115 gm)
8 oz cottage cheese (225 gm)
3 Sunnybisk or Weetabix breakfast cereal
  cakes, crushed

3 tbls parsley, chopped
1 tbls onion, finely chopped
Salt and pepper to taste

Combine the cottage cheese, nuts, parsley, onions and sufficient salt and pepper to taste. Shape the mixture into six 'cakes'. Coat in crushed cereal and refrigerate until required (minimum 1 hour).

90

COUNTRY PIE
Nanette R. Stolerman

Serves 6   **Preparation 30 mins.**   **Cook 30 mins.**   **Advance**

10 oz wholemeal shortcrust
  pastry (285 gm) (see page 232)
12 oz potatoes, diced (340 gm)
1 lb onions, chopped (450 gm)
4 oz cheese, grated (115 gm)
1 oz butter (30 gm)

Chopped parsley
1 dsp oil
1 tbls milk
Salt and pepper
2 cloves garlic, crushed
9″ flan tin (23 cm)

Roll out pastry and line flan tin. Boil potatoes until tender and drain. Sauté onions in oil until soft. Combine potatoes, onions, butter, parsley, half the cheese, garlic, milk and season well. Cool mixture then fill pastry case. Sprinkle remaining cheese and bake in oven Gas No.7, 425°F, 220°C for 20 minutes until golden.

 ## FENNEL, ALMOND AND GRUYERE BAKE
Marion Cohen

Serves 6   **Preparation 10 mins.**   **Cook 1 hour**

6 very small fennel, trimmed
1 pt single cream (560 ml)
1 large egg
2 oz Gruyère, grated (55 gm)

2 oz parmesan, grated (55 gm)
Salt and pepper
2 oz flaked almonds (55 gm)

Set oven at Gas No.4, 350°F, 180°C. Cook the fennel for 20 minutes in boiling salted water. Drain and arrange in small ovenproof dish. Whisk together the cream, egg, half the Gruyère and parmesan. Season and pour the mixture over the fennel and sprinkle with the remaining cheese and the almonds. Bake for 30–40 minutes until the fennel is tender, the custard is set and the nuts are golden brown.

HERB SPONGE ROULADE
WITH TUNA SALAD
Bettina Bradfield

Serves 8   **Preparation 30 mins.**   **Cook 15 mins.**

ROULADE

1 tbls oil
4 eggs, separated
$\frac{1}{2}$oz sugar (15gm)
$2\frac{1}{2}$ floz vegetable stock (70ml)
$\frac{1}{3}$ cup fresh parsley
2 tbls fresh dill
3 tbls parmesan cheese

*$3\frac{3}{4}$oz flour, (105gm)
*1 tsp baking powder
*Pinch salt
*(sieved together)

SALAD FILLING

3 x 7oz tins tuna in brine,
   drained (600gm)
2oz celery, finely chopped (55gm)
2oz spring onions, finely
   chopped (55gm)
1 tbls lemon juice
Salt and pepper
2 tbls fresh dill, chopped
2 tbls parsley, chopped
8–10 tbls mayonnaise

Swiss roll tin 13 x 9" (32 x 23cm)

Preheat oven to Gas No.5, 375°F, 190°C. Line a Swiss roll tin with buttered and floured paper. Combine flour, baking powder, salt, parsley and dill and set aside. Beat egg yolks until light and fluffy. Gradually add sugar and beat until they are light lemon in colour. Fold in a little flour and the vegetable stock. Beat the egg whites to stiff peaks and fold into the yolk mixture, alternating with the flour. Pour into Swiss roll tin, spread evenly and bake until just cooked, about 12 minutes. Place a damp tea towel on work surface, sprinkle with parmesan and turn out Swiss roll onto it. Remove paper and roll up in the towel. Prepare the salad filling by mixing all the ingredients together. When the roll is cold, spread the filling over it and roll up together.

For variety you can substitute chicken stock for the vegetable stock and use chopped chicken in the salad instead of the tuna fish. Omit the parmesan cheese.

MUSHROOM ROULADE   Michelle Davidson

Serves 6   Preparation 45 mins.   Cook 15 mins.   Advance   Freezable

FILLING

2 oz fresh breadcrumbs (55 gm)
¾ lb mushrooms, chopped (340 gm)
2 tbls single or soured cream
2 tbls parsley, chopped
1 clove garlic, crushed
Salt and pepper
2 oz butter or margarine (55 gm)

ROULADE

2 oz fresh breadcrumbs (55 gm)
3 oz cheddar cheese, grated (85 gm)
4 eggs, separated
4 tbls single or soured cream
Salt and pepper
2 tbls warm water

13 x 9″ Swiss roll tin (32 x 23 cm)
Bakewell paper

Filling: Gently fry breadcrumbs in 1 oz (30 gm) butter until golden. Remove from heat. Heat the rest of the butter, add mushrooms and garlic. Cook for 3–4 minutes. Add seasoning, cream, parsley and cooked breadcrumbs. Keep warm.

Roulade: Line tin with non-stick paper. Mix breadcrumbs and cheese, add egg yolks, cream and seasonings. Stir in warm water, whisk whites until stiff then fold into cheese mixture. Spread evenly in tin and bake for 15 minutes. Turn roulade out onto non-stick paper. Remove lining and add mushroom mixture. Leave on non-stick paper and roll up. To freeze, wrap up in foil. To re-heat, cook for 20–30 minutes Gas No.4, 350°F, 185°C.

Mushrooms can be replaced with same quantity of either spinach or broccoli.

PARSLEY EGGS   Sybil Sinclair

Serves 4   Preparation 30 mins.   Cook 5–10 mins.

4 eggs hardboiled, quartered
2 oz margarine (55 gm)
2 heaped tbls flour
1 or 2 oz cheese, grated, (30–55 gm)

1 pt milk (560 ml)
Salt and pepper
2 heaped tbls parsley, finely chopped

GARNISH: mashed potato and croûtons

Place eggs in a buttered casserole. Melt margarine in a pan, stir in flour and slowly add milk. Cook, stirring constantly, until thickened and add parsley and seasoning. Pour over eggs, sprinkle with grated cheese. Place under moderate grill to melt cheese and heat everything through. Serve with piped potato and garnish with croûtons.

PISSALADIRE

Marion Cohen

Serves 6   **Preparation 20 mins.**   **Cook 1 hour**   **Advance**

8 oz shortcrust pastry (225 gm)
1 lb onions, thinly sliced (450 gm)
4 tbls oil
2 garlic cloves, crushed
1 lb tomatoes, peeled and
   chopped (450 gm) *or*
14 oz tin tomatoes, chopped (400 gm)
1 tsp caster sugar

1 bouquet garni
2 tbls tomato purée
Black pepper
2 oz tin anchovy fillets,
   drained (55 gm)
8–10 black olives

8–9″ flan tin (20–23 cm)

Line the flan tin with pastry and bake blind for 15 minutes on Gas No.6, 400°F, 200°C. Remove the paper and weights. Meanwhile make the filling by heating the oil in a large frying pan. When hot, add the onions and garlic and fry gently for about 10 minutes. Stir in the tomatoes, sugar, bouquet garni, tomato purée, salt and pepper and bring the mixture to the boil. Reduce the heat and simmer, uncovered, for about 30 minutes, stirring occasionally. Remove the bouquet garni and spoon the tomato mixture into the flan case. Lattice the surface with the anchovy fillets and place an olive in each square. Bake for a further 20 minutes, brushing the anchovies and olives with a little oil if they become dry. Serve with a fresh green salad.

QUIZZA

Michelle Davidson

Serves 5   **Preparation 20 mins.**   **Cook 40 mins.**   **Advance**   **Freezable**

12 oz plain or wholemeal
   flour (340 gm)
8 oz tin tomatoes, chopped (225 gm)
1 oz fast action yeast (30 gm)
1 oz margarine (30 gm)
2 eggs
$\frac{1}{2}$ pt milk (280 ml)
4 oz cheese, grated (115 gm

1 onion, chopped
1 clove garlic, chopped
Salt, pepper and mixed herbs
6 black olives
2$\frac{1}{2}$ oz tin anchovy fillets (70 gm)
$\frac{1}{3}$ pt milk/water mixed
   together (180 gm)

7–8″ flan tin (19 cm)

Sieve flour and rub in fat. Add yeast. Stir in milk and water. Gather into a ball and knead until smooth and firm. Roll out into an 8″–9″ (20–23 cm) circle and place in flan tin. Make edges slightly thicker. Fry onion and garlic and add tomatoes, beaten eggs, milk, cheese and seasonings. Pour onto base. Decorate with anchovy fillets and olives. Sprinkle with herbs and cook Gas No.6, 400°F, 200°C for 15 minutes then Gas No.4, 350°F, 180°C for 25 minutes.

The anchovies and olives can be replaced with either tuna and onions or red and green peppers, sliced tomato, mushrooms and mozzarella cheese if preferred.

94

CREAMY SPINACH QUICHE   Beverly Stopler

Serves 8–10   Preparation 20 mins.   Cook 35 mins.   Advance   Freezable

8oz shortcrust pastry (225gm)
1lb frozen spinach (450gm)
2¾oz Boursin with herbs (78gm)
3oz Philadelphia cream cheese (85gm)

5 floz sour cream (140ml)
4 large eggs, beaten
1 tsp nutmeg, grated
Salt and black pepper

Line a flan case with the pastry. Defrost and drain the spinach well. Beat together the cheeses, sour cream and drained spinach, then add the eggs, nutmeg and seasoning. Bake at Gas No.4, 350°F, 185°C.

SPINACH AND COTTAGE CHEESE QUICHE   Avril Kleeman

Serves 4   Preparation 10 mins.   Cook 45 mins.   Advance   Freezeable

8″ (20cm) pastry flan case, uncooked
8oz frozen spinach, defrosted (225gm)
8oz plain cottage cheese (225gm)
3 eggs, beaten

1oz cheddar cheese, grated (30gm)
4 tbls cream or milk
Salt and pepper

Mix spinach and cottage cheese. Add eggs, cheese and milk or cream and seasoning. Pour into the flan case and cook at Gas No.5, 375°F, 190°C for 45 minutes.

SPINACH ROULADE
WITH CHEESE SAUCE
Bianca Roden

Serves 3–4   **Preparation 30 mins.**   **Cook 25 mins**

1½lb frozen chopped spinach,
   thawed and drained (700gm)
4 eggs, separated
Pinch nutmeg
Salt and black pepper

Swiss roll tin 8" x 12" (20 x 30cm)

GARNISH: 1oz cheddar cheese, grated
   (30gm)

CHEESE SAUCE
1½oz butter (42gm)
1oz flour (30gm)
½ pt milk, warmed (280ml)
4oz cheddar cheese, grated (115gm)
Pinch nutmeg
¼ tsp cayenne pepper
Salt and black pepper

Pre-heat oven to Gas No.6, 400°F, 200°C. Mix lightly beaten egg yolks with the drained spinach and season with nutmeg, salt and black pepper. Whisk egg whites until moist in appearance and form soft peaks. Stir just 1 tablespoon egg whites into the spinach mixture then fold in remainder in two batches. Put this mixture into lined and greased Swiss roll tin and bake for 10–15 minutes until beginning to brown.

Sauce: Melt butter then sprinkle over the flour and cook roux for 2–3 minutes stirring. Pour in the warmed milk slowly and bring sauce to the boil stirring continuously. When boiled, let simmer for 5 minutes. Remove pan from heat and stir in grated cheese and season with nutmeg, cayenne pepper and salt and pepper. When roulade is cooked take it out of oven, turn out onto greaseproof paper and peel off the lining paper. Spread some of the sauce over it and roll up the roulade. Pour remaining sauce over the top and sprinkle with extra grated cheese. Put roulade back into oven for 5–10 minutes until cheese has melted. Serve immediately.

SPINACH ROULADE
WITH TARAMASALATA
Jo Luck

Serves 6   **Preparation 15 mins.**   **Cook 20 mins.**

ROULADE

8oz frozen spinach (225gm)
4 medium eggs, separated
½ pint béchamel sauce (280ml)
   (see Sauces section page 156)
Salt, pepper, nutmeg
Parmesan cheese

FILLING

7oz taramasalata (200gm)
5 floz soured cream (or creme fraiche)
   (142ml)
Spring onions, chopped

GARNISH: radishes or tomato rosettes

Swiss roll tin

Mix the cooked, drained spinach with the egg yolks and the white sauce. Fold in the stiffly beaten egg whites. Spread mixture onto greased paper on a Swiss roll tin and cook for 15–20 minutes Gas No.6, 400°F, 200°C. When light and spongy turn onto another sheet of greaseproof paper that has been liberally sprinkled with Parmesan cheese. Spread with a layer of soured cream and chopped spring onions, then a layer of taramasalata. Roll up and serve warm, garnished with radishes or tomato rosettes.

TARTE BARCELONA
Meriel Joseph

Serves 6   **Preparation 10 mins.**   **Cook 20 mins.**

12oz shortcrust pastry (340gm)

WHITE SAUCE

1¾oz butter (50gm)
2oz flour, sifted (55gm)
½ pt hot milk (280ml)
½ tsp nutmeg
10″ tart tin (25cm)

FILLING

3½lb fresh spinach (1.5k)
3½oz sultanas (100gm)
2oz pine kernels (55gm)
¾oz butter (25gm)
Salt
Black pepper, freshly ground
6 poached eggs (optional)

Line tart tin with pastry and bake blind for 15 minutes on Gas No.5, 375°F, 190°C. Cook spinach in boiling salted water for 5 minutes. Drain thoroughly and chop.

White sauce: Melt butter in saucepan. Stir in flour and cook gently for one minute. Slowly stir in the hot milk until thickened and season to taste with salt, pepper and nutmeg. Add the spinach and boil for 2 minutes. Meanwhile, heat remaining butter in small pan and toss the sultanas and pine kernels in it. Drain them and add to the spinach mixture. Pour into the warm pastry shell and serve immediately. If desired place 6 poached eggs on top.

TUNA AND EGG PASTIES
Janet Williams

Serves 6   **Preparation 20 mins.**   **Cook 25–30 mins.**   **Advance**   **Freezable**

7oz tin tuna (200gm)
4 hard boiled eggs
½ lemon rind, grated
3 tbls lemon juice
2 tbls parsley, chopped
12oz shortcrust pastry (350gm)
Beaten egg to glaze

WHITE SAUCE

1oz margarine (25gm)
3 level tbls flour
½ pt milk (280ml)
Salt and ground black pepper

Drain tuna and flake fish into basin. Chop eggs and mix with lemon rind, juice, parsley and fish. Make white sauce and mix into fish and eggs. Season to taste and cool. Roll pastry and cut into 12 squares. Divide filling equally onto pastry. Fold into triangles. Seal edges well to prevent oozing. Glaze. Place on greased baking sheet. Cook at Gas No.5, 375°F, 190°C for 25–30 minutes or until golden.

TUNA AND SALMON
DELIGHT
Michelle Davidson

Serves 4   Preparation 20 mins.   Cook 15–20 mins.   Advance   Freezable

3½oz tin salmon, drained (100gm)
3½oz tin tuna, drained (100gm)
12 stuffed green olives
1lb 10oz frozen puff pastry (730gm)
Milk to glaze

SAUCE
½oz butter (15gm)
½oz flour (15gm)
¾ pt milk (425ml)
¼ tsp dried tarragon (optional)
Seasoning

Drain fish, remove skin and bones, mash with fork. Make sauce by melting butter in pan, stir in flour until combined, add milk slowly stirring until thickened. Mix fish with sauce, add seasonings and cool. Roll out pastry, cut into 8 fish shapes. Add mixture to top of 4 shapes and dampen edges. Cover with remaining shapes. Use pastry to decorate shapes to look like fish. Glaze with milk and cook until risen and golden brown on Gas No.7, 425°F, 220°C. Serve hot or cold.

MIXED VEGETABLE
STRUDEL
Sandra Rubinstein

Serves 6–8   Preparation 40 mins.   Cook 35 mins.   Freezable

1lb filo pastry (450gm)
2oz butter (55gm)

SAUCE

8oz Greek yoghurt *or*
3 rounded tbls Hellman's mayonnaise
1 tsp caster sugar
1 tbls chives, snipped
Parsley
Pinch of salt
Speck of white pepper

FILLING

1lb frozen stir fry vegetables (450gm)
½lb broccoli florets (225gm)
4oz mange-tout cut in half lengthways
   (115gm)
1oz butter (30gm)
1 tbls parsley, finely chopped
6oz strong flavoured cheddar cheese,
   grated (180gm)
2 eggs, beaten
Seasoning to taste
2 tbls sesame seeds

Filling: Pre-heat oven to Gas No.5, 375°F, 190°C. Melt the butter in a wok or a frying pan and stir-fry the vegetables until tender about 3–4 minutes then stir in the beaten eggs, cheese, seasonings and parsley. Slightly cool the mixture. Brush the baking tray with some of the 2oz (50gm) butter which has been melted. Cover with a layer of filo pastry, brush the pastry immediately with more of the melted butter and continue in this way until you have used 4 sheets of filo pastry. Spoon the cooled filling onto the pastry leaving 1″ (2.5cm) border all round, making a band of filling about 3″ (7.6cm) across. Turn in the sides to enclose the filling, then roll up the pastry into a strudel and brush the top with melted butter and scatter thickly with sesame seeds. Bake for 35 minutes until golden. Slice and serve within 30 minutes accompanied by the sauce

Sauce: Stir all the ingredients together and serve with the strudel.

VEGETABLE TART
Simone Ross

Serves 4   **Preparation 15 mins.**   **Cook 30 mins.**   **Freezable**

4oz shortcrust pastry (115gm)
4oz vegetables, blanched (115gm)
   (e.g. broccoli, courgettes, carrots)
1 tbls fresh herbs, chopped

1 whole egg
3 egg yolks
8 floz double cream (225ml)
Salt and black pepper

10 x 8″ oblong flan dish (25 x 20cm)

Line the flan dish with the pastry and bake blind for 12–15 minutes on Gas No.4, 350°F, 180°C. Meanwhile beat the eggs and cream together to make a custard. Put the blanched vegetables into the flan pastry and sprinkle with chopped herbs and seasoning. Pour over the custard and bake for 15 minutes or until the custard is set, on Gas No.3, 325°F, 160°C.

N.B. Leftover vegetables may be used instead of fresh.

VOULAS PIE
Phyllis Horal

Serves 6   **Preparation 45 mins.**   **Cook 30 mins.**

2.2lb courgettes, coarsely grated (1k)
6 eggs
Salt and black pepper

Filo pastry
10oz Feta cheese, grated (300gm)
Greased oval ovenproof dish

Salt the courgettes and leave to drain in a colander for 30 minutes; squeeze dry. Beat the eggs and add the cheese, courgettes and pepper. Lay 3 pieces of filo pastry on the bottom of an oval ovenproof dish, oiling lightly between each sheet. Cover with half the courgette mixture, then add another layer of the filo sheets. Pour on the remaining mixture and finish with the pastry; always lightly oiling between the sheets. Cook at Gas No.6, 400°F, 200°C for 10 minutes, then at Gas No.1, 275°F, 150°C for 20 minutes.

Vegetable Main Dishes

AUBERGINE BAKE Susan Gelb

Serves 6   Preparation 45 mins   Cook 30–45 mins.   Advance   Freezable

2 large aubergines, sliced with
  skins on
½lb mushrooms, chopped (225gm)
6oz cheese, grated (170gm)
1 tbls sesame seeds

SAUCE

1 tbls Vecon or other vegetable extract
14oz tin plum tomatoes (395gm)

4¾oz tin tomato purée (140gm)
1 onion, chopped
2 cloves garlic, chopped
2 tbls oil
1 green pepper, chopped (optional)
1 stick celery, chopped (optional)
1 tsp oregano
1 tsp basil

Sprinkle aubergines with salt and leave for 30 minutes. Wash and dry. Brush with oil and place under hot grill until well browned. Turn over and repeat.

Sauce: Fry onion and garlic in oil until golden. Add peppers and celery if used. Fry 2–3 minutes. Add all remaining sauce ingredients plus 3 tins water (use tomato tin). Bring to boil and simmer until thick – about 25 minutes. Season well. Place thin layer of sauce in large ovenproof dish, then a layer of aubergines, then chopped mushrooms. Sprinkle with a little cheese and repeat layers ending with cheese. Sprinkle sesame seeds on top and bake for 30–45 minutes at Gas No.4, 350°F, 180°C until golden and bubbly. Serve with brown rice and green salad.

N.B. For extra nutrition add 4oz (115gm) washed red lentils to sauce when adding tinned tomatoes.

Microwave instructions
Cook on power 7 for 10–12 minutes.

BUCKWHEAT PANCAKES Lynne Goldwyn

Serves 4   Preparation 5 mins. Refrigerate 30 mins.   Cook 10 mins.

3oz strong white flour (85gm)
3oz buckwheat flour (85gm)
½ tsp sea salt
A little oil

2 eggs
¼ pt milk (115ml)
¼ pt water (115ml)

Process all the ingredients together (except the oil) and leave to rest in the refrigerator. Cover the bottom of a small crepe pan with a film of oil and heat until smoking. Pour in enough batter to cover the bottom of the pan and swirl it around until it forms an even layer. Cook until the bottom is just golden then turn it over and cook the other side. Repeat until all the mixture is used. Serve flat with sour cream, or cream cheese and chopped chives, or chopped spring onion.

BUDDHIST MIX OR STIR-FRIED
MIXED VEGETABLES
Jane Finestone

Serves 4   Preparation 15 mins.   Cook 7–10 mins.   Freezable

2 tbls groundnut oil
1 dsp fresh ginger, finely chopped
1 dsp fresh garlic, finely chopped
1 tbls dry sherry
2 tbls soy sauce
1 fl oz water (30 ml)
2 tsp sugar
3 tbls spring onion finely chopped

2 lb any combination of vegetables
  (900 gm)
e.g. 3 courgettes, chopped
  $\frac{1}{2}$ lb whole green beans (225 gm)
  4 large carrots, sliced
  1 tin baby sweet corn
  $\frac{1}{4}$ cauliflower head in florets
  4 large spinach leaves
  3 oz mushrooms (85 gm)

Heat the oil in a wok, or cast iron casserole and sauté onions, ginger and garlic. After about 2 minutes add sherry, sugar, soy sauce and water and stir well. Add the carrots and any of the firmer vegetables and coat well. Then add all the softer vegetables, e.g. mushrooms. Stir well and reduce heat. Simmer for about 5 minutes with the lid on. Cooking time will depend on the types of the vegetables selected. Serve with pasta or baked potato.

Microwave instructions

If this is microwaved it becomes a Chinese vegetable casserole. Simply combine all the sauce ingredients and cook on full power for $1\frac{1}{2}$ minutes. Mix and coat vegetables well. Cover completely and cook on full power for 9 minutes in a shallow dish, and stand for 4 minutes.

BROCCOLI AND CHEESE
GOUGERE
Naomi Greenwood

Serves 4   Preparation 20 mins.   Cook 1 hour

GOUGERE
$\frac{1}{2}$ pt water (280 ml)
4 oz butter cut into pieces (115 gm)
4 oz flour (115 gm)
Salt and black pepper
4 eggs

FILLING
1 lb broccoli, roughly chopped (450 gm)
2 tsp cornflour
$\frac{1}{4}$ pt cream or yoghurt (140 ml)
$\frac{1}{4}$ pt pint milk (140 ml)
4 oz cheddar cheese, grated (115 gm)

Pre-heat oven to Gas No.7, 425°F, 220°C. Heat water and butter in saucepan until butter has melted and then bring mixture to the boil. Remove from heat and immediately beat in the flour and a pinch of salt with a wooden spoon until mixture comes away from the sides of the pan. Beat in eggs one at a time and continue beating until mixture is satin smooth. Spoon mixture around edges of heatproof flan dish. Bake for 40 minutes until risen and golden. Boil broccoli until just beginning to soften, then drain. Mix cornflour to a smooth paste with a little of the cream/yoghurt, add to the heated milk and stir until boiling. Remove from heat and stir in the remainder of the cream/yoghurt, seasonings and most of the cheese. Remove gougere from the oven, and arrange broccoli in the centre and pour sauce over the broccoli. Sprinkle with the remaining cheese and return to oven for 10 minutes until cheese has melted and is brown on top.

STIR FRIED CHINESE LEAVES
WITH ALMONDS
Naomi Greenwood

Serves 4 Preparation 10 mins. Cook 3 mins.

6 oz Chinese noodles, cooked (170 gm)
½ small head of Chinese leaves, diced
½ red pepper, shredded
2 spring onions, shredded
2″ piece root ginger, peeled and finely
shredded (5 cm)
1 sprig fresh rosemary

2 tbls oil
1 tbls soy sauce
1 tbls dry sherry
Pinch of ground cardamom
Salt and pepper
2 oz blanched almonds, shredded
(55 gm)

Heat oil until very hot in a wok or large saucepan. Add almonds, ginger and rosemary and cook, stirring, for one minute. Add the rest of the vegetables and noodles and stir fry for 2 minutes. Meanwhile mix soy sauce, sherry and cardamom. Pour into the pan, season and cook stirring for a few more seconds. Remove rosemary and serve immediately.

LAYERED CASHEW
AND MUSHROOM ROAST
Bianca Roden

Serves 6–8 Preparation 20 mins. Cook 1 hour Standing time 10 mins. Advance

1 tbls oil
1 small onion, finely chopped
2 cloves garlic, crushed
8 oz cashew nuts (225 gm)
4 oz fresh breadcrumbs (115 gm)
1 egg
3 medium parsnips, cooked and
    mashed with a little butter

1 tsp fresh rosemary
1 tsp fresh thyme
1 tsp yeast extract
¼ pt hot water/stock (140 ml)
Salt and black pepper
1 oz butter (30 gm)
8 oz mushrooms, chopped (225 gm)
2 lb loaf tin (900 gm)

Pre-heat oven to Gas No.4, 350°F, 180°C. Heat oil and fry onion and garlic until soft. Grind cashew nuts in a nut mill/blender/mincer, then mix with the breadcrumbs. Beat egg and add it to the dry ingredients. Mix in the mashed parsnips and herbs. Add the fried onion. Dissolve yeast extract in hot water/stock and add to the other ingredients. Season well. Melt butter in frying pan and sauté mushrooms until soft. Grease the loaf tin with butter then press in *half* the nut mixture. Cover with a layer of mushrooms and top with the rest of the nut mixture. Cover with foil and bake for 1 hour. When cooked, remove loaf from oven and let it stand for 10 minutes before turning it out. Serve hot or cold.

CHESTNUT ROAST

Sybil Sinclair

Serves 4–6   Preparation 1 hour 10 mins.   Cook 1 hour

½lb dehydrated chestnuts (225gm)
1 large onion, stuck with 1 clove
2oz margarine (55gm)
3oz soft breadcrumbs (85gm)
1 pt milk (570ml)

2 eggs
1 bay leaf
Nutmeg
Salt and pepper
1lb loaf tin (450gm)

Put the chestnuts, onion, bay leaf and milk in a pan. Heat to boiling point then remove from heat. Cover and leave for 30 minutes to infuse. Remove bay leaf and clove and cook chestnuts and onion until tender about 30 minutes, and liquid is reduced to ¼ pt (145ml). Sieve or liquidise. Add margarine, breadcrumbs, eggs, nutmeg, salt and pepper and mix well. Turn into 1lb loaf tin that has been lined with buttered greaseproof paper. Bake for 1 hour at Gas No.4, 350°F, 180°C. Serve with roast potatoes and a green vegetable.

STUFFED CHESTNUT
AND CHEESE ROAST

Gillian Carmel

Serves 6   Preparation 20 mins.   Cook 45 mins.   Advance

CHESTNUT MIXTURE

1lb fresh chestnuts (450gm)
or ½lb dried soaked chestnuts (225gm)
2 large onions, chopped
2oz breadcrumbs (55gm)
1 tsp dried sage
1 tsp yeast extract
Salt and pepper
1 tbls oil

STUFFING

1 large onion, chopped
4oz cheese, grated (115gm)
2 tbls milk
1 egg
1 tbls oil

Chestnut mixture: Sauté onion in oil until soft, approx. 10 minutes. Slit chestnuts and roast for 10 minutes (Gas No.8, 450°F, 230°C) until able to be peeled. Cook shelled chestnuts in water until soft; drain and purée. Mix purée with onion and remaining chestnut mixture ingredients.

Stuffing: Sauté onions in oil and mix with remaining stuffing ingredients. Spread half the chestnut mixture in a baking dish. Spread the stuffing mixture on top and cover with remaining layer of chestnut mixture. Bake in moderate oven Gas No.5, 375°F, 185°C. for 40–50 minutes.

GATEAU ROTHSCHILD

Anne Moss

Serves 6   **Preparation 40 mins.**   **Cook 30 mins.**   **Advance**

8 oz green peppers, thinly sliced
  (225 gm)
12 oz ripe tomatoes, peeled and sliced
  (340 gm)
12 oz aubergines or courgettes (340 gm)
2 oz cheese, grated (55 gm)
Salt and pepper
3 oz butter (85 gm)
Oregano

8 oz onions or shallots, chopped
  (225 gm)
2 cloves garlic, crushed
6 oz mushrooms, finely chopped
  (170 gm)
3 oz breadcrumbs (85 gm)
3 fl oz oil (85 ml)
1 tsp parsley

Heat butter and oil in pan. Cut aubergines in half and score, sprinkle with salt and leave for about 20 minutes. Rinse and cut into slices. Fry peppers gently until tender. Turn into sieve and squeeze out all the oil and butter with the back of a spoon. Turn onto a plate. Fry each vegetable separately and remove excess oil and place on a separate plate. Fry the tomatoes with the oregano. Season each vegetable with salt and pepper. Place a layer of the peppers in a greased ovenproof dish, sprinkle with breadcrumbs and cheese and parsley. Cover with onions and garlic and sprinkle with cheese mixture, then tomatoes followed by mushrooms and finally aubergines. Sprinkle a layer of cheese mixture in between each layer, ending with the cheese mixture. Press down well. Allow to set in fridge. Just before serving bake on Gas No.4, 350°F, 185°C for about 15 minutes. Courgettes may be used instead of aubergines.

HAZELNUT AND WALNUT ROAST

Sybil Sinclair

Serves 6   **Preparation 30 mins.**   **Cook 30 mins.**

3 large Spanish onions, finely chopped
3 oz margarine (85 gm)
6 oz hazelnuts, ground (170 gm)
2 oz walnuts, ground (55 gm)
5 oz breadcrumbs (140 gm)
1 dsp yeast extract (marmite)

1 egg
1 tsp sage
Seasoning to taste
2 lb loaf tin (1 k)

GARNISH: tomato, cauliflower and
  parsley

Sauté onions in the margarine until golden brown. Add the ground nuts, crumbs, egg, sage, yeast extract and seasoning and mix well. Place the mixture in a well-greased tin and bake for about 30 minutes Gas No.5, 375°F, 190°C. Remove from oven and leave in tin for a few minutes. Turn out onto hot plate and garnish with slices of tomato and sprigs of cauliflower and parsley.

MUSHROOM CROUSTADE
Anna Cohen

Serves 4   **Preparation 15 mins.**   **Cook 20 mins.**

BASE

4 oz soft breadcrumbs (115 gm)
4 oz ground almonds (115 gm)
4 oz butter/margarine, cut in pieces
 (115 gm)
4 oz mixed flaked almonds/pine kernels/
 chopped hazelnuts (115 gm)
1 clove garlic, crushed
$\frac{1}{2}$ tsp mixed herbs

TOPPING

1 lb mushrooms (450 gm)
2 oz butter (55 gm)
2 heaped tbls flour
12 fl oz milk (340 gm)
Salt, pepper, nutmeg
8″ ovenproof dish (20 cm)

Base: Mix breadcrumbs and ground almonds. Rub in butter (as for pastry). Add flaked almonds, pine kernels and hazelnuts. Add garlic and herbs and mix well. Press down firmly in greased ovenproof dish. Bake in oven Gas No.8, 450°F, 230°C until golden (10–15 minutes).

Topping: Chop half the mushrooms and slice the rest. Saùté in butter. Stir flour into the mushrooms until the butter froths, then remove from the heat and gradually stir in the milk. Return to the heat and stir until thickened. Simmer over low heat for 5–10 minutes, add seasonings to taste. Spoon on top of base and serve immediately.

PIPERADE
Elissa Bennett

Serves 4–6   **Preparation 20 mins.**   **Cook 45 mins.**   **Sauce may be made in advance**

1 large Spanish onion, finely chopped
1 fat clove garlic, crushed
4 large tomatoes, skinned and
 chopped
4 tbls olive oil
5 large eggs

*1 red pepper
*1 green pepper
*1 yellow pepper
* *Skinned, deseeded and finely*
 chopped
Salt and pepper

Soften onions and garlic in closed saucepan in olive oil for about 15 minutes. Add peppers and cook for further 15 minutes. Add tomatoes and cook until all are tender, but not mushy. If very wet reduce liquid by boiling gently with lid off. Season. Beat eggs lightly and scramble into the mixture. Serve at once with crusty bread.

PASSOVER VEGETARIAN ROAST   David Burr

Serves 4   Preparation 8 mins.   Cook 45 mins.   Advance

6 oz ground mixed nuts (170 gm)
2 eggs, beaten
1 onion, chopped
1 carrot, grated
2 cloves garlic, crushed

2 tbls tomato purée
2 oz fine matzo meal (55 gm)
1 onion, sliced
1 pt vegetable stock (570 ml)
Salt and black pepper

Put all the ingredients except the sliced onion and vegetable stock, into a bowl and mix well. Grease an ovenproof casserole and place a layer of sliced onions on the base and around the sides. Put the nut mixture in the casserole, pour on the vegetable stock, and bake at Gas No.4, 350°F, 180°C. Can be served hot or cold.

SABZI KUKU   Naomi Greenward
(Scrumptious green pancakes)

Serves 4–6   Preparation 10 mins.   Cook 5 mins.   Advance   Freezable

4 cups spinach, chopped
2 sprigs fresh parsley, finely chopped
2 sprigs each fresh coriander and
    dill, finely chopped
2 leeks, finely chopped

6 eggs
Salt and black pepper
1 cup fine matzo meal
4 tbls oil

Place eggs in a large bowl with the vegetables and herbs, then season to taste. Stir in the matzo meal. The mixture should have the consistency of thick cream, if it is too thick add a little water. Heat the oil in a pan over high heat until very hot. Drop 1 or 2 tablespoons of the mixture into it to make pancakes about 3″ (7½ cm) in diameter. Cook for 2 minutes, then turn them and cook for another 2 minutes. Drain the pancakes on absorbent paper, and continue to make more until batter is used up. Serve warm or cold with sour cream or cottage cheese.

SHEPHERD'S PIE I   Zoe Sorkin

Serves 4   Preparation 15 mins.   Cook 25 mins.

2 onions, chopped
6 oz mushrooms, sliced (170 gm)
4 sticks celery, chopped
1½ lb potatoes, mashed (700 gm)
½ pt vegetable stock (280 ml)

Juice of ½ lemon
2 oz margarine (55 gm)
1 heaped dsp wholemeal flour
Salt and pepper

Sauté the onions, mushrooms and celery in margarine until transparent. Stir in the flour, gradually add the stock and lemon juice and stir until thickened. Transfer to ovenproof dish and cover with mashed potatoes. Bake in moderate oven Gas No.4, 350°F, 185°C for 20 minutes.

SHEPHERD'S PIE II

Susan Gelb

Serves 6   Preparation 25 mins.   Cook 30 mins.   Advance   Freezable

2 cups unflavoured T.V.P. mince or chunks
2 tbls tomato purée
1 large carrot, chopped
2 large onions, chopped
1 stick celery, chopped
1 red pepper, chopped
1 green pepper, chopped

1 tbls oil
1 tbls mixed herbs
4 cups strong stock approx.
5 large potatoes
Seasoning
1 tbls sesame seeds or
   sunflower seeds

Soak the T.V.P. in well flavoured stock. Fry onions in oil until brown, then add remaining vegetables. Sweat for about 7 minutes in covered saucepan. Add T.V.P. with any left over stock, tomato purée and herbs. Season well. The mixture should be quite wet, if not, add more stock. Pour into pie dish. Boil potatoes and mash, season well. Smooth potatoes on top and sprinkle with sesame seeds and bake until golden for approx. 30 minutes at Gas No.4, 350°F, 180°C. If desired sprinkle cheese on top before baking. Serve hot with vegetables e.g. cauliflower, beans etc.

SHEPHERD'S PIE III

Wendy Grossmith

Serves 4   Preparation 10 mins.   Cook 1 hour   Advance   Freeze without potatoes

4oz split red lentils (115gm)
2oz pearl barley (55gm)
8oz carrots, grated (225gm)
1 medium onion, finely chopped
14oz tin of tomatoes (400gm)
1½ pt oven proof dish (850ml)

½ pt vegetable stock (280ml)
1½lb potatoes (750gm)
6 tbls milk
3oz cheddar cheese, grated (85gm)
N.B. Low fat cheese may be used

Put lentils, barley, carrots, onion, tomatoes and their juice and stock into a saucepan. Bring to the boil, cover pan and simmer for 40 minutes or until the lentils and barley are soft. Season to taste. Boil potatoes until soft and mash with milk and cheese. Preheat oven to Gas No.6, 400°F, 200°C. Put lentil mixture into an ovenproof dish and pile potatoes on top in an even layer. Make pattern on top with fork. Put pie in oven for 20 minutes or until golden around the edge.

PROVENCALE VEGETABLE CASSEROLE
Helen Meller

Serves 6   **Preparation 30 mins.**   **Cook 45 mins.**

$2\frac{1}{4}$lb aubergine, diced (1k)
$2\frac{1}{4}$lb tomatoes, peeled and
  quartered (1k)
2 large spanish onions, chopped
$5\frac{1}{4}$ fl oz olive oil (150ml)
3 cloves garlic

8 anchovy fillets in oil
1 tbls flour
$2\frac{1}{2}$ fl oz milk (70ml)
Parsley, chopped
2oz fresh white breadcrumbs (55gm)
Salt

Put aubergines into a sieve, sprinkle with salt and leave to sweat for 30 minutes. Heat oil and fry onions until transparent. Remove seeds from tomatoes. Wash aubergines and dry on kitchen paper. Add to onions, together with tomatoes and one chopped clove of garlic. Cook gently stirring frequently. In a mixing bowl make a roux of anchovy fillets mashed in their oil with the flour and milk. Add to the vegetables mixing well. Crush remaining garlic and mix with parsley and breadcrumbs. Put vegetables into ovenproof dish and cover with breadcrumb mixture. Put into very hot oven Gas No.8, 450°F, 230°C until a crust is formed.

VEGETABLE CRUMBLE I
Sylvia Webber

Serves 4   **Preparation 15 mins.**   **Cook 40 mins.**   **Advance**

1 cauliflower, divided into florets
12oz carrots, thinly sliced (340gm)
12oz parsnips, sliced (340gm)
12oz leeks, sliced (340gm)

$1\frac{1}{2}$ pt white sauce made from water
  vegetables are cooked in (850ml)
5oz breadcrumbs (140gm)
3oz soft margarine (85gm)
2oz rolled oats (55gm)

Preheat oven to Gas No.6, 400°F, 200°C. Cook the vegetables together until tender in boiling salted water. Put in ovenproof dish and cover with the sauce. Rub the margarine into the breadcrumbs with the rolled oats. Sprinkle over the vegetables and bake for 20–25 minutes.

VEGETABLE CRUMBLE II
Maralyn Fraser

Serves 6   Preparation 25 mins.   Cook 1 hour   Advance   Freezable

CRUMBLE TOPPING

4 oz butter or margarine (115 gm)
6 oz 100% wholemeal flour (170 gm)
4 oz cheddar cheese, grated (115 gm)
2 oz mixed nuts, chopped (55 gm)
2 tbls sesame seeds (optional)

BASE

1½ lb mixed root vegetables, chopped (675 gm)
1 large onion, chopped
2 oz butter or margarine (55 gm)
1 oz 100% wholemeal flour (30 gm)
8 oz tomatoes, skinned, chopped (225 gm)
½ pt vegetable stock (280 ml)
¼ pt milk (140 ml)
3 tbls parsley, chopped
Salt and pepper to taste

Crumble topping: Rub the butter into the flour until the mixture resembles fine crumbs. Mix in the cheese, nuts and sesame seeds.

Base: Melt the butter in a large saucepan and sauté the onion until transparent. Add the prepared vegetables and cook over a gentle heat, stirring occasionally, for 10 minutes. Stir in the flour, then add the remaining ingredients. Bring to the boil, reduce heat, cover and simmer for about 15 minutes until the vegetables are just tender. Transfer to an ovenproof dish. Press the crumble topping over the vegetables and bake in the oven at Gas No.5, 375°F, 190°C for about 30 minutes until golden.

VEGETABLE HOT POT
Eve Barry

Serves 4–6   Preparation 15 mins.   Cook 1 hour   Advance

1 large potato
1 large onion
1 medium swede
1 large parsnip
2 large or 3 medium carrots
5 oz tin baked beans (140 gm)
Salt and pepper

1 or 2 sticks celery
4 oz fresh breadcrumbs (115 gm)
4 oz cheddar cheese, grated (115 gm)
1¼ cups boiling water
1 vegetable cube
1 bouquet garni, *or*
½ tsp mixed herbs

Slice all vegetables and put in layers, together with bouquet garni or mixed herbs. Dissolve vegetable cube in water and pour over vegetables. Bake, covered, until soft (approx. 45 minutes) on Gas No.4, 350°F, 180°C. Remove bouquet garni. Pour on baked beans. Shake cheese and breadcrumbs together in plastic bag and spread on top of vegetables. Bake, uncovered, for 15 minutes on Gas No.6, 400°F, 200°C.

VEGETABLE LAYER BAKE　　Lilian Bloch

Serves 4　　　Preparation 35 mins.　　　Cook 45 mins.　　　Advance

½lb potatoes, sliced (225gm)
4oz swede and parsnips,
　cubed (115gm)
4oz carrots (115gm)
2 sticks celery, sliced
2oz mushrooms, sliced (55gm)
4oz onions, sliced (115gm)
1oz frozen peas (30gm)
1oz frozen corn (30gm)

½ pt milk (280ml)
4oz cheese, grated (115gm)
Salt and pepper
Vegetable oil
2 eggs
1 tbls dried herbs
2 pt oven dish (1.14l)

GARNISH: watercress
　　　　　 2–3 tomatoes

(You can use any combination of vegetables as long as you have a good mix of colour and texture.) Gently cook potatoes, carrots, celery, swede, and parsnip, in salted water until just cooked. Drain and reserve. Sauté onions in a little vegetable oil until soft. Preheat oven Gas No.4, 350°F, 185°C. Grease oven dish. Alternate layers of all vegetables, chopped herbs and grated cheese. Repeat until all the ingredients are used, finishing with a layer of cheese. Beat together eggs, milk and seasoning. Pour over ingredients in dish. Bake for 45 minutes until set and golden. Serve hot, garnished with watercress and tomato.

 ## VEGETARIAN MOUSSAKA　　Kate Williams

Serves 10–12　Preparation 1 hour　Cook 45 mins.–1 hour　Advance　Freezable

8oz hazelnuts – toasted, skinned and
　finely ground (225gm)
8oz walnuts, finely ground (225gm)
4oz sunflower oil (115ml)
8oz granary or wholemeal bread-
　crumbs (225gm)
1 medium onion, finely chopped
2 cloves garlic, crushed
1 pt vegetable stock (570ml)

1 pt tomato sauce (570ml)
　(see Sauce section page 159)
2 tbls parsley, chopped
Salt and freshly ground black pepper
2lb aubergines (1k)
Bechamel cheese sauce
　(see Sauce section page 156)
Vegetable oil for frying

Ovenproof dish 12″ x 10″ x 2½″
　(30cm x 25cm x 6cm)

Slice aubergines lengthways, score and sprinkle with salt – leave for 1 hour then rinse and dry with paper towel. Fry aubergines in vegetable oil until crisp. Drain on paper towel to get rid of any excess oil. Soften chopped onion in sunflower oil until transparent, add garlic, ground nuts, breadcrumbs, stock and parsley. Bring to the boil slowly, then reduce the heat and simmer gently for about 15 minutes, stirring occasionally to prevent mixture from sticking. Add tomato sauce to nutmeat mixture, adding more stock if necessary. Put half the aubergines in a layer on base of large ovenproof dish. Cover with the nutmeat mixture then top with the remaining aubergine slices. Pour over the bèchamel sauce. Bake in preheated oven Gas No.6, 400°F, 200°C for 45 minutes–1 hour until golden.

Poultry

My doctor's a darling — he told me to keep the sling for another month!

HINTS

Turkey has less fat than any other meat.

Grilled chicken is particularly tasty but only use young chickens or poussins. They may be marinaded in chopped onion, a little oil, salt, pepper and cinnamon for at least 2 hours before cooking.

CHINESE CHICKEN HAMPSTEAD STYLE
Colin Aaronson

Serves 4 Preparation 10 mins. Cook 10 mins.

4 chicken breasts, skinned and cut into 1" cubes (2.5 cm)
2 green peppers, cut into 1" cubes (2.5 cm)
1 clove garlic, chopped
Vegetable oil for frying
Salt
3 slices peeled fresh ginger
½ chicken stock cube

½ tbls sugar
½ red chilli, sliced
Plain flour to coat

SAUCE

6 tbls sherry
2 tbls white wine vinegar
2 tbls soya sauce
1 tbls caster sugar

Mix together sauce ingredients. Coat chicken in flour and fry in hot oil until golden. Remove chicken and add peppers, garlic, ginger, chilli, sugar and crumbled cube into pan and fry. As peppers soften return chicken to pan. Add sauce and stir. Serve on a bed of rice.

CHICKEN DO PIAZZA (CURRY)
Mireille Dessau

Serves 4 Preparation 15 mins. Cook 10 mins.

4 chicken breasts, boned
1 large onion, finely chopped
2 skinned tomatoes or 1 tsp tomato purée
1 tbls water
1½ tsp ground coriander
1 tsp turmeric
1 tsp cayenne
1 tsp cumin
Garam Masala

CURRY PASTE

Garlic
Ginger
Chilli

(See Sauce section page 160)

GARNISH: fresh coriander leaves

Cut chicken into small pieces and fry quickly to seal. Remove from pan. Fry onion, then add curry paste and fry for 1 minute. Add spices, cook, add chicken and water. Cover and cook. Add tomatoes when ready. Garnish with coriander leaves.

CHICKEN WITH EGGPLANT   Barbara Green

Serves 4   Preparation 1¼ hours   Cook 1½ hours

2 medium or 1 large eggplant (aubergine)	½ cup margarine or oil
3 lb chicken (1.35 kg)	2 tomatoes, sliced
Salt and pepper	or 8 oz tin chopped tomatoes (225 gm)
Turmeric	½ cup lemon juice
	1 medium onion, peeled

Peel the eggplants in strips from top to bottom, alternating ½" (1.25 cm) wide peeled and unpeeled strips. Cut eggplant lengthwise into 4 slices. Sprinkle with salt and let it stand for 1 hour. Wash and dry with paper towelling. Wash the chicken and sprinkle with salt, pepper and turmeric. Add the onion to the pan. Roast the chicken in a preheated oven Gas No.3, 325°F, 180°C for 1 hour, or until just done. Meanwhile fry the eggplant slices in the margarine or oil until golden, and dry on paper towelling. Remove chicken from oven and increase the temperature to Gas No.6, 400°F, 200°C. Cut chicken into serving pieces and arrange in the centre of the same baking dish. Arrange the eggplant slices on the sides and the tomato slices on the top of the eggplant. Season the eggplant with salt and sprinkle with lemon juice. Cover with foil and bake for 20 minutes. Then bake uncovered for a further 10 minutes.

GRILLED CHICKEN   Jennifer Davis

Serves 4   Preparation 10 mins.   Marinate 2 hours   Cook 10 mins.

2 poussins, halved	French mustard
or	Olive oil
1 roasting chicken, jointed	Lemon juice
3 bunches watercress	

Paint chicken pieces all over with mustard and pour equal parts of lemon juice and olive oil over them. Leave to marinate at least 2 hours or as long as convenient, turning occasionally. Heat grill and when very hot place chicken close to heat, skin side up, for 5 minutes or until skin is very well browned. Baste with marinade and grill further from heat for another 5 minutes or slightly longer if necessary. Turn pieces over and baste with more oil and lemon juice and repeat the process. The chicken should be charred on the outside without being overcooked on the inside. Serve on a bed of watercress sprinkled with oil and lemon juice and with boiled new potatoes.

CHICKEN LIMA   Debby Winter

Serves 4   **Preparation 15 mins.**   **Marinate 1 hour**   **Cook 1½ hours**

½lb baby lima beans (225gm)
3 cups water
2½lb chicken, diced (1.15k)
2 tbls oil
1 clove garlic, chopped
1 cup carrots, coarsely chopped

1 large onion, chopped
1 green pepper, chopped
1 tsp paprika
1¾ tsp salt
¼ tsp pepper

Wash lima beans and then boil in a pot of water for a few minutes. Remove from heat and let stand for 1 hour. Heat oil in pan, add chicken pieces and brown well. Remove and drain off fat, leaving 1 tablespoon in pan. Add garlic, onions, green pepper and carrots to same pot and sauté until lightly browned. Add paprika, cook for 2 minutes stirring constantly. Add browned chicken, sautéed vegetables, salt and pepper to lima beans and cover. Bring to the boil. Cook for 1 hour or until chicken is tender.

MOROCCAN CHICKEN WITH PRUNES Gillian Burr

Serves 4–6   **Preparation 30 mins.**   **Cook 1¼ hours**

3½lb–4lb chicken (1.6–1.8 k)
¼ pt hot water (142ml)
¼ tsp saffron
2oz margarine (55gm)
1 stick cinnamon
A little oil
4oz large plump prunes (115gm)

1 tsp cinnamon powder
4 tbls thin honey
1oz flaked almonds (30gm)
1 tbls sesame seeds
1 onion, finely chopped
Salt and pepper

Soak the saffron in the hot water for 30 minutes. Joint the chicken and brown the pieces in margarine in a frying pan or casserole with a few drops of oil to stop the margarine from burning. Remove, fry the onion, return the chicken and season with plenty of salt and pepper. Add the soaked saffron and the cinnamon stick. Cover closely and simmer gently for 35–45 minutes until the chicken is nearly cooked. Remove the chicken pieces, add the prunes to the juice and simmer for 10–15 minutes. Add the powdered cinnamon and honey and boil down until thick and syrupy; degrease if necessary. Return the chicken to the pan and simmer together for 10–15 minutes until hot through and the flavours are well blended. Toast the sesame seeds in a hot, dry frying pan. Fry the flaked almonds in a speck of oil and have ready to scatter over the dish with the sesame seeds. Serve with rice.

LEFTOVER CHICKEN CURRY   Audrey Jacobs

Serves 4–6   Preparation 15 mins.   **Cook 45 mins.**

$\frac{1}{2}$ chicken, cooked and shredded
1 large pepper, diced
1 large onion, diced
2 cooking apples, diced
14 oz tin apricot halves (400 gm)
$\frac{1}{2}$ pt chicken stock (280 ml)
1$\frac{1}{2}$ cups rice
2 tbls white wine (optional)

1 tbls sugar or equivalent
1 tbls flour
1 tbls vinegar
Curry powder to taste
1 tbls soya sauce
Squeeze of lemon
Salt
Freshly ground black pepper

Simmer onion, apples and pepper together until soft in a little of the chicken stock (2–3 tablespoons). Add curry powder, rest of chicken stock and flour and bring gently to the boil. Add apricots, sugar, vinegar, lemon juice, soya sauce and wine and return to a gentle boil then simmer for 30 minutes. Add chicken for 10 minutes before end of simmering time. Serve with rice cooked as on packet directions.

 LEMON AND MUSTARD CHICKEN Sandy Prevezer

Serves 4   Preparation 15 mins.   **Cook 15 mins.**

4 boned chicken breasts, diced
2 tbls lemon juice
2 tbls coriander leaves, chopped
2 oz margarine (55 gm)

2 tsp French mustard
1 green chilli, chopped
1 tsp toasted ground cumin seeds
Salt to taste

Brown the cumin seeds in a frying pan and dry. Heat margarine in heavy shallow pan. Add mustard, salt, lemon juice and chopped chilli. Fry for a few seconds then add cumin powder and coriander leaves. Add chicken pieces and fry quickly for a few minutes until brown outside and cooked through. Serve immediately.

PEANUT CHICKEN   Professor Ian Aaronson

Serves 4   Preparation 10 mins.   Cook 10 mins

4 chicken breasts, filleted and skinned
2 egg whites
1 tsp salt
1½ tbls cornflour
* Chopped peanuts or mixed nuts
1 small red hot chilli, sliced into 6 rings
Vegetable oil to fry

SAUCE
⅓ cup white wine vinegar
⅔ cup water
4 tsp sugar
2 tbls cornflour

GARNISH: 6 spring onions

(* same volume as chicken)

Mix sauce ingredients and retain in a bowl. Cut chicken into small strips less than ½″ (1.25 cm) thick. Mix in another bowl, chicken, egg whites, salt and cornflour until sticky. Shallow fry this mixture for approx 5 minutes in hot oil and keep separating strips of chicken. Add chilli, peanuts and the sauce to frying pan and keep stirring until nice and sticky. Serve on a bed of white rice.

Garnish: Slice green portions of spring onions into thin rings and sprinkle on top of chicken.

POULET PORTUGAISE   Lilian Bloch

Serves 4–6   Preparation 30 mins.   Cook 45 mins.   Advance   Freezable

2 small onions, chopped
½ lb mushrooms, sliced
1 oz margarine (30 gm)
2 tbls oil
8 chicken joints
1 clove garlic, crushed

¼ pt dry white wine (142 ml)
¼ pt stock or water (142 ml)
4 tbls tomato purée
1 chicken cube
Salt and black pepper

Heat the margarine and oil and sauté chicken until browned, add onions and garlic. Cook until tender. Add mushrooms, wine, stock or water, tomato purée and stock cube. Cover pan and cook 5 minutes. Season well and cook at Gas No.5, 375°F, 190°C.

CHICKEN QUENELLES   Rosanna Burr

Serves 4   Preparation 10 mins.   Cook 15 mins.

1 lb chicken breasts, minced (450 gm)
2 eggs
1 cup stock

Margarine
2 oz breadcrumbs (50 gm)
Salt and pepper

Mince chicken and mix with beaten eggs. Add breadcrumbs, salt and pepper and sufficient stock to moisten. Form into egg shaped quenelles with 2 dessertspoons and place in a greased omelette pan. Pour hot water round quenelles, cover with greased paper and cook gently for 15 minutes. Remove carefully and serve.

SPICED POUSSIN WITH ALMONDS   Lisa Rose

Serves 4   **Preparation 15 mins.**   **Marinate 2 hours**   **Cook 45 mins.**

3–3½lb poussin or chicken
  (1.35–1.6 k)
2 oz margarine (55gm)
¼ tsp whole cumin seeds
2 tsp whole coriander seeds
4 whole shelled cardamoms
½″ grated fresh root ginger (1cm)
1 clove garlic, crushed
Grated rind of ½ lemon
½ tsp freshly ground black pepper
1–1½ tsp sea salt

SAUCE
1 onion, finely chopped
2 oz margarine (55gm)
1 tsp turmeric
1 tbls ground almonds
1 tbls currants
¼ tsp cornflour
9 tbls chicken stock

Pound all the whole spices in a mortar until finely powdered. Cream the margarine and add the spices, ginger, salt, pepper, garlic and lemon rind. Slip your fingers between the skin and the flesh of the chicken breast to loosen it and also loosen the skin from the legs. Pack the spiced margarine over the chicken breast and legs under the skin. Cut the chicken down the back from neck to tail, snip through the wishbone and press the chicken out flat. Leave breast upwards for the flavours to penetrate for 2 hours, then roast in a hot oven Gas No.7, 425°F, 220°C for 35–45 minutes.

Sauce: Melt the margarine and gently fry the onion until golden brown. Add the turmeric, almonds and currants and fry for 1–2 minutes. Then moisten with the combined cornflour and stock. Simmer down a little and then spoon over roasting chicken after 15 and again after 25 minutes of the cooking time. Serve with plain boiled rice over which you spoon the roasting juices.

 STICKY CHICKEN   Sally Rosenthal

Serves 4 Preparation 15 mins. Marinate 1 hour Cook 1 hour Advance Freezable

4 chicken pieces
1 medium onion, chopped
2 fl oz soya sauce (60ml)
2 fl oz Worcester sauce (60ml)
2 oz brown sugar (55gm)

2 fl oz tomato purée (60ml)
2 fl oz vinegar (60ml)
2 fl oz lemon juice (60ml)
1½ fl oz oil (45ml)

Heat the oil until hot and then gently fry chicken pieces until golden brown. Place in a casserole dish. Mix together the soya sauce, Worcester sauce, tomato purée, vinegar and onion and pour over chicken pieces. Allow to marinate for at least 1 hour. Sprinkle surface with lemon juice and brown sugar and cook on Gas No.4, 350°F, 185°C for 1 hour.

Microwave instructions

Brown chicken in browning dish, or in normal manner. Cover with soya sauce mixture and cook in microwave oven on full power for 6–7 minutes, or roast for 8 minutes.

STIR FRY CHICKEN
GINGER AND NUTS
Miki Hildebrand

Serves 4   Preparation 10 mins.   Cook 15 mins.

4 chicken breasts, sliced into strips
1 clove garlic, chopped
4 oz mushrooms, sliced (115 gm)
2 tbls soya sauce
12 oz beanshoots (340 gm)
3 spring onions, chopped

1″ fresh ginger, peeled and
  chopped (2.5 cm)
1 tbls oil
1 onion, sliced
1 red pepper, sliced
1 stick celery, sliced
Salt and pepper

Heat oil. Add chicken strips and sauté until evenly cooked, approx. 10 minutes. Add onion, pepper, celery, spring onions, mushrooms, garlic and ginger and cook for a further 2 minutes. Finally add sauce, beanshoots and nuts and cook for 2 minutes. Season. Serve with brown rice or noodles.

280 calories per portion.

STIR FRY LEMON CHICKEN
Miki Hildebrand

Serves 4   Preparation 10 mins.   Cook 15 mins.

4 chicken breasts, cut into thin strips
5 fl oz chicken stock (140 ml)
2 tbls soya sauce
Rind of 1 lemon
1 oz pine kernels (30 gm)

4 spring onions, chopped
1 red pepper, chopped
1 stick celery, chopped
4 oz mushrooms, sliced (115 gm)
Salt and pepper
1 tbls oil

Heat oil in large pan or wok and sauté chicken for 8 minutes. Add vegetables and cook for a further 4 minutes. Finally add remaining ingredients and cook for 2 minutes. Season. Serve with brown rice or noodles.

280 calories per person.

CHICKEN TURBIE
Suzy Landes

Serves 4   Preparation 15 mins.   Cook 1 hour approx.   Advance   Freezable

4 chicken legs
1 green pepper, chopped
14 oz tin peeled tomatoes (400 gm)
2 tbls tomato purée
3 onions, chopped

2 tsp oregano
2 tsp basil
Salt
Pepper
Margarine

Brown onions and pepper in ovenproof dish. Brown chicken pieces in frying pan with margarine. Combine both in the ovenproof dish. Add spices, peeled tomatoes and tomato purée. Cook in the oven Gas No.6, 400°F, 200°C for about 1 hour.

Chicken Salads

IRANIAN CHICKEN SALAD
Margaret Lewis

Serves 4   Preparation 20 mins

4 chicken breasts, cooked and diced
4 medium potatoes, cooked and diced
3–4 eggs, hard boiled and chopped
8 oz tin petits pois, drained (225 gm)

3 pickled cucumbers, chopped
Mayonnaise to bind
Salt and pepper

Mix ingredients together. Add mayonnaise to bind. Place on a bed of lettuce and serve cold.

MEXICAN CHICKEN SALAD
Sandra Seifert

Serves 4–6   Preparation 15 mins.   Advance

4 chicken breasts, cooked and diced
12 oz tin sweetcorn, drained (340 gm)
$\frac{1}{2}$ red pepper, chopped
$\frac{1}{2}$ small cucumber, diced

2 celery sticks, chopped
6 spring onions, chopped
Coleslaw dressing (see Sauce section)
Chopped parsley

Mix together all the ingredients and enough coleslaw dressing to coat the chicken. Place in serving dish and decorate with chopped parsley. This is delicious with jacket potatoes. This salad is best served fresh but will keep for 24 hours.

Turkey

 ## TURKEY SCHNITZELS
Rosanna Burr

Serves 4   Preparation 5 mins.   Standing time 50 mins.   Cook 12 mins.

4 turkey breasts, skinned
1 egg, beaten
1 cup fine dry breadcrumbs
Juice of $\frac{1}{2}$ orange

4 tbls oil
Flour for coating
Salt and pepper

Flatten turkey breasts and dip in a mixture of juice, salt and pepper. Leave in fridge for 20 minutes before coating in flour then a thin layer of egg. Dip into breadcrumbs and leave turkey breasts in fridge for a further 30 minutes. Heat oil and cook turkey breasts for 5–6 minutes on each side. If necessary they can be kept hot in oven Gas No.1, 275°F, 150°C for a short time.

Duck

DUCK WITH ARTICHOKES
Gillian Burr

Serves 4   Preparation 30 mins.   Cook 50 mins.

2 x 3lb ducks (900 gm)
3 tbls margarine
12 small new potatoes
Salt
Freshly ground black pepper
3 cups water
Potato flour (optional)

$\frac{1}{2}$ cup dry white wine

GARNISH: pitted black olives
2 artichokes
2 tomatoes, peeled, seeded
and chopped

Make stock with necks, wings and giblets plus 3 cups of water. Simmer for 30 minutes. Truss the ducks and season. Rub lightly with the margarine. Roast for 50 minutes on Gas No.4, 350°F, 185°C. Baste well then remove from oven and keep warm.

Artichokes: Simmer artichokes in enough salted water to cover them for 30–45 minutes until the leaves are easily removed. Separate artichoke hearts and retain.

Potatoes: Boil until cooked.

Sauce: Deglaze the roasting pan with the wine, add the strained stock and continue cooking until reduced by a half. Remove all fat. Thicken if desired with a little potato flour. Adjust seasoning.

To serve: Arrange quarters of the artichokes and whole potatoes around the ducks. Decorate the platter with the chopped tomatoes and olives. Serve the sauce separately.

ROAST DUCK
WITH SAUCE CHAMPIGNONS
Gloria Cohen

Serves 2–3   Preparation 20 mins.   Cook 1$\frac{1}{4}$ hours

4lb duckling (1.81 k)
3 tbls apple purée
$\frac{3}{4}$ pt rich brown stock or consommé (425 ml)

6 oz mushrooms (170 gm)
2 tbls brandy
2 tbls vermouth
2 bay leaves

Ensure that most of the fluid has been boiled away from apple purée. Stuff the duckling carcass with the apple purée and sew up firmly. Prick the skin of the duckling all over and put into an ovenproof dish with a lid. Put into the oven Gas No.7, 425°F, 220°C for 20 minutes. Drain the fat from the dish, pour the brandy over the bird and light. Pour the stock around the bird, add the bay leaves and roast with the lid on the dish in oven Gas No.5, 375°F, 190°C until the bird is tender. This will take about 40 minutes, but will vary according to the size and age of the bird. Drain all the liquor into a saucepan, slice the mushrooms and add to the pan, season well and boil quite rapidly until the mushrooms are tender and the sauce reduced by one third. Pour in the Vermouth, check seasoning and serve with the roast bird.

ROAST DUCK WITH CHERRY SAUCE Gillian Burr

Serves 4–6   Preparation 10 mins.   Cook 1¾ hours

4–5 lb duck (1.8–2.25 k)
½–1 tsp arrowroot or potato flour
40 fresh cherries or a 1 lb jar of
   stoned morello cherries
½ oz margarine (15 gm)
Lemon juice
Salt and pepper

4 tbls port or red wine

SAUCE
½ pt duck stock made from giblets
   (280 ml)
3–4 tbls red wine vinegar
3 tbls granulated sugar

Make the duck skin as dry as possible for a nice crisp finish. Place the duck on a rack in a roasting pan, prick the skin with a fork to let the fat out, and roast in a hot oven Gas No.6, 400°F, 200°C for 1¼–1½ hours. Do not baste, but cover lightly with tinfoil if it is getting too brown. Joint the duck by snipping down the breast bone and the backbone with a good pair of scissors, then cutting each half into two or three pieces. Use a knife for the skin and flesh and scissors for the bone. This makes a large looking portion, but there is never much meat and it is the best way for crispy skin. Duck is best fairly well cooked and served straight from the hot oven for crispness, though it will keep warm for 30 minutes or so, as will the sauce.

Sauce: Reduce the stock down to ¼ pt (150ml) to make it stronger. Sprinkle the sugar into a small frying pan and heat gently until it melts and turn to brown caramel. Add the vinegar and then the reduced stock, watch out – it spits like mad, but caramel should bubble straight off. Toss the stoned cherries in margarine in a frying pan for 2–3 minutes. Then pour the port over and boil up. Add the sauce and thicken lightly with potato flour mixed with a little water. Season, simmer a few minutes, and set aside covered. Finish with a few drops of lemon juice and serve in a sauceboat with the jointed duck.

DUCK WITH COGNAC   Gloria Cohen

Serves 4   Preparation 20 mins.   Cook 65 mins.

5 lb duck (2.25 k)
1 duck's liver
Margarine
1 tsp allspice

½ glass cognac
½ glass port
¼ pt stock (140 ml)
Salt and pepper

Roast duck in oven Gas No.5, 375°F, 190°C for 55 minutes. Sauté liver in margarine until firm. Add pan juices from duck, mash liver and season. Warm cognac and port add to sauce, ignite and reduce over high heat to three quarters original quantity. Remove drumsticks and wings and sauté in margarine until completely cooked. Remove breast, cutting into strips, sauté and arrange in centre of heated dish, with drumsticks and wings on either side. Heat sauce, strain through a sieve and pour over duck.

LEMON DUCK
Ann Cohen

Serves 4　　　　　　**Preparation 20 mins.**　　　　　　**Cook 1½ hours**

$\frac{3}{4}$pt stock (425 ml)
2 lemons
$\frac{1}{2}$ cup sugar
5 lb duck (2.25 k)
1 cup dry white wine
1 cup water
Salt and pepper

$\frac{1}{2}$ cup vermouth
1 tbls cornflour
1 egg
$\frac{1}{2}$ cup breadcrumbs

GARNISH: 1 lemon, thinly sliced

Peel lemons, reserving peel, and cook flesh in pan with cup of water and sugar. When tender, press through sieve to squeeze all juice from the pulp. Set aside. Cook lemon peel in the water until tender and cut into fine strips. Set aside. Roast duck for 65 minutes in oven Gas No.5, 375°F, 185°C. Add half a cup white wine to pan juices, boil and reduce to half. Reserve. Put lemon syrup mixture, remaining white wine and vermouth in saucepan, reduce to half, thicken stock with cornflour and add to saucepan. Cook for 15 minutes and add reserved duck sauce with the strips of lemon. Decorate with lemon slices.

ROAST DUCK WITH FRUIT AND
GREEN PEPPERCORN STUFFING
Gloria Levy

Serves 4　　　　　　**Preparation 20 mins.**　　　　　　**Cook 1 hour 20 mins.**

2 ducks
4 oz plump dried apricots (115 gm)
$\frac{1}{4}$ pt white wine or water (140 ml)
1 oz walnuts (30 gm)
2 lemons

2 oz margarine (55 gm)
1 tsp green peppercorns
1 lb pasta (450 gm)
Salt and pepper

Soak the apricots in the minimum of white wine or water overnight. Take tiny julienne strips of rind from 1 lemon and blanch in boiling water for 4–5 minutes. Cut the pith and skin from this lemon and remove the flesh in segments. Mix with the drained chopped apricots (reserve the liquid), the chopped walnuts and the julienne lemon strips. Add $\frac{1}{2}$ tsp green peppercorns and stuff the ducks. Prick all over with a fork and place in a roasting tin. Roast in hot oven Gas No.7, 425°F, 220°C for 5 minutes without basting to seal in the juices, then turn down to moderately hot Gas No.5, 375°F, 190°C. Cover the breast with margarine and add 4 tablespoons of the apricot soaking juice and the remaining peppercorns to the pan. Roast for 65 minutes. Baste frequently with juices and see they do not burn, add more liquid if the fat seems to be over-browning. Remove the ducks and keep warm. Rest for at least 10 minutes before carving. Cook the pasta in plenty of boiling salted water and drain. Mix 3–4 tablespoons of the juices with the cooked pasta and serve the remaining juices separately. Toss well and heap on a serving dish. Carve the ducks and arrange onto the pasta with the spooned out stuffing. Cut the remaining lemon into wedges for squeezing over ducks. Serve at once.

Vegetables

So tell me Walter, which end do you light?

HINTS

Nuts of all kinds add important food value to vegetables.

Fillings for baked potato (serves 2)

- **Tuna and onion:** Scoop out flesh from potatoes and mix with small tin of drained tuna, chopped spring onions, grated lemon rind, 2 tablespoons of mayonnaise, salt and pepper.
- **Sour cream and chives:** Cut a deep cross in the centre of each potato, hold the potato in a tea towel and press in the sides to open up the cross, spoon in the soured cream and sprinkle with chives.
- **Cheese and pickle:** Scoop out potato flesh and mix with 3 tablespoons of grated cheddar cheese, 2 tablespoons of pickle, chopped fresh parsley and black pepper.

Aubergines are bulky but not calorific.

If potatoes are cooked in their skins and peeled afterwards less nutrients are lost.

To skin chestnuts easily see page 127.

JERUSALEM ARTICHOKE
PUREE

Miki Hildebrand

Serves 4   Preparation 5 mins.   Cook 25 mins.

1½lb Jerusalem artichokes (675gm)
1½oz butter or margarine (45gm)
½ pt water (280ml)

1 tbls cream
Salt and pepper

Scrape artichokes, cut into quarters, and sweat in 1oz (30gm) butter, shaking pan every few minutes. After 5 minutes add water and cook gently until tender. Drain, mash with ½oz (15gm) butter and add cream and seasoning to taste.

BREADED EGGPLANT

Elaine Knobil

Serves 2–3   Preparation 5 mins.   Cook 10–15 mins.

1 large eggplant (aubergine)
1 cup breadcrumbs
1 egg, beaten

Oil for frying
Salt and pepper

Peel eggplant and slice into ¼″ (6mm) thick slices. Season with salt and pepper. Dip into breadcrumbs, beaten egg and into breadcrumbs again. Fry in hot oil on both sides until golden brown. Drain on paper towel. Serve right away.

AUBERGINE CURRY
(BRINJAL BHARTHA)

Sandy Prevezer

Serves 3–4   Preparation 15 mins.   Cook 20–30 mins.   Advance

1 large aubergine
1 onion, chopped
1 green chilli, chopped (optional)
2 tomatoes, skinned and chopped
1 tsp cumin seeds
1 tsp turmeric powder

Salt
2 tsp coriander powder
½ tsp chilli powder
1 tbls oil

GARNISH: coriander leaves, chopped

Rub a little oil on the aubergine and grill until soft and the skin crackles. Open skin and scoop out pulp. Put oil in pan and when hot add cumin seeds. Add chopped onion and brown slightly. Add tomatoes and spices and cook and stir for a few minutes. Add aubergine pulp and mash it with a fork. Cook for a few more minutes on a low heat and cover. Decorate with chopped fresh coriander leaves and serve.

SWEET AND SOUR
AUBERGINES

Naomi Greenwood

Serves 6   **Preparation 20 mins.**   **Cook 20 mins.**   **Advance**

$2\frac{1}{2}$lb aubergines ($1\frac{1}{4}$k)
6–8 tbls vegetable oil
Salt
Freshly ground black pepper

3 tbls lemon juice
2 tbls sugar
1 tsp ground cumin seeds
$\frac{1}{4}$ tsp cayenne pepper (optional)
10" ovenproof dish (25cm)

Preheat the grill. Cut aubergines diagonally into slices $\frac{1}{3}$" (9mm) thick. Brush both sides with oil and sprinkle each side lightly with salt and pepper. Grill the slices on both sides until they are golden red, then remove from grill. Preheat the oven to Gas No.4, 350°F, 180°C. Mix together the lemon juice, sugar, cumin, cayenne, $\frac{1}{2}$ tsp salt and some black pepper. Arrange slices in the dish in slightly overlapping rows. When the bottom of the dish has been covered dribble a third of the lemon juice mixture evenly over them. Continue in this way until all ingredients have been used with the lemon mixture over the top. Cover with foil and bake for 20 minutes.

GREEN BEAN RAGOUT

Gillian Burr

Serves 4–6   **Preparation 10 mins.**   **Cook 50 mins.**

1lb fresh or other green beans (450gm)
1lb tomatoes, peeled and thinly sliced
   (450gm)
2 medium onions, peeled and thinly sliced

Salt and pepper
2 tbls oil

GARNISH: parsley and chives,
         chopped

Prepare the beans and cook for 10 minutes only in seasoned boiling water, strain and reserve $\frac{1}{4}$ pt (150ml) of the liquid. Toss onions and tomatoes in hot oil for 10 minutes until a fairly soft purée. Add the beans and liquid, together with a little more seasoning. Cook steadily, with the lid off the pan, until the excess liquid has evaporated and the beans are tender. Garnish with parsley and chives. Serve hot or cold as a vegetable dish or starter.

BROCCOLI AND SHALLOTS
WITH BLACK OLIVES

Bondi Zimmerman

Serves 6   **Preparation 5 mins.**   **Cook 15 mins.**

1lb broccoli, washed and trimmed
   (450gm)
8oz shallots, peeled (225gm)
1 tbls lemon juice

1 tbls olive oil
12 black olives, stoned
Salt and black pepper

Cook the broccoli in boiling salted water for about 7 minutes until 'al dente'. Drain well. Heat the oil in a large frying pan and add the rest of the ingredients. Fry for 2 minutes and serve immediately.

BRUSSELS SPROUTS
AU GRATIN WITH BASIL
David Burr

Serves 4   **Preparation 5 mins.**   **Cook 20 mins.**

1lb brussels sprouts (450gm)
8oz courgettes, sliced (225gm)
4oz button mushrooms, sliced (115gm)
2 tbls oil
1 tsp dried basil

2oz cheddar cheese, grated (55gm)
2oz wholemeal breadcrumbs (55gm)
1oz flaked almonds (30gm)
Salt and pepper

Cook sprouts in boiling salted water for 10 minutes until almost tender. Drain and reserve. Heat oil in pan, add courgettes and fry for 4 minutes approx. Add mushrooms and basil and fry for a further 2 minutes. Stir in the sprouts and cook for a minute until heated through. Add seasoning and spoon into a hot ovenproof dish. Mix cheese, breadcrumbs and almonds and sprinkle over the vegetables. Place under grill for 5–6 minutes until golden.

BURGHUL WITH BROWN
LENTILS
Lesley Bennett

Serves 8   **Soak 1 hour**   **Preparation 10 mins.**   **Cook 1½ hours**   **Advance**

½lb burghul (225gm)
½ Spanish onion, chopped
½lb brown lentils (225gm)
Salt and pepper

Oil for frying
½–1 pt water or chicken stock
(280ml–560ml)
1 tsp cumin

Soak lentils for 1 hour and then drain. Boil lentils in water to cover for 1 hour approx. until soft. Drain. Sauté chopped onions in a little oil until transparent and golden. Add burghul and fry lightly for 7 minutes. Season to taste with salt and pour in stock to cover burghul by ½" (13mm). Mix and simmer covered, over a low heat until all liquid is absorbed. Add a little more water if it seems too dry during cooking. This should take approx 30 minutes. Add cooked lentils to burghul and sprinkle with cumin and mix. This is nice to serve instead of rice. Burghul can be purchased from Indian and Greek stores.

RED CABBAGE WITH CHESTNUTS
Gloria Greenberg

Serves 4–6   Preparation 10 mins   Cook 3 hours   Advance

2lb red cabbage (900gm)
2oz butter (55gm)
2 large onions, sliced
3 cooking apples, peeled and diced
1 clove garlic, chopped
1 bay leaf
Nutmeg

$\frac{1}{4}$ pt strong red wine (140ml)
$\frac{1}{4}$ pt good stock (140ml)
2–3 tbls wine vinegar
2 tbls redcurrant jelly
16–20 chestnuts (fresh or tinned)
Ground cloves
Salt and pepper

Gently fry onion in the butter in a large casserole. Thinly slice the cabbage, removing the core, stir in and turn until every slice glistens. Add the apples, garlic and bay leaf and season with pepper, nutmeg, ground cloves and plenty of salt. Pour over the wine, stock and vinegar and simmer for about $1\frac{1}{2}$ hours on the stove or in a very moderate oven Gas No.3, 325°F, 170°C.

To skin fresh chestnuts: Cut halfway round the skin of the chestnuts on the rounded side and drop a few at a time into boiling water; boil for 3 minutes and remove one at a time to peel off the outer and inner skins together (if you get it just right you should be able literally to squeeze them and they will pop out of their shells). Add the chestnuts to the cabbage with the redcurrant jelly and a little more stock if needed and cook slowly for another $1-1\frac{1}{2}$ hours until the chestnuts are tender and the liquid all but gone. Correct the seasoning and serve. This dish reheats beautifully and often tastes even better on the second occasion.

CARROT RING MOULD
Stephanie Brahams

Serves 8   Preparation 15 mins.   Cook 35 mins.   Advance

$2\frac{1}{2}$lb new carrots, thickly sliced
   ($1\frac{1}{4}$k)
$\frac{1}{4}$ pt vegetable stock (140ml)
1 tbls sugar
Salt
2 tbls butter or margarine

2 eggs
6–8 tbls cheddar cheese, grated
Fresh pepper

GARNISH: cooked peas and button onions or any other vegetables

Boil carrots for 2 minutes, then drain. Simmer blanched carrots in vegetable stock, sugar and salt to taste, until liquid is absorbed. Liquidise carrot mixture and mix well with eggs, butter, cheese, salt and ground pepper to taste. Press into a well-greased ring mould, and heat slowly in the oven Gas No.1, 275°F, 150°C for 35 minutes. Turn carrot ring out onto serving dish, and fill centre with cooked peas and onions.

CARROT AND COURGETTE STREAMERS
Naomi Greenwood

Serves 4   Preparation 10 mins.   Cook 3 mins.

12 oz carrots, peeled (350 gm)
12 oz courgettes, trimmed (350 gm)
Salt and pepper

Knob of butter or 1 tbls sesame oil
Pinch of ground coriander

Coarsely grate the carrots and courgettes. Just before serving fry in butter or sesame oil for 2–3 minutes.

29 calories per serving

HOT SPICY CARROTS – TERSHI
Dinny Charkham

Serves 10   Preparation 20 mins.   Cook 40 mins.   Freezable

1 lb carrots, sliced (450 gm)
2 tbls oil
1 tbls garlic paste (see opposite)
1½ tbls tomato purée
1 tbls vinegar
1 tsp cumin
Salt to taste

GARLIC PASTE
6 cloves garlic, crushed
1 tsp salt
2 tbls red hot paprika
1 tbls oil
Lemon juice to bind

Garlic paste: Liquidise all ingredients until smooth.

Boil carrots until soft and reserve liquor. In another saucepan heat oil, stir in garlic paste and tomato purée, add 3 tablespoons of water from the boiled carrots and continue to stir. Add boiled carrots with enough of the water to cover (if not enough add more water). Bring to the boil then add vinegar and cumin. Can be served hot or cold as an accompaniment to any dish.

Microwave instructions
Place carrots in a shallow dish with a little water. Cover with pricked cling film and cook on high for 6 minutes. Then proceed with the recipe as above.

CAULIFLOWER LATKES
Elaine Knobil

Serves 4   Preparation 10 mins.   Cook 15 mins.

1 head cauliflower
1 egg
3 tbls matzo meal
Salt and pepper to taste

Oil for frying
Pinch of baking powder (optional to fluff up mixture)
1 medium potato, grated (optional for a variation)

Cook cauliflower in salted water until soft. Mash and add remaining ingredients except oil. Heat oil in frying pan and drop mixture into hot oil by spoonfuls. Brown on both sides.

CAULIFLOWER WITH WATERCRESS
SAUCE
Gloria Greenberg

Serves 4–6 **Preparation 10 mins.** **Cook 15 mins**

1 firm cauliflower
2 oz butter (55 gm)
1½ oz flour (45 gm)
¾ pt milk (450 ml)

2–3 tbls double cream
1 bunch watercress
Salt and pepper

Melt 1½ oz (45 gm) butter in a saucepan, add the flour and cook for 2–3 minutes over moderate heat. Draw the pan off the stove and when the sizzling ceases add all the milk, then return to the heat and bring to the boil, whisking hard. Season, add the cream and simmer for 2–3 minutes. Keep warm and covered until needed. Pick over the watercress, discarding the tough stalks, then throw into a pan of boiling salted water and blanch for 4–5 minutes. Drain into a sieve and refresh under the cold tap to set the colour. Set aside. Wash the cauliflower and break into large florets. Boil these gently in salt water for 10–15 minutes until just tender but still crisp. Drain and arrange in a serving dish. Liquidise the hot sauce with the watercress until it is a beautiful green, add the rest of the butter, pour over the cauliflower and serve at once.

CELERIAC WITH MUSTARD
SAUCE
Marion Cohen

Serves 4 **Preparation 15 mins.** **Cook 35 mins.**

1¼ lb celeriac, peeled and diced (675 gm)
1 oz butter or margarine (30 gm)
1 small onion, finely chopped
½ oz plain flour (15 gm)
1 tsp dry mustard
1 tbls vinegar

1 tsp sugar
¼ pt milk and vegetable stock, mixed (140 ml)
Salt and black pepper
2 tbls fresh breadcrumbs
1 oz cheese, grated (30 gm)

Cook the celeriac pieces in boiling salted water until just tender. Drain, reserving some of the water for the sauce. Heat the butter or margarine in a pan, add the onion and stir until tender and just starting to brown. Mix in the flour and mustard powder. Remove from heat and add the vinegar and sugar, then gradually blend in the mixed milk and vegetable water. Bring mixture to the boil, stirring, then simmer for 3 minutes. Season. Stir the cooked celeriac into the sauce and spoon the mixture into an ovenproof dish. Sprinkle top with cheese and breadcrumbs and brown in preheated oven Gas No.5, 375°F, 190°C for 15 minutes.

CORN CROQUETTES
Rosanna Burr

Serves 4–6   Preparation 10 mins.   Standing time 1 hour   Cook 20 mins.   Advance

12 oz whole kernel sweetcorn (340 gm)
2 oz butter (55 gm)
2 oz flour (55 gm)
¾ pt milk (450 ml)
Slice of onion
Blade of mace
5 peppercorns
1 bay leaf
Several parsley stalks

2 egg yolks
1 tbls parsley, finely chopped
Salt and pepper

COATING

2 whole eggs
1 tbls oil
Flour for coating
6 oz stale white breadcrumbs (170 gm)
Deep fat for frying (optional)

Heat and infuse milk for 10 minutes with slice of onion, mace, peppercorns, bay leaf and parsley stalks. Fresh or frozen corn needs boiling or steaming for 10–15 minutes; tinned corn is ready to use. Melt the butter in a saucepan, add the flour and cook gently for 2–3 minutes. Draw the pan off the stove, wait for the sizzling to cease and add the strained milk. Return to the heat, bring to the boil whisking with a wire whisk, and simmer for 1–2 minutes. Remove from the heat, beat in the egg yolks one at a time and simmer for 1 minute before stirring in the corn, parsley and seasoning. Pour into a greased 1″ (2.5 cm) deep dish, cover with cling film and leave to cool. Chill until firm. Beat the two whole eggs with the oil and seasoning in a soup plate, place some flour on another plate and the breadcrumbs on a third. Form the chilled mixture into cork-shaped croquettes, roll in flour, then in egg, and finally in breadcrumbs; pat the crumbs on firmly and lay on greaseproof paper. Preferably refrigerate for an hour or so before frying. Either deep fry a few at a time in hot oil or shallow fry, turning once. The croquettes should be a good brown. Drain on kitchen paper and serve at once or keep hot for up to an hour. They can be fried in advance, then re-heated for 30–40 minutes in a moderate oven Gas No.4, 350°F, 180°C.

COURGETTES SAUTEES
Mia Simmons

Serves 4   **Preparation 20 mins.**   **Cook 12 mins**

1½ lb small courgettes (675 gm)
4 tbls flour
4 tbls grated parmesan
Salt and black pepper

2 oz butter (55 gm)
4 tbls olive oil
1 Spanish onion, roughly chopped
4 tomatoes, skinned, seeded and chopped

Cook courgettes in boiling salted water until tender, 6–8 minutes. Drain, cool and cut in thick slices. Dry with kitchen towel. Mix flour, parmesan, salt and a few grinds of black pepper to taste. Coat the sliced courgettes lightly with the flour mixture. Heat the oil in a heavy pan, sauté the courgettes until golden brown all over. Remove them from the pan and drain them on kitchen paper and keep them hot. Sauté the onion in butter until soft and transparent. Add the chopped tomatoes and simmer for 2–3 minutes. Heat a serving dish, pile the courgettes in the middle and surround them with the onion and tomato mixture.

COURGETTE AND TOMATO
WITH FRESH BASIL
Marion Cohen

Serves 4   **Preparation 1 hour 5 mins.**   **Cook 20 mins.**   **Advance**

1½lb courgettes, sliced (675gm)
1 small onion, chopped
1 clove garlic, crushed
2 tbls wine vinegar
1 tbls fresh basil, chopped

Salt and freshly ground black pepper
2 tbls olive oil
1lb tomatoes, peeled and sliced (450gm)
1 tbls lemon juice
1 tbls castor sugar

Place the courgette slices in a colander and sprinkle with salt and leave to drain for 1 hour then dry well. Heat the oil in a large pan and sauté the onion and garlic for 5 minutes, add the courgettes and cook gently for about 10 minutes stirring occasionally. Add the tomatoes and stir in the vinegar and lemon juice, sugar and basil. Season to taste and cook for a further 5 minutes.

HERBED FENNEL
Miki Hildebrand

Serves 2   **Preparation 5 mins.**   **Cook 10–12 mins.**

1 head fennel
1 dsp oil
3 tbls stock or 1½ tbls stock and 1½ tbls wine
Parsley

2 tbls breadcrumbs
1 tsp Herbes de Provence
½ tsp lemon rind, grated
Salt and pepper

Slice through fennel and fry in oil to colour. Add stock, season with herbs, lemon rind, salt and pepper, and simmer. Drain and place on serving dish. Brown breadcrumbs and scatter over top. Serve.

BRAISED LETTUCE
Marion Cohen

Serves 4   **Preparation 5 mins.**   **Cook 25 mins.**

1 iceberg lettuce
2oz butter or margarine (55gm)
¼ pt parev chicken stock (140ml)

2oz cheese, grated (55gm)
Breadcrumbs
Salt and pepper

Cut iceberg lettuce into 4–8 wedges and place in ovenproof dish. Put knob of butter on each wedge. Pour over stock and season slightly. Bake, covered, for 20 minutes in hot oven Gas No.6, 400°F, 200°C. Uncover, sprinkle with grated cheese and breadcrumbs. Place under hot grill until brown.

LEEK AND WATERCRESS PUREE   Jennifer Davis

Serves 4   Preparation 25 mins.   Cook 13 mins. approx.   Freezable

1 lb leeks, sliced finely (450 gm)
5 fl oz double cream (140 ml)

3 oz butter (85 gm)
Bunch of watercress, washed, drained
    and chopped

Cook leeks in 2 oz (55 gm) butter with a little salt for 8–10 minutes until tender, stirring now and again. There should be very little liquid left, if necessary raise heat to evaporate it. Purée leeks with cream in food processor or blender. The mixture should be smooth but thick. Melt remaining butter and add the watercress. Stir over moderate heat for 1–2 minutes until watercress has collapsed but is still bright green. Stir into leek purée and serve or reheat later, covered, in a hot oven.

MANGE-TOUT WITH ORANGE
AND ALMONDS   Lynne Goldwyn

Serves 8   Preparation 10 mins   Cook 6 mins.

1 lb mange-tout, trimmed (450 gm)
2 oranges, peeled and sliced
4 oz flaked toasted almonds (115 gm)

Salt and freshly ground black pepper

GARNISH: knob of butter

Cook the mange-tout in boiling salted water for 5 minutes. Drain well and transfer to a warm serving dish. Place the orange slices in a small saucepan and warm slightly then add to the mange-tout with the remaining ingredients. Mix well and serve immediately garnished with a knob of butter.

 BAKED PEPPER AND ONIONS   Anna Cohen

Serves 4   Preparation 10 mins.   Cook 45 mins.

8 oz onions, thinly sliced (225 gm)
1 red pepper, seeded and finely sliced
1 green pepper, seeded and finely
    sliced

½ tsp dried thyme *or*
    a few sprigs of fresh thyme
2 oz butter (55 gm)
Salt and black pepper

Put butter into ovenproof dish, cover and melt in preheated oven Gas No.4, 350°F, 180°C. Stir in onions, peppers, herbs and seasonings. Cover the dish, return it to the oven and cook for 45 minutes.

PASTA SPECIAL   Gerda Doll-Steinberg

Serves 4–6   Preparation 10 mins.   Cook 10 mins.

6oz pasta bows (170gm)   2 tbls oil
Salt   Poppyseeds
Black pepper   2 tbls flaked almonds

Toast flaked almonds on a greased baking tray on Gas No.4, 350°F, 180°C for 10 minutes approx. until they are golden brown. Cook pasta in boiling water as directed on packet using 1 tsp salt. When pasta is cooked, drain and gently heat in some butter or oil. Sprinkle well with poppyseeds and the toasted flaked almonds. Delicious served with any casserole dish.

Potato Time

POTATO AND CELERIAC PUREE   Gillian Burr

Serves 4–6   Preparation 15 mins.   Cook 20 mins.

2–3 potatoes   Up to $\frac{1}{4}$ pt cream or milk (140ml)
1–1$\frac{1}{2}$lb celeriac root (450–675gm)   Salt and pepper
2–4oz butter (55–115gm)   Parsley, chopped

Boil the potatoes in their skins. Slice, skin and cube the celeriac. Simmer in salt water until nearly tender, about 10 minutes. Drain well and return to the pan with the butter. Leave over very gentle heat for 10 minutes or so. Peel and slice the potatoes and add to the celeriac. Mash well together, adding enough cream to make a firm texture. Season and add the parsley. Serve at once or, to keep warm, smooth the top, pour over a little cream, cover closely and stand in a pan of hot water. Beat in the cream on serving.

POTATO BASKET
Sybil Sinclair

Serves 8 Preparation 1 hour

2 eggs
1 egg, beaten
4 lb potatoes, boiled and sieved (1.8 k)
$\frac{1}{2}$ pt cheese sauce (280 ml)
(see Sauce section page 157)

$1\frac{1}{2}$–2 lb of cooked vegetables
  (e.g. peas, French beans, carrots,
  cauliflower, parsnips)
Sesame seeds (optional)
1 oz pine kernels (30 gm)

Beat the 2 eggs, add to potatoes and season well. On a greased baking dish make a base with the potatoes, dinner plate size, and pipe the rest round the sides leaving a hollow centre. Mark the sides with lines with a fork, and then brush the potato with a little egg, and put in the oven to brown on Gas No.4, 350°F, 180°C for about 10 minutes. Toss the vegetables in the hot cheese sauce and add the pine kernels. Remove the potato basket from the oven and empty the vegetables into it. Sprinkle if wished with sesame seeds.

CITRUS POTATOES
Marion Cohen

Serves 4–6   Preparation 10 mins.   Cook 1 hour

$2\frac{1}{4}$ lb potatoes, cut into small chunks
  (1 k)
1 lemon, grated rind and juice
$1\frac{1}{2}$ oz butter (45 gm)

Salt
1 onion, finely chopped

GARNISH: 2 tbls chives, chopped

Cook the potatoes in boiling salted water for 5 minutes. Drain and reserve. Melt butter in a saucepan and sauté the onion until soft but not brown. Mix in the lemon rind and juice then add the potatoes and shake all the ingredients together. Turn mixture into ovenproof dish and cook in preheated oven for about 1 hour Gas No.4, 350°F, 180°C. Sprinkle with chopped chives before serving.

CURRIED POTATOES
Michelle Dessau

Serves 4   Preparation 15 mins.   Cook 20 mins.

1 lb small potatoes (450 gm)
1 medium onion, chopped
1 tsp black mustard seeds
1 tsp turmeric powder
Salt
$\frac{1}{2}$ pt water (280 ml)

$\frac{1}{2}$ tsp ground cumin seeds
2 green chillies, finely chopped
Oil for frying

GARNISH: coriander leaves, chopped

Fry mustard seeds in hot oil until they pop; add the onion and spices and cook for 2 minutes; (if a mild curry is desired remove seeds from chillies). Add the whole potatoes in salt water and cook slowly until the juice evaporates. The dish is ready when the potatoes are cooked and the pan is fairly dry. Decorate with coriander leaves.

GRATIN DAUPHINOIS Gloria Ross

Serves 4–6 Preparation 15 mins. Cook 40 mins. Advance

2½lb potatoes, peeled and thinly sliced (1.1k)
½ pt milk (280ml)
1 clove garlic
2oz butter (55gm)

2oz gruyere cheese, grated (55gm)
¼ pt double cream (140ml)
Salt and pepper
Nutmeg

Rub a shallow gratin dish with the cut clove of garlic, then crush it, add it to the milk in a pan and heat. Generously butter the dish and put in a layer of the potatoes. Dot with butter, sprinkle with cheese and season with salt, pepper and a little freshly grated nutmeg. Continue the layers and finish with the cream and seasoning. Remove the garlic from the milk and pour carefully over, then sprinkle with the remaining cheese and dot with the last of the butter. Bake in hot oven Gas No.6, 400°F, 200°C until golden brown and tender.

HASH BROWNS Naomi Greenwood

Serves 4 Preparation 10 mins. Cook 45 mins.

1lb potatoes, scrubbed (450gm)
3 tbls oil

1 egg, beaten
Salt and black pepper
9″ (23cm) non-stick round tin

Grate potatoes coarsely into a large bowl of cold water. Pour the oil into the tin and place in the oven Gas No.7, 425°F, 220°C for 5 minutes. Drain the potatoes in a sieve and press gently to remove the excess water. Place the potatoes in a bowl and mix in the beaten egg and seasonings. Press the potato mixture evenly into the tin and bake for 45 minutes until a brown crust forms on the underside. To serve, turn out the potatoes so that the brown side is uppermost. Delicious with eggs.

 POTATO KUGEL Valerie Halpern

Serves 6 Preparation 20 mins. Cook 1 hour approx. Advance Freezable

6 potatoes, grated
3 carrots, grated
1 onion, grated
2 eggs
1 slice wholemeal bread made into crumbs

2 tbls parsley, chopped
2 tbls oil
4oz mushrooms, sliced (115gm)
Salt and pepper
2oz cheddar cheese, grated (55gm)
½oz butter (15gm)

Mix all the ingredients together and put in a well greased dish with cheese and butter on top. Cook in oven Gas No.4, 350°F, 180°C. for 1 hour.

135

POTATO PATTIES
Zoe Sorkin

Serves 4   **Preparation 15 mins.**   **Cook 10 mins.**

1½lb cooked potatoes (675gm)
4 small carrots, diced
1 onion, diced
2 small courgettes, diced
½ cup frozen peas (optional)

2oz Tomor margarine (55gm)
1oz plain flour (30gm)
Salt and black pepper
Oil for shallow frying

Mash potato. Sauté carrots, onions and courgettes with a little Tomor. Add the lightly fried vegetables to the mashed potato. Season then make into patties and coat lightly with flour and then fry lightly in oil.

 # POTATOES ROSTI
Gillian Burr

Serves 4–6   **Preparation 10 mins.**   **Cook 30–40 mins.**

2.2lb potatoes (1k)
Salt and black pepper

3oz butter or margarine (85gm)

Cook potatoes in their skins in boiling salted water for 10 minutes. Drain, rinse in cold water and peel off skins. Coarsely grate the potatoes into a bowl and mix in salt and pepper. Heat the butter in a good sized frying pan. Add the potato and stir until all butter has been absorbed. Press the mixture down so that it forms a solid 'cake' and cook slowly for 20–30 minutes, until evenly browned. Invert the potato cake onto a serving dish and cut into wedges.

SUZY'S TEMPTATION
Suzy Landes

Serves 4–6   **Preparation 15 mins.**   **Cook 40 mins.**   **Advance**   **Freezable**

8 medium potatoes
2 medium yellow onions, thinly sliced
4½oz anchovies, filleted (125gm)

¾oz butter (20gm)
Breadcrumbs
5 floz cream or milk (140ml)

Cut potatoes into thin strips. Brown potatoes and onions in a little butter. Alternate layers of potatoes and onions with filleted anchovies in a buttered ovenproof dish. The top layer should be potatoes. Pour cream or milk over the dish. Sprinkle with breadcrumbs. Dot with 1 teaspoon butter. Bake in oven Gas No.6, 400°F, 200°C for approx 40 minutes.

Microwave instructions

Cook on full power, covered, for 15–20 minutes or until potatoes are soft. Then brown under grill.

RUMBLEDETHUMPS Hannah Buchanan

Serves 6 Preparation 10 mins. Cook 15–20 mins.

1 lb potatoes, cooked and
mashed (450 gm)
1 lb cabbage, shredded and
cooked (450 gm)

2 oz butter or margarine (55 gm)
4 spring onions, finely chopped
Salt and black pepper

Mix the mashed potatoes and cooked cabbage together. Beat in the butter with plenty of salt and freshly ground black pepper. Stir in the onions and turn the mixture into a serving dish.

  POTATO SOUFFLE Miki Hildebrand

Serves 4–6 Preparation 10 mins. Cook 40 mins.

1 lb potatoes, boiled and mashed (450 gm)
2 fl oz double cream (55 ml)
2 oz cheddar cheese, grated (55 gm)
Salt and pepper

2 egg yolks
3 egg whites
Chives, chopped

Add cream, cheese, chives, salt and pepper and yolks to the potatoes. Beat the egg whites until stiff and fold in carefully. Either pour mixture into 6 individual greased ramekins or 1 pt (560 ml) soufflé dish. Bake large dish in oven on Gas No.6, 400°F, 200°C for 25–30 minutes or the 6 ramekins on Gas No.7, 425°F, 220°C for 15–20 minutes.

SPICED NEW POTATOES Gwen Neviss

Serves 4–6 Preparation 20 mins. Cook 15 mins.

24 small, even-sized new potatoes, washed
$\frac{1}{4}$ pt oil (140 ml)
$\frac{1}{2}$ level tsp nutmeg

1 level tsp ground coriander
$\frac{1}{4}$ tsp hot paprika
Black pepper and 1 level tsp salt

Blanch the potatoes in boiling salted water for 2 minutes. Drain. Mix the oil, spices and seasoning together. Add the warm potatoes and leave to cool, turning occasionally. Thread onto oiled satay sticks or skewers. Grill or barbecue until crisp and cooked 10–15 minutes depending on the size. Turn and baste during cooking.

RATATOUILLE NICOISE Sybil Sinclair

Serves 4–6   Preparation 15 mins.   Cook 30 mins.

2 onions, cut into rings
2 red or green peppers, sliced
2 tbls olive oil
½ marrow, peeled and diced
2 aubergines, peeled and diced

2 shallots, finely chopped
2 tomatoes, roughly chopped

GARNISH: parsley
          Toast triangles

Fry onions and peppers lightly in the olive oil. Add the marrow and aubergines, mix well, then add the shallots, tomatoes and seasoning. Put lid on pan and cook slowly for 30 minutes. Garnish with toast and parsley. Also very good with plain boiled rice and a green salad.

BROWN RICE WITH
ALMONDS AND RAISINS   Jane Cohen-Setton

Serves 4–6   Preparation 10 mins.   Cook 1½–2 hours

2 oz butter (55 gm)
12 oz long grain brown rice (340 gm)
4 oz mushrooms, sliced (115 gm)
3 tbls flaked almonds

1 onion, finely chopped
2 tbls raisins
1 pt chicken stock (600 ml)
Salt and pepper

Fry the onions in the butter in a casserole until softened, add the mushrooms and fry for a minute before adding the rice, almonds and raisins. Fry for another 2–3 minutes cover with boiling stock, season and cook, very well covered, in a slow oven Gas No.2, 300°F, 150°C for about 1½–2 hours, or simmer very gently until done.

 PERSIAN STEAMED RICE Lesley Bennett

Serves 8   Preparation 30 mins.   Cook 1 hour

12 oz long grain rice (340 gm)
2 carrots, chopped
½ Spanish onion, chopped
1½ tbls dill

2 large potatoes, coarsely sliced
3 fl oz oil (85 ml)
2 tbls salt

Soak rice for 30 minutes. Rinse well. Place in a large pan of boiling salted water. Boil vigorously for 7–8 minutes only. Strain and rinse thoroughly. Heat 2 fl oz (55 ml) oil in the bottom of a heavy pan. Place a double layer of sliced potato in the hot oil. Add rice, chopped vegetables and dill. Stir, being careful not to disturb potatoes. Pour remaining oil over rice. Cover with a damp tea towel and place lid on top, folding ends over the lid. Cook over a low heat. The potatoes on the bottom should be brown and crispy. Put rice in serving dish and place browned potatoes on top.

SALSIFY IN BUTTERY
HERB SAUCE
Marion Cohen

Serves 4–6   Preparation 10 mins.   Cook 35 mins.

1½lb salsify, scraped (675gm)
1 dsp wine vinegar
2oz butter or margarine (55gm)

1½ tbls chopped fresh mixed herbs
   (marjoram, thyme, sage, parsley)
Salt

Put salsify in boiling salted water, add vinegar and cook for about 30 minutes until tender. Drain thoroughly. Melt butter in the pan, return salsify to it, cover and cook over a high heat, shaking the pan frequently until the salsify starts to brown. Sprinkle over the herbs and a little extra salt.

STIR-FRIED SUMMER
MEDLEY
Naomi Greenwood

Serves 4   Preparation 10 mins.   Cook 5 mins.

2 sticks celery, ⎫
4 small carrots, ⎬ cut into juliennes
4 spring onions, ⎭
4oz button mushrooms, thinly sliced (115gm)
4 tbls lemon juice

4oz beansprouts (115gm)
4 tsp soya sauce
2 level tsp sugar
Salt and pepper
Oil for frying

Toss the celery, carrots and onions in a little very hot oil for 2–3 minutes. Remove and drain. Toss the mushrooms and beansprouts in hot oil for 1 minute. Remove and drain. Mix vegetables together and heat through in a pan with lemon juice, soya sauce, seasoning and sugar. Serve immediately.

CREAMED SWEDE AND CARROT
Anna Cohen

Serves 4–6   Preparation 10 mins.   Cook 40 mins.   Advance

1½lb swedes, peeled and diced (675gm)
8oz carrots, peeled and sliced (225gm)
1oz butter (30gm)
2 tbls milk

7oz tin corn niblets, drained (200gm)
Salt and black pepper
3 large tomatoes, sliced
1oz fresh breadcrumbs (30gm)

Boil the carrots and swedes together in salted water for about 10 minutes. Drain well then roughly mash together. Beat in half the butter with the milk, sweetcorn, salt and pepper. Turn the mixture into a 2 pt (1.21) casserole dish. Arrange the sliced tomatoes on top, sprinkle the surface with breadcrumbs, then dot the remaining butter on top. Put under preheated hot grill until top is crisp and brown.

Salads

Don't panic – it's only a baby Lesser Spotted Bolivian Maneater!

HINTS

A cold salad may be just as nourishing as a hot meal and is often more so.

Watercress supplies vitamin A, as well as iodine, iron and calcium.

Raw mushrooms added to salads are a useful source of fibre, protein and B vitamins.

Hazelnuts are lower in fat than many other nuts.

Chop fruit and vegetables just before using to prevent the loss of nutrients, as there is less time for the enzyme that destroys nutrients to work on the food.

To ensure that artichoke hearts stay white during cooking, boil them in water which has had the juice of $\frac{1}{2}$ lemon and some vegetable oil added.

ASPARAGUS SALAD

Ruth Smilg

Serves 4 Preparation 5 mins.

12oz raw asparagus, trimmed, pared,
   chopped and blanched (340 gm)
4 tbls yoghurt
2 tbls double cream

2 tbls lemon juice
Mixed herbs, sea salt and
   chopped parsley
Pepper to taste

Mix the yoghurt with the lemon juice, herbs and salt, add the beaten cream and pour over the asparagus.

65 calories per serving.

AUBERGINE SALAD

Naomi Pope

Serves 4   Preparation 10 mins.   Advance

1 aubergine
$\frac{1}{2}$ fl oz lemon juice (15 ml)
$\frac{1}{2}$ onion, finely chopped
$\frac{1}{2}$ green pepper, chopped
3 tomatoes, chopped
2oz pineapple, chopped (55 gm)
$\frac{1}{2}$oz sultanas (15 gm)

DRESSING

1 tbls natural yoghurt
1 tbls low calorie mayonnaise
Pinch of curry powder
1 tsp sweet pickle
Pinch of tandoori powder

GARNISH: red lettuce leaves and fresh
              coriander leaves

Cut the aubergine into bite-sized pieces. Sprinkle with lemon juice. Add the onion, pepper, tomatoes, pineapple and sultanas. Mix the dressing ingredients together and pour over the salad. Toss. Spoon salad into a serving dish and garnish with lettuce and coriander.

45 calories per serving.

AUSTRALIAN PICNIC SALAD

Muriel Sherwood

Serves 4   Preparation 15 mins.

1 large avocado, skinned and chopped
1–2 hard boiled eggs, chopped
1 red or sweet onion, chopped

1 cooked beetroot, chopped
Mayonnaise to taste
Salt and pepper to taste

Mix all the vegetables, add mayonnaise and seasoning and serve immediately.

135 calories per serving.

CAESAR SALAD
Miki Hildebrand

Serves 4   Preparation 10 mins.

1 cos lettuce washed, dried and
   coarsely shredded
1 bunch watercress, trimmed
1 beef tomato, chopped
1 medium onion, chopped

1 egg
1 oz parmesan cheese, grated (30 gm)
3 slices crustless wholemeal bread,
   cubed and toasted
6 tbls low calorie French dressing

Toss together the salad vegetables and dressing. Boil the egg for 1 minute only, break into the salad and toss again well. Add the cheese and croûtons just before serving.

203 calories per serving.

CANNELLINI SALAD
Gillian Burr

Serves 3–4   Preparation 5 mins.   Refrigerate 2 hours   Advance

1 lb tin cannellini beans (450 gm)
1 small to medium green pepper,
   thinly sliced
1 very small onion, thinly sliced

DRESSING

2 tbls oil
$\frac{1}{4}$ tsp salt and pepper
2 tbls red wine vinegar
1 tsp sugar

Drain the beans in a colander, wash well and drain completely. Put into a bowl with pepper and onion. Mix dressing ingredients together and pour over the vegetables. Chill for at least 2 hours and serve.

100 calories per serving.

CARROT SALAD
Ruth Smilg

Serves 2–3   Preparation 10 mins.

8 oz carrots, grated (225 gm)
4 tbls yoghurt
2 tbls honey

Juice of 2 lemons
1 medium apple, grated

Make a dressing from the yoghurt, honey, lemon and apple and pour over the carrots.

54 calories per serving.

CAULIFLOWER SALAD   Rennie Mendelssohn

Serves 6   Preparation 5 mins.

1 small cauliflower (about 1½lb)
   (675 gm)
6 radishes, sliced
¼ cup Spanish onion, chopped

DRESSING
3 tbls chilli sauce
¼ cup mayonnaise
1 tsp fresh or dried dill, chopped

Divide the cauliflower into florets and cut into ¼″ to 1″ (1.5–2.5 cm) pieces. A 1½lb (675 gm) cauliflower will yield about 5–6 cups of pieces. Put the vegetables in a bowl. Stir the chilli sauce, mayonnaise and dill together, add to the vegetables and toss until thoroughly mixed. Garnish with chopped parsley if desired.

115 calories per serving.

CELERIAC SALAD   Bernice Burr

Serves 4   Preparation 35 mins.   Advance

1 large celeriac
1 tbls gherkins or dill cucumber,
   finely chopped
2 tbls parsley, finely chopped
1 tbls capers
1 tbls lemon juice or wine vinegar

1 tin anchovies with oil
2 spring onions, finely chopped
3 hard boiled egg yolks
4 tbls mayonnaise

GARNISH: chopped stuffed olives

Finely grate the celeriac and soak in water to which you have added lemon juice or vinegar for half an hour then strain. Place the drained anchovies into a food processor or blender (reserving the oil), and process to a purée. Add egg yolks and process again, then add mayonnaise, lemon juice, anchovy oil and black pepper. Blend this mixture until smooth and then add the cucumbers, parsley and onions and mix well. Pour this mixture into a bowl. Combine celeriac and dressing and mix thoroughly so that the celeriac is well coated. Transfer to a serving dish and scatter with sliced, stuffed olives and capers.

120 calories per serving.

CELERIAC AND TOMATO SALAD   Caroline Smilg

Serves 4   Preparation 15 mins.

2 medium sized celeriac roots, grated
8 oz tomatoes, thickly sliced (225 gm)
1 medium onion, finely chopped

DRESSING
4 tbls salad oil
4 tbls wine or raspberry vinegar
Pinch of celery salt and onion salt and a
   little chopped herbs

Arrange the celeriac on top of the tomatoes. Mix the onion with the rest of the dressing ingredients and pour over the salad.

179 calories per serving.

CHEESE, EGG AND ASPARAGUS SALAD

Ruth Smilg

Serves 2   Preparation 5 mins.

5 oz Gouda cheese, cubed (140 gm)
2 hard boiled eggs, roughly chopped
4 spears of asparagus, cut into strips
Culpepper salad seasoning salt

DRESSING

4 tbls yoghurt
1 tsp sour cream
Juice of 1 lemon
Mustard
Parsley, chopped

Mix all the ingredients together with the prepared dressing.

122 calories per serving.

CHEESE, GRAPE AND NUT SALAD

Ruth Smilg

Serves 3   Preparation 10 mins.

5 oz Gouda cheese (140 gm)
2 oz black grapes, halved and
    deseeded (55 gm)
2 tbls hazelnuts, grated

DRESSING

1 tbls single cream
Culpepper salad seasoning salt
Juice of 1 lemon

Mix all salad and dressing ingredients together.   147 calories per serving.

CHEESE AND MUSHROOM SALAD

Caroline Smilg

Serves 3   Preparation 10 mins.

5 oz Gouda cheese, cut into cubes (140 gm)
4 tbls mushrooms, finely sliced
1 tbls sour cream

4 tbls yoghurt
Sea salt
Parsley, chopped

Place cheese and mushrooms in a bowl and pour over them the dressing made from the remaining ingredients.

83 calories per serving.

CHICKPEA AND PINE KERNEL SALAD

Anna Cohen

Serves 6   Preparation 10 mins.   Soaking time 8 hours   Cook 1 hour   Advance

8 oz chickpeas (225 gm)
3 oz pine kernels (85 gm)
Generous bunch of parsley, chopped
1½ tsp tomato paste

Dried basil
1 tbls sunflower oil
14 oz tin tomatoes (400 gm)
Salt and pepper to taste

Soak chickpeas for 8 hours overnight. Change water. Add salt, boil rapidly for 10 minutes then simmer for 50 minutes – chickpeas swell, so water level should be checked. Drain and transfer to serving bowl.

Sauce: place oil in saucepan and heat. Add tomato paste and stir; add tinned tomatoes and mash slightly. Add black pepper (no salt) and basil. Bring to the boil, cover and simmer for 10 minutes. Add parsley to sauce stirring well. Remove from heat and pour over chickpeas. Mix well. Add pine kernels. Serve warm or cold.

400 calories per serving

CHINESE SALAD

Marion Cohen

Serves 4   Preparation 10 mins.

4 oz Chinese leaves, shredded (115 gm)
4 oz beansprouts (115 gm)
3 oz red cabbage, shredded (85 gm)
1 yellow pepper, deseeded and sliced

6 radishes, sliced
1 kiwi fruit, peeled and sliced
4 tbls vinaigrette

GARNISH: 1 tbsp sesame seeds

Toss together the salad vegetables and kiwi fruit. Stir the vinaigrette into the salad and sprinkle with sesame seeds before serving.

126 calories per serving.

CONTINENTAL PLATTER

Rose Levy

Serves 4   (P)   Preparation 10 mins.

1 small radicchio, torn into pieces
1 small bulb of fennel, cubed
1 yellow pepper, deseeded and cubed
1 head curly endive, shredded

4 tbls mayonnaise
1 paw-paw, peeled, deseeded and cubed

GARNISH: fresh oregano or sage

Arrange the endive and radicchio around the edge of a serving plate. Toss together the fennel, pepper and paw-paw, arrange in the centre and pipe the mayonnaise over the top. Garnish with herbs.

260 calories per serving.

COURGETTE VINAIGRETTE SALAD

(P)   Lynne Goldwyn

Serves 8   Preparation 10 mins.   Refrigerate 1 hour

2 lb small courgettes, thinly sliced (1 k)
1 clove garlic, crushed
½ cup red onion, chopped

1 tsp oregano or basil
¼ cup parsley, chopped
¾ cup basic French dressing

Drop the courgettes into a large pan of boiling salted water and cook for 2 minutes only. Drain in a colander and run cold water over the courgettes to stop the cooking. Place the courgettes in a bowl and add the onion, oregano and parsley. Beat the garlic into the French dressing and pour over the courgette mixture. Toss well and chill.

40 calories per serving.

CRUNCHY SALAD

Mirelle Dessau

Serves 8–10   Preparation 40 mins.   Advance (dressing)

¼ red cabbage, chopped
¼ white cabbage, chopped
2 carrots, sliced
2 sticks celery, sliced
¼ Chinese cabbage, shredded
6 small brussels sprouts, sliced
½ small cauliflower in florets
2 small leeks, sliced (discard green
   parts)
2 tbls peanuts
2 tbls sultanas

DRESSING

6 floz sunflower oil (170 ml)
2 floz olive oil (55 ml)
2 floz wine vinegar (55 ml)
2 tsp sugar
3 tsp lemon juice
1 tsp wholegrain mustard
1 tsp sea salt
1 clove garlic, crushed
20 grinds black pepper
GARNISH: 1 tbls sesame seeds, toasted

Dressing: Shake all ingredients together until it emulsifies. Half an hour before serving coat all vegetables with the dressing. Toss in the peanuts and sultanas. Just before serving, sprinkle with the sesame seeds.

220 calories per serving.

DANISH SALAD

Ruth Smilg

Serves 6   Preparation 10 mins.

6 oz wholemeal noodles, cooked (170 gm)
2 tbls petit pois, cooked
2 tbls mushrooms, sliced
2 tbls green beans, sliced and cooked
2 tbls asparagus tips

DRESSING

4 tbls yoghurt
1 tbls sour cream
Mixed herbs
Sea salt to taste
Chives

Mix the vegetables with the cooked and strained noodles and pour over the dressing made with the rest of the ingredients.

192 calories per serving.

EGG AND MUSHROOM SALAD   Ruth Smilg

Serves 4   Preparation 5 mins.

4 hardboiled eggs, sliced
4 tbls mushrooms, finely sliced

DRESSING

4 tbls yoghurt
1 tsp single cream
1 tsp vinegar
$\frac{1}{2}$ tsp mustard
Pinch of Culpepper salad seasoning salt
Chives

Mix together all the dressing ingredients. Arrange the eggs on a flat dish with the mushrooms, and pour over the dressing.

93 calories per serving.

FENNEL SALAD I   Ruth Smilg

Serves 4   Preparation 10 mins.

2 fennel bulbs, grated
1 apple, grated
2 tbls walnuts, chopped
4 tbls yoghurt

2 tbls sour cream
Lemon juice
Pinch of sugar or substitute

Mix the fennel and apple. Made a dressing with the rest of the ingredients and mix thoroughly. Decorate with the feathery tops of the fennel cut into small pieces.

126 calories per serving.

FENNEL SALAD II   Yaffa Wagner

Serves 8–10   Preparation 15 mins.

2lb fennel, thinly sliced lengthways
  (900gm)
2lb Spanish onions, thinly sliced,
  lengthways (900gm)
Juice of 4 large lemons

Mayonnaise
Salt and pepper

GARNISH: 1 avocado, sliced lengthways
           Parsley

Mix the fennel and onion. Dress with lemon juice, salt and pepper and some mayonnaise to taste. Decorate with dish with sliced avocado and parsley.

82 calories per serving.

147

FISH SALAD
Elissa Bennett

Serves 6   Preparation 30 mins.   Cook 35 mins.   Refrigerate 1 hour

½lb best button mushrooms, sliced (225 gm)
1½lb skinned fillets of lemon sole (675 gm)
Tabasco sauce
4 tbls single cream

4 tbls olive oil
Juice of ½ lemon
¼lb black olives (115 gm)
½ cup parsley, chopped
1 clove garlic, crushed (optional)

Lightly grease an enamel plate and place fish fillets on it, season and cover. Steam the fish gently until cooked. Allow them to cool. Place the mushrooms in a bowl, add olive oil, lemon juice, a couple of shakes of Tabasco sauce and a little crushed garlic if desired. Stir in and allow to stand in a cool place for 1 hour. Add the black olives, single cream, salt and pepper. Finally, add the parsley and stir in the pieces of fish.

495 calories per serving.

FRIED FISH SALAD
Sheila Kustow

Preparation 15 mins.

Left over fried fish
Celery, chopped
Apples, chopped
Tomatoes, quartered
Mushrooms, sliced
Cucumber, sliced

DRESSING
Tomato ketchup
Mayonnaise
Worcester sauce
Salt and pepper

As this is a way of using left over fried fish, exact quantities cannot be given.

Chop up fried fish and make a dressing using ketchup, mayonnaise, Worcestershire sauce, salt and pepper. Mix fish and vegetables into sauce and serve.

Not slimming!

FRUIT AND CHEESE SALAD
Andrew Hildebrand

Serves 4   Preparation 15 mins.

2 oz lamb's lettuce, washed and dried (55 gm)
¼ watermelon, peeled, deseeded and cubed
½ pineapple, peeled and chopped

1 punnet mustard and cress
3 tbls French dressing
8 oz cottage cheese (225 gm)
1 mango, stoned and cubed

Toss together the lettuce, fruit, mustard and cress and dressing. Arrange in a serving dish with the cottage cheese in the centre.

229 calories per serving.

GREEK CHEESE SALAD WITH WALNUT
AND MUSTARD DRESSING   Jane Finestone

Serves 6   Preparation 10 mins.

1 little gem lettuce
1 radicchio head
1 bunch watercress
1 small curly endive
8 oz fresh feta cheese, thinly sliced
   (225 gm)

DRESSING

2 oz chopped walnuts (55 gm)
3 tbls olive oil
1 tbls white wine vinegar
2 tsp Dijon mustard
$\frac{1}{2}$ tsp fresh basil, chopped

Wash and drain salad leaves, arrange them on a large oval serving platter, lay cheese slices along centre, cover and chill until ready to serve. Combine all dressing ingredients and pour over just before serving.

238 calories per serving.

GRAPEFRUIT SALAD   Lisa Rose

Serves 4–6   Preparation 15 mins.   Refrigerate 1$\frac{1}{2}$ hours

$\frac{1}{2}$ oz envelope unflavoured gelatine (15 gm)
$\frac{1}{2}$ cup water
2 tbls sugar
16 oz tin grapefruit segments (450 gm)
Fruit juice

$\frac{1}{4}$ cup white wine
1 tbls fresh lemon juice
1 cup raw vegetables, diced:
   cauliflower, green pepper,
   carrot, etc.

In a small saucepan, sprinkle the gelatine over the water and allow to stand for 5 minutes. Bring the water slowly to the boil, stirring until the gelatine is dissolved. Drain the tin of grapefruit sections, saving the syrup. Add enough fruit juice to the syrup to make one cup of liquid. Add the fruit juice – syrup mixture, white wine and lemon juice to the gelatine mixture. Refrigerate until just beginning to thicken. Cut the grapefruit into $\frac{1}{2}$" (1 cm) pieces and add with the diced vegetables to the gelatine. Pour into a 1$\frac{1}{2}$–2 pt (800 ml–1.2 l) mould and chill until firm.

175 calories per serving.

LENTIL SALAD

Anna Cohen

Serves 4–6   Preparation 10 mins.   Cook 35 mins.   Cool 1 hour

2 cups lentils
1 stalk celery
1 small onion
4 cups water
1 tsp salt
½ large Spanish onion, chopped
½ green pepper, chopped

DRESSING

5 tbls oil
3 tbls vinegar
¾ tsp salt
¼ tsp pepper

Pour the dry lentils, one cup at a time, on a large baking sheet and pick over carefully to remove any foreign particles. Then wash well in a colander. Place the lentils, small onion and celery with the salt and water in a saucepan, bring to the boil and simmer covered until the lentils are tender but not mushy – about 35 minutes. Drain, remove onion and celery and place lentils in a bowl. Whisk the dressing ingredients together and pour over the warm lentils. Leave until the lentils are cool and then stir in the green pepper and Spanish onion.

260 calories per serving.

PASTA, BEAN AND
ARTICHOKE SALAD

Sheila Fraser

Serves 6   Preparation 10 mins.   Cook 10 mins.   Advance

4 oz pasta bows or shells (115 gm)
14 oz tin artichoke hearts, drained 400 gm)
3 heaped tbls red kidney beans, drained
3 heaped tbls green flageolet, drained
3 heaped tbls chick peas, drained
3 tbls sweetcorn, drained
1 tbls parsley, chopped
Salt
Black pepper

DRESSING

3 tbls olive oil
1 tbls wine vinegar
½ tsp Dijon mustard
1 tbls mild mayonnaise
Seasoning to taste

Cook pasta in boiling salted water until al dente. Cut artichoke hearts into quarters and mix with the pasta, beans and sweetcorn. Season with pepper and salt.

Dressing: Combine all the ingredients and pour over the pasta mixture. Decorate with the chopped parsley.

275 calories per serving.

150

RED CABBAGE AND
BANANA SALAD
Gillian Burr

Serves 4   Preparation 10 mins.

8oz red cabbage, shredded (225gm)
2 bananas, thickly sliced
2 tsp lemon juice

DRESSING
½oz brown sugar (15gm)
1 floz vinaigrette dressing (30ml)
Salt and pepper

GARNISH: parsley, chopped
                watercress

Sprinkle the bananas with lemon juice as you slice them. Mix the brown sugar and vinaigrette together and season to taste. Gently mix the red cabbage and bananas together and pour the dressing over. Toss lightly. Sprinkle the salad with the parsley and garnish with watercress.

80 calories per serving.

BROWN RICE SALAD
Ruth Smilg

Serves 4   Preparation 10 mins.   Refrigerate

4oz brown rice, cooked and drained (115gm)
2oz frozen peas, cooked and drained (55gm)
1 small dessert apple, diced and tossed in
    lemon juice
½ yellow pepper, deseeded and diced

¼ cucumber, diced
2 tomatoes, diced
1 tbls chives, finely chopped
2 tbls French dressing

Stir all the ingredients together in a bowl until thoroughly coated with the dressing. Chill before serving.

143 calories per serving.

RICE SALAD
Caroline Smilg

Serves 3   Preparation 5 mins.

5oz cooked rice (170gm)
1 tomato, diced
½ cucumber, diced
1 apple, diced

DRESSING
2 tbls yoghurt
1 tsp single cream
Parsley, chopped
Sea salt

Mix the rice with the tomatoes, cucumber and apple and pour the dressing over.

137 calories per serving.

151

SPINACH AND ORANGE SALAD   Diane Taylor

Serves 6   Preparation 10 mins.

10 oz fresh spinach (280 gm)
3 oranges, peeled and sectioned

1 medium red Spanish onion, thinly sliced
½ cup French dressing

Thoroughly wash the spinach and drain in a colander. Dry in a towel and tear into bite size pieces. Place the spinach, orange sections and onion slices in a salad bowl. Just before serving, toss with the dressing.

156 calories per serving.

SPRING SALAD   Ruth Smilg

Serves 4   Preparation 10 mins.

5 oz cauliflower, grated (145 gm)
5 oz Emmenthal cheese, cubed
  (145 gm)
2 tomatoes
¼ cucumber, cubed
1 head of lettuce

DRESSING
2 tbls salad oil
2 tbls wine or raspberry vinegar
Mustard
Sea salt
Sugar or substitute
Fresh chopped herbs

Cut lettuce and tomatoes in strips. Mix with the cucumber, cheese and cauliflower. Mix the dressing ingredients and stir carefully into the salad.

115 calories per serving.

TABBOULEH   Ruth Starr

Serves 6   Preparation 30 mins.   Refrigerate overnight   Advance

7 oz bulgar wheat (195 gm)
1 tsp salt
12 fl oz boiling water (340 ml)
1 lb tomatoes, chopped (450 gm)
½ cucumber, diced

DRESSING
2 fl oz olive oil (50 ml)
2 fl oz lemon juice (50 ml)
2 tbls fresh mint, chopped
1–2 cloves garlic, crushed
6 tbls fresh parsley, chopped

Mix wheat with salt. Pour boiling water over. Leave 15–20 minutes. Mix dressing ingredients together and pour over soaked wheat. Leave overnight in refrigerator to absorb flavours. Before serving, stir in chopped salad ingredients.

157 calories per serving.

TOMATOES WITH LEMON
CREAM DRESSING
René Geison

Serves 4–6　　　　　　　　Preparation 10 mins.

1½lb tomatoes, peeled and thickly
　　sliced (675gm)
Chives, finely chopped
Pepper and salt

DRESSING
3 floz cream (85ml)
3 tbls oil
1 tsp sugar
Juice and rind of ½ lemon
Salt and pepper

Arrange the tomato slices in a wide serving dish. Season with salt and pepper. Whisk all the dressing ingredients together until thick and pour over the centre of the tomatoes leaving a border showing. Scatter liberally with chives. Can be served as a starter with crusty French bread.

190 calories per serving.

TUNA FISH PLATTER
Bernice Burr

Serves 4–6　　　　　　　　Preparation 20 mins.　　　　　　　　Advance

16oz tinned tuna fish (450gm)
4 hard boiled eggs, quartered
4–6 spring onions, sliced
½ green pepper, diced
1 tin anchovies, drained
8oz new potatoes, cooked and sliced
　　(225gm)
2–4 sticks celery, sliced

10 stuffed olives, halved
10 black olives
½ pt vinaigrette (280ml)
1 tsp mustard

GARNISH: chives, snipped
　　　　　　parsley, chopped
　　　　　　watercress
　　　　　　radishes

Drain and flake the fish, add the celery, spring onion and pepper and spread onto a platter. Add mustard to vinaigrette and sprinkle enough over fish mixture to moisten it. Cover surface of fish mixture with the potatoes. Decorate with eggs, anchovies and olives. Cover with cling film and chill until required. Before serving, garnish with the chives, parsley, watercress and radishes.

Not slimming.

TUNA, TOMATO AND MACARONI SALAD

John Hildebrand

Serves 4–6   Preparation 10 mins.   Cook 7 mins.   Refrigerate 2 hours

8 oz quick macaroni (225 gm)
2 cups tomatoes, diced
1 cup cucumber, diced
½ cup celery or green pepper, diced
½ cup scallions or red onions, diced

¼ cup fresh parsley, minced
7 oz tin tuna fish, drained and flaked (200 gm)
½ cup mayonnaise
¼ pt vinaigrette dressing (140 ml)

Cook the quick macaroni according to package directions. Drain. Rinse thoroughly with cold water and drain well again. Transfer the macaroni into a large bowl, add the vegetables and the tuna fish. Stir the mayonnaise and vinaigrette together and spoon over the other ingredients. Toss well and serve chilled.

425 calories per serving.

VEGETARIAN SALAD

Anna Cohen

Serves 4–6   Preparation 10 mins.

8 oz new potatoes, cooked (225 gm)
3 tomatoes, sliced
¼ cucumber, diced
7½ oz tin red beans, drained and rinsed (215 gm)
8 oz tin chick peas, drained and rinsed (225 gm)
2 oz mushrooms, sliced (55 gm)

DRESSING

4 tbls mayonnaise
1 clove garlic, crushed
1 tsp wholegrain or French mustard

GARNISH: 1½ oz dry roasted peanuts (40 gm)

Place all salad and vegetable ingredients in a bowl. Mix the mayonnaise, garlic and mustard together. Stir into the vegetables to coat thoroughly. Sprinkle with the nuts before serving.

416 calories per serving.

Sauces

Just waiting for the devil sauce!

HINTS

All freezable sauces should be frozen in ice cube trays for easy use.

PICKLING MARINADE FOR CUCUMBERS: 5 cloves garlic, 1 tbls pickling spice, 1 tsp sugar, 1 tbls salt, 4 bay leaves, 2 tbls acetic acid, 3 pt (1.7 litres) boiling water.

LESS FATTENING MAYONNAISE: Add half quantities of yoghurt to mayonnaise being used.

GHERKIN BUTTER: Blend 1 tsp made-up mustard with 2oz (55gm) butter; then add 4 finely chopped cocktail gherkins and some cayenne pepper.

HERB BUTTER: Cream 2oz (55gm) butter with 1 tsp lemon juice, then add any chopped fresh herbs and salt and black pepper.

Savoury Sauces

BECHAMEL SAUCE

Lesley Bennett

Serves 6   **Preparation 10 mins.**   **Cook 20 mins.**

2 tbls butter
½ onion, finely chopped
1 stalk celery, finely chopped
2 tbls flour
1 pt hot milk (560 ml)

1 small sprig thyme
½ bay leaf
White peppercorns
Nutmeg

Melt butter in thick or double saucepan. Cook finely chopped onion and celery over low heat until onion is soft but not brown. Remove from heat and stir in flour. Return to heat and cook gently for 3–5 minutes, stirring until flour is cooked through. Add quarter of the boiling milk and cook over water, stirring continuously. As sauce thickens add the remaining milk stirring with a wooden spoon until the sauce bubbles. Add thyme, bayleaf, pepper and nutmeg to taste. Simmer for 15 minutes. Strain through fine sieve and dot with butter.

Cream sauce: To one pint béchamel sauce add 4 tablespoons double cream, bring to boiling point and add a few drops of lemon juice. Ideal for fish, eggs or vegetables.

BROCCOLI SAUCE FOR PASTA SHELLS

Jennifer Davis

Serves 4   **Preparation 5 mins**   **Cook 30 mins.**

14 oz pasta shells (400 gm)
4 tbls olive oil
½ pt milk (280 ml)
Salt

1 lb broccoli heads (450 gm)
3 cloves garlic, sliced
2 oz parmesan cheese, freshly grated (55 gm)
Freshly ground black pepper

Wash broccoli and boil in lightly salted water until soft, 12–15 minutes. Drain and chop finely. Leave aside. Heat oil in fairly large saucepan and add finely sliced garlic cloves. Allow to soften but not brown. Next add chopped broccoli heads and milk and cook for 10–15 minutes over high heat stirring quite often, the broccoli should be reduced to a creamy texture by the end of this time. Cook chosen pasta, dried gnocchi shells are good with this sauce, until al dente. Drain, reserving a little of the cooking water, then add to saucepan with the broccoli mixture, adding the parmesan, salt and black pepper. Add a spoonful or two of reserved cooking water so that the mixture is creamy rather than stiff. Stir well over a moderate heat for just a moment. Serve in warm dishes with extra parmesan cheese.

BUTTERY HERB SAUCE

Marion Cohen

Serves 2–4   Preparation 3 mins.   Cook 7 mins.

2 oz butter/margarine (55 gm)   2 tbls chopped fresh mixed herbs
Salt   (thyme, sage, marjoram, parsley)

Melt butter in pan until it just begins to brown. Sprinkle in the herbs and a little salt.
Serve with vegetables or grilled or poached fish.

CHEESE BECHAMEL SAUCE

Kate Williams

Serves 6–8   Preparation 5 mins.   Cook 25 mins.   Advance

6 oz butter (170 gm)   4 oz cheddar cheese, grated (115 gm)
6 oz white flour (170 gm)   4 eggs, lightly beaten
1½ pt milk (850 ml)   Nutmeg, freshly grated
2 tsp Dijon mustard   Salt and pepper

In a saucepan melt butter, stir in flour; cook gently for 1 minute stirring to prevent
burning. Gradually add the milk whisking constantly to blend the mixture smoothly.
Add the mustard, seasoning and nutmeg to taste. Add the grated cheese and simmer
very slowly for about 15 minutes, stirring occasionally to prevent sauce sticking to
bottom of the pan. Cool slightly, then whisk in the beaten eggs.

SAUCE GRIBICHE

Helen Meller

Serves 6   Preparation 20 mins.   Advance

3 hard boiled eggs   Sprig of parsley, finely chopped
1 tbls Dijon mustard   3 sprigs tarragon, finely chopped
1 tbls wine vinegar   6 chives, finely chopped
Salt and pepper   1 shallot, finely chopped
9 fl oz olive oil (255 ml)   1 tbls capers, finely chopped
1 chilli, chopped (optional)

Shell the eggs and separate yolks from whites. Chop the whites. Put yolks into mixing
bowl and mash. Mix in the mustard, vinegar and seasoning. Add oil drop by drop,
making a mayonnaise. Add herbs, the shallot and capers. Mix into the sauce together
with chopped egg whites. If a hotter taste is liked then mix in a crushed chilli. Serve
with cold fish.

157

MUSTARD SAUCE
Marion Cohen

Serves 4   Preparation 5 mins.   Cook 15 mins.   Advance

1 oz butter/margarine (30 gm)
1 small onion, finely chopped
$\frac{1}{2}$ oz plain flour (15 gm)
$\frac{1}{4}$ pt milk/vegetable stock, mixed (140 ml)

1 tsp dried mustard
1 tbls vinegar
1 tsp sugar
Salt and pepper

Heat the fat in a saucepan and add the onion and stir until tender and just starting to brown. Mix in the flour and mustard powder. Remove from the heat and add the vinegar and sugar, then very gradually blend in the milk and vegetable stock mixture. Bring to the boil stirring constantly, then simmer for 3 minutes. Season. Delicious with celeriac and other root vegetables.

PESTO SAUCE
Wendy Grossmith

Serves 2–3   Preparation 5 mins.   Advance   Freezable

1 oz fresh basil leaves (30 gm)
2 cloves garlic
2 oz pine kernels (55 gm)

Seasoning
2 oz grated parmesan cheese (55 gm)
3 fl oz oil (85 ml)

Put basil, garlic and kernels in blender and mix. Add cheese. Then add oil a little at a time whilst mixing. Season to taste.

SAFFRON SAUCE
Bondi Zimmerman

Serves 4–6   Preparation 5 mins.   Cook 5–10 mins.   Advance

1 oz butter/margarine (30 gm)
1 tbls flour
1 pt good fish or vegetable stock (570 ml)

Lemon juice to taste
1 tsp saffron shreds
5 fl oz cream (140 ml) (optional)

Soak saffron shreds in the hot stock and leave to infuse. Melt the butter in a pan until bubbling. Add the flour and mix well. Remove from the heat and slowly pour in the stock and lemon juice, stirring constantly. Return to the heat and bring to the boil, stirring all the while, until the sauce thickens. Strain it to remove any remaining shreds of saffron. Return to the heat and add the cream, if desired, just before serving. Delicious with all fish and with vegetables.

TOMATO SAUCE
Kate Williams

Serves 6   **Preparation 5 mins.**   **Cook 35 mins.**   **Advance**   **Freezable**

14 oz tin tomatoes (400 gm)
1 medium onion, chopped
2 carrots, grated
1 small red pepper, chopped

½ vegetable stock cube
3 tsp tomato purée
2 oz butter (55 gm)
2 tsp sugar

Soften onion, carrot and pepper in the butter. Add tomatoes, tomato purée, sugar and stock cube and simmer for 30 minutes. Liquidise and serve.

CONCENTRATED TOMATO SAUCE
Bernice Burr

Serves 8   **Preparation 10 mins.**   **Cook 40 mins.–1 hour**   **Advance**   **Freezable**

2–3 beef tomatoes, skinned and
   chopped
14 oz tin Italian tomatoes (400 gm)
4 oz dried Italian tomatoes, cut into
   small pieces (115 gm)
3 tbls tomato paste
8 oz onion, finely diced (225 gm)
1 green pepper, finely chopped

Salt and black pepper
1 clove garlic, finely chopped
2 tsp sugar
2 tsp basil
2 tsp parsley
2 tsp Italian seasoning
2 tbls oil

Heat the oil in a pan, add the onion, pepper and garlic, sprinkle with salt and pepper, cover and lower heat to sweat the vegetables. When soft, add the fresh and dried tomatoes and the tinned tomatoes with their juice (break up the tinned tomatoes with a fork). Add all the spices and herbs and the tomato paste and bring the sauce to the boil, stirring constantly. Turn down the heat and cook uncovered, stirring occasionally until most of the juice has evaporated. Cool and store in fridge or freezer.

YOGHURT AND CUCUMBER SAUCE
Jill Summers

Serves 6   **Preparation 15 mins.**

1 cucumber
2 tbls olive oil

5 fl oz plain yoghurt (140 ml)
Garlic salt

Grate the unpeeled cucumber in a food processor or by hand on a coarse grater. Drain in a colander for 5 minutes, pressing out as much liquid as possible. Put cucumber in a bowl and mix with olive oil. Add a good sprinkling of garlic salt. Add yoghurt. Mix well.

Pastes

 GARLIC PASTE   Dinny Charkham

Preparation 5 mins.   Advance

6 cloves garlic, crushed   1 tbls oil
1 tsp salt   2 tbls hot paprika powder
Lemon to taste

Blend all ingredients together until smooth. Can be stored in a jar in the fridge for months.

CURRY PASTE   Mirelle Dessau

Preparation 5 mins.   Freezable

*Fresh ginger   *Green chillies (the seeds provide the
*Garlic   strength so omit some if desired)
*Use in equal quantities

Liquidise ingredients together. Freeze mixture in ice cube trays. When needed, 1 or 2 cubes can be used.

Sweet Sauces

  ICED BRANDY SAUCE   Rosanna Burr

Serves 4–6   Preparation 10 mins.   Freeze 2 hours

6 oz sugar (170 gm)   1 lemon
¼ pt water (140 ml)   4 tsp white wine
1 orange   4 tbls brandy

Dissolve the sugar in the water, boil for 5 minutes and chill. Add grated rind of half an orange and half a lemon to the syrup, together with the juice of the whole orange and whole lemon. Add the wine and brandy and freeze to a mush. Stir once or twice.

CASHEW CREAM
Miki Hildebrand

Serves 8–10 **Preparation 5 mins.** **Advance** **Freezable**

8oz unsalted cashew nuts (225gm) 8tsp concentrated apple juice
6 tbls water

Liquidise nuts with a little of the water, adding more of the apple juice until you have a cream of the consistency you require – fairly thick is delicious and suitable to sandwich 2 cakes together; thinner is delicious with vanilla ice cream.

HOT CHOCOLATE SAUCE
Gillian Burr

Serves 6 **Preparation 4 mins.** **Cook 10 mins.**

2oz bitter chocolate (55gm)   * 8oz sugar (225gm)
$\frac{1}{2}$ pt water (280ml)   * 1 tbls cornflour
2 tbls butter   * Salt
2 tbls cognac   (* *mixed together*)
$\frac{1}{2}$ tsp orange rind, grated very finely

Combine the chocolate with the water and melt over a gentle heat. When smooth, add the combined sugar, cornflour and salt. Cook, stirring constantly, until the sugar is dissolved and sauce is thick. Boil for 3 minutes, then add butter and cognac. Stir again then remove from heat. Add the finely grated orange rind.

Microwave instructions

Place chocolate and water in bowl and cook on high for 1 minute at a time, stirring after each minute until melted. Add cornflour mixture and cook on medium for 1 minute. Stir. Sugar should now have dissolved. Cook on high for 1 to 2 minutes then add butter and cognac. Heat for 30 seconds. Stir again and add the finely grated orange rind.

COFFEE SAUCE
Lisa Rose

Serves 6 **Preparation 5 mins.** **Cook 10 mins.** **Advance**

6 egg yolks   3 tbls sugar
1 tbls strong instant coffee $1\frac{3}{4}$ tbls coffee liqueur
1 pt hot milk (570ml) $1\frac{1}{2}$ floz double cream whipped (45ml)

Whisk together the yolks, sugar, coffee and liqueur. Add the hot milk and cook in a bowl over a pan of hot water until the liquid coats the back of a spoon. When the sauce has cooled, whisk in the cream. This sauce is delicious with chocolate mousse.

161

ORANGE RUM SAUCE   Marion Cohen

Serves 6   Preparation 10 mins.   Advance

3 tbls butter
6 oz icing sugar (170 gm)
$\frac{1}{2}$ pt sour cream (280 ml)
1 tsp orange rind, grated

2 tbls orange juice
1 tbls lemon juice
2 tbls rum

Cream together the butter and sugar until smooth. Combine all the other ingredients and add to the butter/sugar mixture. Mix well together. Serve cold, with cake or hot puddings.

RASPBERRY SAUCE   Gillian Burr

Serves 6   Preparation 5 mins.   Advance

$\frac{1}{2}$ lb frozen or fresh raspberries (225 gm)   3 tbls icing sugar
1 tsp brandy

Place all ingredients in liquidiser and process until smooth. If desired, sieve sauce to remove pips. Delicious with ice cream or meringues.

 ## CREME VANILLE   Rosanna Burr

Serves 8   Preparation 5 mins.

1 cup double cream
1 tsp vanilla essence

1 tbls sugar
1 cup softened vanilla ice cream

Whip cream, sugar and vanilla essence until stiff. Fold into the ice cream and refrigerate. May be stored for 2 hours.

Salad Dressings

COLESLAW DRESSING   Gillian Burr

Serves 8–10   Preparation 5 mins.   Advance

$\frac{1}{2}$ pt mayonnaise (280 ml)
Juice of $\frac{1}{2}$ lemon
1 tsp sugar

1 tbls white vinegar
Salt and pepper

Mix all ingredients together. Enough for $1\frac{1}{2}$ lb (675 gm) white cabbage.

CURRY DRESSING

David Burr

Serves 4–6   Preparation 2 mins.   Advance

3 tbls natural yoghurt
2 tbls mayonnaise

Pinch of curry powder
Pinch of Tandoori powder

Mix all ingredients together and beat well.

HERBY YOGHURT DRESSING   Lynne Goldwyn

Serves 6   Preparation 5 mins.   Refrigerate 1 hour   Advance

$\frac{1}{2}$ pt natural yoghurt (280 ml)
$\frac{1}{2}$ tsp mixed herbs
Pinch of onion salt

1 clove garlic, crushed
Clear honey to taste

Combine the yoghurt with the herbs, garlic and seasoning. If a sweeter dressing is required, add the honey as desired. Refrigerate for at least 1 hour before using.

HONEY LEMON DRESSING   Bondi Zimmerman

Serves 4–6   Preparation 10 mins.   Advance

$\frac{1}{2}$ tsp salt
$\frac{1}{2}$ tsp lemon rind, grated
2 tbls honey

2 tbls red wine vinegar
2 tbls fresh lemon juice
$\frac{1}{2}$ cup oil

Beat together the salt, grated lemon rind, honey, vinegar and lemon juice. Gradually beat the oil and keep refrigerated. Beat again or shake in a covered jar before serving. Delicious with green salad and blintzes, and sweetened berries.

LEMON CREAM DRESSING   Lynne Goldwyn

Serves 4–6   Preparation 2 mins.

3 fl oz single cream (85 ml)
3 tbls oil
1 tsp sugar

$\frac{1}{2}$ lemon, rind and juice
Salt and pepper

Whisk all ingredients together until thick and use immediately.

LOW CALORIE DRESSING (1)　　Ruth Smilg

Serves 4　　　　　　Preparation 5 mins.　　　　　Advance

$\frac{1}{2}$ tsp sea salt
$\frac{1}{2}$ tsp mixed herbs
$\frac{1}{2}$ tsp fresh chopped or dried basil
$\frac{1}{2}$ tsp sugar or substitute
A few chives, chopped

Juice of 1 lemon
$\frac{1}{2}$ pot yoghurt or 4 tbls buttermilk
Little mustard
Little parsley, chopped
Little dill, chopped

Shake together well or blend in a blender.　　　　21 calories per serving.

LOW CALORIE DRESSING
FOR GREEN SALADS (2)　　Ruth Smilg

Serves 4　　　　　　Preparation 5 mins.　　　　　Advance

$\frac{1}{2}$ pot yoghurt
1 tsp mustard
$\frac{1}{2}$ tsp garlic powder

2 tbls sour cream
$\frac{1}{2}$ tsp wine or raspberry vinegar
$\frac{1}{2}$ tsp onion salt

Shake together well or blend in blender.　　　　30 calories per serving.

LOW CALORIE DRESSING
FOR GREEN SALADS (3)　　Ruth Smilg

Serves 4　　　　　　Preparation 5 mins.　　　　　Advance

4 tbls salad oil
1 tsp fresh or dried herbs
1 tsp herb salt
Pinch of garlic salt

4 tsp wine or raspberry vinegar
A little mustard
1 tsp sugar or substitute

Shake together well or blend in blender.　　　　102 calories per serving.

ORIENTAL DRESSING

Jane Cohen-Setton

Serves 8–10　　　　Preparation 10 mins.　　　　Advance

1 clove garlic, finely chopped
A little fresh ginger, grated
1 small slice onion, finely chopped
3 tsp sugar
1 tsp tomato purée

1 tsp French mustard
1 tsp dried mint
2 tbls wine vinegar
$\frac{1}{4}$ pt oil (140ml)
Salt and pepper

Combine all the ingredients except the oil and stir well to dissolve the salt. Gradually beat in the oil or use a liquidiser or a food processor. Serve sliced Chinese leaves or white cabbage or lettuce tossed in some of this dressing.

POPPY SEED DRESSING

Anna Cohen

Serves 6–8　　　　Preparation 5 mins.　　　　Advance

$\frac{2}{3}$ cup oil
$\frac{1}{4}$ cup red wine vinegar
1 tbls poppy seeds

$\frac{1}{2}$ tsp dry mustard powder
$\frac{1}{3}$ tsp salt
$\frac{1}{4}$ cup sugar

Beat together with a fork, or whisk, the vinegar, poppy seeds, mustard, sugar and salt until the salt and the sugar dissolve. Gradually beat in oil. Shake before serving.

WALNUT AND MUSTARD
DRESSING

Jane Finestone

Serves 4　　　　Preparation 5 mins.　　　　Advance

2 oz walnuts, chopped (55gm)
3 tbls olive oil
1 tbls white wine vinegar

2 tbls French mustard
$\frac{1}{2}$ tbls fresh basil, chopped

Combine all ingredients and mix or shake together well. Pour over salad just before serving.

Desserts

You can eat it off after the school play!

HINTS

Sprinkle fresh strawberries with freshly ground black pepper to bring out their full flavour.

Fruit Crudités: Mix some stem ginger and syrup into a pot of sour cream and use as a dip with a choice of fresh fruit cut into fingers.

If watching your fat and sugar intake, you can make fruit fools, creamy ice creams, fruit compôtes, etc. using fresh or dried fruits, yoghurt, low fat white cheese and a little honey for sweetening.

Muesli: Mix together 1lb of oats (450gm), 6 crushed Weetabix, 4 handfuls of cornflakes 1 cup sultanas, $\frac{1}{2}$ cup brown sugar, $\frac{1}{2}$ cup chopped nuts and $\frac{1}{4}$ cup chopped dried fruit.

Naturally sweet fruit such as bananas may be used to cut down the amount of sugar required in a dessert.

Rhubarb provides fibre, calcium and potassium.

Use 1% fat crème fraiche instead of cream.

Light Desserts

(mostly decadent)

APPLE CHARTREUSE
Barbara Green

Serves 4–6   **Preparation 15 mins.** Cook $2\frac{1}{2}$–3 hours

3 lb apples (cookers, or eaters that
  keep their shape) (1.35 k)
5 oz sugar (140 gm)
$\frac{1}{4}$ tsp mixed spice
5 tbls quince jelly or apricot jam

CARAMEL
4 oz granulated sugar (115 gm)
3 tbls cold water

Caramel: Dissolve the sugar in the water in a small pan over gentle heat, stirring. Once every grain of sugar has dissolved stop stirring, turn up the heat and boil fast to a good brown caramel. Pour at once into a warmed $1\frac{1}{2}$–2 pt (900 ml–1.1 l) soufflé dish and coat the bottom and sides with the caramel. Peel, core, quarter and slice the apples. Layer them with the mixed sugar and spice in the soufflé dish until full, pressing well down. Cover with greaseproof paper and bake (standing the dish in a pan of hot water to come halfway up) in a hot oven Gas No.6, 400°F, 200°C for $2\frac{1}{2}$–3 hours. Cool, and when lukewarm turn out on to a serving dish and spoon over the jelly or jam. Serve cold with cream.

TANGY APPLE SWIRL Barbara Green

Serves 4   Preparation 15 mins. Advance

1 lb cooking apples (450 gm)
1 oz butter or margarine (30 gm)
2 oz raw brown sugar (55 gm)

Pinch, ground cloves
½ lemon rind, grated
½ pt natural yoghurt (285 ml)

Peel, core and chop the apples. Place all the ingredients, except yoghurt in a saucepan. Cook over gentle heat, stirring occasionally until the apples are pulpy. Stir thoroughly to give a rough purée. Leave to cool. In a glass serving dish, or individual dishes, spoon alternate spoonfuls of yoghurt and apple until it is all used up. With a knife, swirl the mixtures to give a decorative effect. Serve chilled.

  POMMES MENTHE Jane Finestone

Serves 4 Preparation 30 mins. Marinate 1 hour Cook 15 mins. Chill 2 hours

4 tart green apples (Granny Smiths)
1 handful fresh mint leaves, chopped
3 oz chopped almonds and raisins
  (85 gm)
2 fl oz Cointreau (60 ml)
4 oz sugar (115 gm)

Juice of 2 lemons
½ pt water (280 ml)
1 liqueur glass Crème de Menthe
Drop green colouring (optional)

GARNISH: whipped cream
         frosted mint leaves

Marinate chopped almonds and raisins in Cointreau for as long as possible (minimum 1 hour but better overnight). Peel and core apples and leave whole. Lightly poach with chopped mint leaves, sugar, lemon juice and water for approx 10–15 minutes. Remove, drain and reserve liquid; add green food colouring if desired. Stuff the apples with the raisin and nut mix. Mix the 'apple-poaching juice' with any remaining Cointreau and raisin juice, plus a glass of Crème de Menthe. Boil down and reduce until thick and syrupy. Place apples on shallow serving dish or in individual dishes and coat with the minty green (jelly-like) sauce. If desired, decorate with whipped cream and some whole sugared mint leaves or sprigs. Chill well before serving.

N.B. *For a frosty look*: To sugar any decorative leaves or flowers either dampen them and dip into caster sugar and chill, or dip into stiffly beaten egg white, then caster sugar, and chill.

AVOCADO SYLLABUB — Stephanie Brahams

Serves 6   **Preparation 15 mins.**

2 avocado pears, peeled and stoned $\frac{1}{2}$ pt double cream (280 ml)
2 tbls lemon juice 4 level tbls icing sugar
$\frac{1}{4}$ pt lime cordial (140 ml)

Purée the avocados with lemon juice. Put cream and sugar into a mixing bowl and beat together until quite thick. Slowly add lime cordial and mix for a few minutes. Fold into avocado purée. Chill before serving.

BLACKBERRY MOUSSE — Monica Levinson

Serves 8–10 **Preparation 30 mins.** **Cook 15 mins.** **Advance**

$\frac{1}{2}$ pt double cream (280 ml) $\frac{1}{2}$ oz gelatine (15 gm)
2 lb blackberries (900 gm) 2–3 egg whites
6–8 oz granulated sugar (170–225 gm) Juice of 1 lemon
5 fl oz whipped cream (140 ml)

Sieve the berries and make up to 1 pt (570 ml) with water. Melt gelatine as per packet instructions. Heat half the blackberry liquid and when simmering add the gelatine and sugar and stir well until quite dissolved. Add this to the rest of the blackberry liquid and stir in the lemon juice. When cold, fold in the whipped cream and the stiffly beaten egg whites.

 # BLACKBERRY SYLLABUB — Lynne Goldwyn

Serves 4 **Preparation 10 mins.** **Refrigerate 1$\frac{1}{2}$ hours** **Advance**

8 oz blackberries (225 gm) $\frac{1}{2}$ pt double cream (280 ml)
2 oz brown sugar (55 gm) 2–3 tbls brandy

Warm the blackberries with the sugar very gently, just enough to make the juices run. Then rub through a sieve. Whip the cream lightly and continue beating as you slowly add the blackberry juice and brandy. Pour into ramekin dishes and place in fridge for at least 1$\frac{1}{2}$ hours before serving.

PHENOMENAL CHOCOLATE
MOUSSE
Elizabeth Futter

Serves 8–10   **Preparation 15 mins.**   **Refrigerate 12 hours**   Advance

8 oz butter or margarine (225 gm)   **7 eggs, separated**
7 oz plain chocolate (200 gm)   **8 soupspoons caster sugar**

Melt butter and chocolate slowly together. With a hand whisk mix sugar and egg yolks together. Add melted chocolate mixture and whisk again. Beat the egg whites until stiff and add to the mixture whisking in by hand. Pour into a bowl or individual ramekins and set overnight.

CHOCOLATE MOUSSE
WITH COFFEE SAUCE
Gillian Burr

Serves 6   **Preparation 20 mins.**   **Refrigerate 4 hours**   Advance

4½ oz plain chocolate (125 gm)   **¼ pt double cream (140 ml)**
2 oz milk chocolate (55 gm)   **¼ pt single cream (140 ml)**
1 whole egg   **1¾ tbls Crème de Cacoa**
1 egg yolk   **1 tbls brandy**
    Coffee sauce *(see page 161)*

Melt the chocolate. Whisk the egg yolk over a pan of hot water until it becomes a thick sabayon. In a separate bowl lightly whip the cream and the liqueurs. Fold in the melted chocolate with the eggs making sure that they are of a similar temperature. Lastly fold in the cream. Pour into a bowl and allow to set for approx. 4 hours. To serve as quenelles, use two large spoons that have been dipped in very hot water. With one spoon, take a heaped spoonful of mousse and with the inside of the other spoon round off the top so that the result is slightly egg-shaped. Serve with coffee sauce.

WHITE AND DARK CHOCOLATE TERRINE
Gillian Burr

Serves 10–12   **Preparation 1½ hours**   **Refrigerate 12 hours**   **Advance**

WHITE CHOCOLATE MOUSSE

5 tbls milk
1 vanilla pod, cut lengthways
8oz white chocolate (225gm)
2 egg yolks
¾oz gelatine (22gm), dissolved in
14 tbls water
½ pt sour cream, whipped (280ml)
8oz caster sugar (225gm)

DARK CHOCOLATE MOUSSE

8oz dark chocolate (225gm)
3 floz strong coffee (85ml)
4oz butter (115gm)
½ pt sour cream, whipped (280gm)

DECORATION: 2oz chocolate, grated (55gm)

Bakewell paper to line a 10 x 3 x 2″ terrine tin (25.5 x 7.5 x 5cm)

White mousse: Place the white chocolate with the milk and vanilla in a saucepan and heat gently; do not boil, stir occasionally until melted. Place the egg yolks and sugar into a double saucepan and cook slowly until the mixture thickens beating regularly. Add 5 tablespoons of the dissolved gelatine and add the chocolate mixture discarding the vanilla pod. Cool and stir from time to time. Fold the cream into the chocolate and pour into a lined tin.

Dark chocolate mousse: Place coffee and chocolate in a double saucepan and melt slowly. Stir in the butter and the rest of the dissolved gelatine. Cool the mixture then fold in the cream and chill until it starts to set and then pour the mixture over the white chocolate mousse and leave to set. Keep tightly sealed under cling film. Turn mousse onto a long plate and peel off the paper. Cut into slices and place on individual dishes and decorate with grated chocolate.

FIGUES PRINCESSE
Meriel Joseph

Serves 8   **Preparation 1 hour**

16 large fresh figs
7oz caster sugar (200gm)
¼ pt Grand Marnier (140ml)
8oz fresh almonds, blanched (225gm)

Juice of 1 lemon
1lb fresh raspberries (450gm)

DECORATION: whipped cream

Peel the figs then slice downwards through them into 4 segments without cutting right down to the base. Pull out the 4 points so that the pink inside can be seen. Arrange in a bowl and scatter half the sugar and all the Grand Marnier over them. Leave for an hour. Halve the almonds and leave them in lemon juice to stop discolouration. Blend the raspberries with rest of sugar, then sieve. Arrange the figs on a serving platter and mix their juice with the raspberry pulp. Push some of the almond halves into the figs. Pour over the raspberry mixture. Decorate with whipped cream and the remainder of the almond halves.

FRUIT AND CREAM BRULEE   Maureen Marks

Serves 8   Preparation 30 mins.   Refrigerate 12 hours.   Advance

1 large melon, cubed
4 peaches or nectarines, finely sliced
2 mangos, sliced
1 lb strawberries or raspberries (450 gm)
(or any other fruit combination)

1 pt double cream (570 ml)
8 oz caster sugar (225 gm)
Juice of $\frac{1}{2}$ orange
Flesh of 1 passion fruit (optional)

Place fruit in a large fireproof dish. Sprinkle it with a little fresh orange juice and sugar, plus lemon juice if you have fruits which discolour. Add passion fruit if desired. Whip cream until thick and stiff, then spoon onto the fruit so that it is covered but not smooth. Chill for 12 hours. Dissolve sugar with a few tablespoons of water and bring to the boil. Boil briskly until it reaches a deep caramel colour. Pour on top of cream so that it sizzles and hardens immediately. Chill again.

FRUIT KEBABS   Sandra Seifert

Serves 4   Preparation 15 mins.

1 large pinapple, cut into 16 chunks
16 seedless grapes
2 mangos cut into 16 chunks

15 large whole strawberries
4 nectarines cut into quarters
(or any other fruits of your choice
Allow 2 satay sticks per person

Spear fruits alternately onto a satay stick. Arrange on a platter in a fan design. Looks most attractive on a buffet table when they are fanned out on a platter with flowers as a centerpiece and a dusting of icing sugar over the flowers.

FRUIT SALAD WITH CANDIED KUMQUATS   Bernice Burr

Serves 4–6   Preparation 10 mins.   Cook 20 mins.   Refrigerate 2 hours

8 oz kumquats (225 gm)
14 oz tin lychees (400 gm)
3–4 kiwi fruits, peeled and thinly sliced

3 Sharon fruit, segmented
3 passion fruit
2 oz caster sugar (55 gm)

Slice kumquats into $\frac{1}{4}$" ($\frac{1}{2}$cm) thick slices into a saucepan to catch any juice. Cover with water then remove kumquats from the pan and reserve. Add the sugar to the water and heat until dissolved. Return kumquats to the pan and allow the water to boil, shaking the pan occasionally. When kumquats are shiny and the liquid much reduced, pour into a bowl. Add the Sharon fruit to the kumquats, together with the kiwi fruit. Add the lychees plus their juice and the passion fruit flesh and mix carefully together. Chill until required.

LEMON MOUSSE

Bobbie Tarn

Serves 6–8   Preparation 10 mins.   Advance   Freezable

1 tin frozen orange juice
Rind and juice ½ lemon
Lemon jelly/crystals
3 tbls water
1 tbls Grand Marnier (optional)

3 whole eggs
2 eggs, separated
2 oz caster sugar (55 gm)

GARNISH: lemon peel

Place 3 whole eggs and 2 yolks into a basin and beat until frothy. Add sugar and continue beating until mousse-like. Put jelly in pan with water (use 4 tablespoons if not using Grand Marnier) and dissolve on low heat. Add lemon juice, grated rind and orange juice to eggs while still whisking; then add the melted jelly. Whip up 2 eggs whites until stiff and fold into the mixture. Pour into dish and allow to set. Decorate with lemon peel.

 ## QUICK LEMON MOUSSE   Marian Goodisman

Serves 6   Preparation 5 mins.   Refrigerate 2 hours   Advance

Juice of 1 lemon
Juice of 2 oranges
½ pt single cream (280 ml)

1 lemon jelly
Water to make up to ½ pt (280 ml)

Put fruit juices and enough boiling water to make ½ pint (280 ml) into a bowl. Add jelly, stir until dissolved. When cool, stir in cream. Refrigerate until set.

 ## OEUFS A LA NEIGE   Wendy Max

Serves 4   Preparation 10 mins.   Cook 25 mins.   Advance: Sauce

4 eggs, separated
12 oz caster sugar (340 gm)

1 pt milk (560 ml)
Vanilla essence

Sauce: Beat the egg yolks with 4 oz (115 gm) caster sugar until white. Heat milk in a saucepan until scalding then add vanilla essence. Pour this onto the eggs and return the mixture to the pan. Stir all the time over a gentle heat until the sauce thickens. Do not boil. Cover and keep in refrigerator until needed. (Can be made the day before).

Meringues: Beat egg whites until stiff. Add 2 tablespoons from remaining sugar and beat again until very stiff, then fold in remaining sugar with a metal spoon. In a wide pan heat some water until simmering and drop into it generous tablespoons of the meringue mixture and allow them to cook for 4 minutes on each side.

To serve: Pour the sauce into a bowl or individual dishes and place meringues on top. Makes 8 meringues.

PEACH MARJORIE
Gloria Levy

Serves 4 **Preparation 20 mins.** **Cook 20 mins.**

4 ripe peaches, peeled and thinly sliced
A little kirsch
A little curaçao
$\frac{1}{2}$oz cornflour (15gm)
$\frac{1}{2}$ pt milk (280gm)

$2\frac{1}{2}$oz sugar (70gm)
2 egg yolks
$\frac{1}{4}$ pt whipped cream (140ml)
$2\frac{1}{2}$oz brown sugar (70gm)

Arrange peaches in an ovenproof dish and flavour with some of the kirsch and curaçao. Dissolve the cornflour in a little milk. Boil up the rest of the milk and bind with the cornflour. Mix together the egg yolks and sugar and stir in the boiling milk. Heat until it boils again, strain and place in a bowl. Dust with sugar and allow to cool. When the mixture is cold, carefully fold in the whipped cream and flavour with the remaining kirsch and curaçao. Cover the peaches with this cream, sprinkle with brown sugar and burn a glaze with a hot iron or place under hot grill.

N.B. It is very important that the iron with which the sugar is burnt is very hot so that a proper glaze of sugar forms.

PEAR BAKE
Maureen Marks

Serves 4 **Preparation 10 mins.** **Cook 20 mins.**

2 large dessert pears, almost ripe
$\frac{1}{4}$ pt double cream (140ml)

2oz demerara sugar (55gm)
4 ramekin dishes

Peel, quarter and remove cores of pears. Cut into bite-sized pieces and place in ramekins. Mix cream with all but a sprinkling of the sugar and pour over pears. Bake for 20 minutes at Gas No.4, 350°F, 180°C. Sprinkle with reserved sugar before serving.

RASPBERRY MOUSSE
Thelma Stanton

Serves 6–8 **Preparation 15 mins.** **Advance**

2 raspberry jellies
$\frac{1}{2}$ pt double cream or $\frac{1}{2}$ pt parev whip (280ml)

15 fl oz boiling water (425ml)
$13\frac{1}{2}$oz tin of unsweetened raspberries and juice (385ml)

Dissolve jellies in the water. Break the raspberries up a little and add the jellies. Beat cream until thickened and fold into jelly mixture. Pour in the bowl and leave to set. Any fruit and appropriately flavoured jellies may be substituted for the raspberries.

174

TIRAMI SU
Jennifer Davis

Serves 8   **Preparation 20 mins.**   **Advance**

2 eggs, separated
2 tbls castor sugar
Few drops vanilla essence
1 lb 2 oz carton Mascarpone cheese
  (500 gm)

20–24 sponge finger biscuits
12 fl oz strong black coffee (340 ml)
2 tbls brandy, coffee liqueur or rum
Unsweetened cocoa powder

Beat together egg yolks, sugar and vanilla to a creamy consistency. Add Mascarpone and fold in until well blended. Beat the 2 egg whites until stiff and fold into the cheese mixture. Put coffee and chosen alcohol in a fairly shallow dish and dip sponge biscuits in coffee mixture allowing them to absorb just enough without falling apart. Place a layer of dipped biscuits in base of the serving dish about 2 inches deep or individual dishes if preferred. Then spread with layer of cheese mixture. Cover this with another layer of dipped biscuits and then another layer of cheese. Dust the top with a complete covering of sieved cocoa powder and put in fridge to set and chill.

WINTER DRIED FRUIT
DELIGHT
Miki Hildebrand

Serves 8   **Preparation 5 mins.**   **Advance 48 hours essential**

1 cup dried peaches
1 cup dried apricots
1 cup prunes
6 oz sultanas (170 gm)
6 tbls almonds, blanched

6 tbls pistachio nuts, shelled
4 tbls pine nuts
Water to cover
2 tsp rose water
2 tsp orange flower water

Wash fruit. Place in bowl with nuts, cover with water and add rose water and orange flower water. Stir and allow to soak 48 hours. Serve chilled.

WINTER FRUIT MERINGUE
Sheila Fraser

Serves 6–8   **Soaking time 40 mins.**   **Cook 55 mins.**

8 oz mixed dried fruit (225 gm)
½ pt apple juice (280 ml)
Lemon juice (optional)

MERINGUE

3 eggs whites
6 level tbls caster sugar

Pour boiling water over dried fruit and allow to soak for 40 minutes. Drain. Cook in apple juice and lemon juice for 40 minutes. When soft and cool chop roughly. Pile into dish.

Meringues: Beat egg whites until stiff, beat in 3 tablespoons of sugar until as stiff as before. Lightly fold in the remaining sugar and pile meringue over fruit. Cook 15–20 minutes on Gas No.3, 325°F, 160°C until meringue is set and lightly browned. Serve hot or cold.

Iced Desserts

(Another decadent section!)

Why can you never get it right — we asked for chocolate chip and pistachio!

AVOCADO AND NUT ICE CREAM Marion Cohen

Serves 4　　**Preparation 25 mins.**　　**Stand 3 hours**　　**Freeze 3 hours**

1 large tin evaporated milk
1 large ripe avocado
1 banana, mashed
5 fl oz double cream (140 ml)

2 oz flaked almonds, toasted (55 gm)
Sugar to taste

DECORATION: mint leaves

Cover the unopened tin of milk with water and boil for 20 minutes. Chill, still unopened, for 3 hours. Remove avocado skin and stone and mash flesh, then blend with banana, cream, almonds and sugar to taste. Whisk up the milk until very thick. Fold in the avocado mixture. Freeze for 1 hour then beat thoroughly and freeze again. Serve, decorated with mint leaves that have been dipped in egg white then dusted with sugar.

BANANA YOGHURT ICE
Lynne Goldwyn

Serves 6–8   Preparation 10 mins.   Freeze 3 hours

1lb bananas (450gm)
8oz low fat Greek yoghurt (225gm)
2–3 tbls lemon juice

Few drops of vanilla essence
2 egg whites
3 tbls honey

Blend bananas to a smooth pulp, mix in yoghurt, lemon juice, honey and vanilla essence. Whisk the egg whites until stiff and then fold gently into the mixture. Turn into a plastic box and freeze until firm.

BLACKCURRANT SORBET
Lynne Goldwyn

Serves 6   Preparation 20 mins.   Freeze 3 hours

1lb ripe blackcurrants, topped and
   tailed (450gm)
Juice of 2 oranges

2 egg whites
2tbls icing sugar
6oz caster sugar (170gm)

Purée the blackcurrants and then put through a sieve to get rid of the pips. Place the purée in a bowl together with the orange juice and sugar and stir the mixture until the sugar has dissolved completely. Pour the mixture into a plastic container and freeze until it is a stiff slush. Whisk the egg whites until foamy, then add icing sugar. Continue whisking until the meringue holds stiff peaks. Take the blackcurrant mixture from the freezer and place in a chilled bowl. Whisk thoroughly, then add meringue and beat lightly together. Return to plastic container, cover and refreeze until firm.

CRUNCHY BROWN BREAD, HAZELNUT AND
GINGER ICE
Elissa Isaacs

Serves 6–8   Preparation 5 mins.   Freeze 3 hours

3oz wholemeal breadcrumbs (85gm)
2oz ground hazelnuts (55gm)
2oz preserved stem ginger, finely
   chopped (55gm)

6oz muscovado sugar (170gm)
3 egg whites
10oz natural low fat yoghurt (285ml)
4 floz double cream (optional) (115ml)

Mix together breadcrumbs, hazelnuts and 2oz (55gm) of sugar onto a baking tray. Put under hot grill for 2 minutes until golden brown. Cool. Whisk egg whites until stiff, gradually adding remaining sugar. Fold in all remaining ingredients and bread mixture. Put in freezer container. Freeze. Place in refrigerator 20 minutes before serving.

CARAMEL ICE CREAM   Gillian Burr

Serves 4–6   Preparation 5 mins.   Cook 10 mins.   Freeze 2 hours essential

4 tbls granulated sugar
½ pt double cream (280 ml)

2 egg yolks

DECORATION: broken walnuts

Place sugar in a saucepan with 2 tablespoons of water and cook over moderate heat until sugar has dissolved completely, then let the sugar boil, swirling the pan occasionally, until it turns a light brown colour. Pour 4 tablespoons of water into the pan and simmer, stirring until the caramel has melted. Beat the egg yolks, pour the syrup into them slowly, continuing to beat until the mixture thickens. Whip the cream and fold it into the mixture. Turn it into a mould, cover and freeze for 2 hours approx. Decorate with broken walnuts.

CHOCOLATE ICE CREAM   Michelle Davidson

Serves 6   Preparation 15 mins.   Freeze   3   hours

2 oz caster sugar (55 gm)
4 tbls water
6 oz plain chocolate (170 gm)

3 egg yolks
½ pt double cream (280 ml)
1½ pt container (850 ml)

Place sugar and water in a saucepan over a low heat until dissolved. Bring to the boil and simmer for 2–3 minutes. Break chocolate into pieces, process in liquidiser, add hot syrup and blend until smooth; add egg yolks and blend again. Whip cream to soft peaks and fold gently into chocolate mixture. Pour into a container, cover with lid and freeze. Place in fridge 20–30 minutes before serving.

CINNAMON TOFFEE ICE CREAM   Marion Cohen

Serves 6   Preparation 10 mins.   Freeze 3 hours

1½ oz brown breadcrumbs (43 gm)
1 tsp ground cinnamon
3 oz sugar (85 gm)

2 tbls water
17 oz pack vanilla ice cream (½ k)

Mix together breadcrumbs and cinnamon. Turn the ice cream into a bowl and break up lightly with a fork. Make a caramel by boiling the sugar and water. When golden, stir in breadcrumbs and cinnamon and *immediately* blend the mixture into the ice cream. Turn into a container and freeze (about 3 hours), stirring occasionally during the first hour.

ICED COFFEE SOUFFLES

Sally Bloom

Serves 6   Preparation 15 mins.   Freeze 4 hours

4 eggs
2 tbls powdered coffee
2 tbls rum

$\frac{1}{4}$ tsp sugar
2 oz chocolate (55 gm)
$\frac{1}{2}$ pt double cream (280 ml)

Separate the yolks and beat them with the powdered coffee until thick and creamy. Melt the chocolate with 2 tablespoons of water, add the rum and stir into the coffee mixture. Whip the cream until stiff and fold into the coffee mixture. Fold in 2 tablespoons of grated chocolate and pour the mixture into individual soufflé dishes. Freeze for 4 hours. Decorate with a little grated chocolate.

FANTASTIC ICE CREAM

Charlotte Davis

Serves 6–8   Preparation 15 mins.   Freezable

3 large eggs
3 oz icing sugar (85 gm)
8 fl oz double cream (225 ml)

2 heaped tsp instant coffee
or 2 tsp vanilla essence
or 2 tsp almond essence

Beat cream and leave. Beat egg whites until stiff, then fold in the icing sugar. Dissolve the coffee granules in as little water as possible. Add the chosen flavouring to cream. Add the beaten egg yolks to whites and hand mix all the ingredients together. Pour into the mould and freeze.

N.B. This is nice frozen in a long paté mould and served at the table in slices.

 ## SORBET DE FRAISES

Rosanna Burr

Serves 4–6   Preparation 10 mins.   Freeze 2 hours

4 oz sugar (115 gm)
4 fl oz water (115 ml)
3 oz strawberries, hulled and sieved (85 gm)

Juice $\frac{1}{4}$ lemon
Juice $\frac{1}{4}$ orange

Heat sugar and water together until syrupy. Add strawberry mixture, then stir in the lemon and orange juice. Cool. Freeze for 1 hour, then beat in food processor or mixer then freeze again. 1 mango, pitted and mashed, can be substituted for strawberries, in which case 1 teaspoon of lemon juice is sufficient in place of the orange and lemon juice in this recipe.

FRUIT PUDDING ICE CREAM   Avril Kleeman

Serves 8   **Preparation 2 hours**   **Cook 5 mins.**   **Freezable**

8 egg yolks
½lb sugar (225gm)
1½ pt single cream (850ml)
Pinch salt
2 tsp vanilla essence
3 level tbls currants
3 level tbls raisins
3 level tbls chopped peel
3 level tbls chopped cherries

MARINADE
2 level tbls brandy
½ tsp ground cloves
½ tsp ground nutmeg
½ tsp mixed spice
½ tsp cinnamon

Mix marinade ingredients together and marinade all fruit for 1–2 hours. Cream the yolks and the sugar with the salt, until they are white and creamy. Scald the cream. Add to the mixture and beat. Pour it all into a double saucepan, and cook stirring continuously until it is like thick custard. Put ice cream mixture in bowl in the deep freeze until it is semi-frozen and thick, but still stirrable. Add the marinated mixture. Stir well. Spoon into loaf tin, or suitable container, and freeze until you wish to serve.

GUAVA SORBET   Gloria Levy

Serves 6   **Preparation 10 mins.**   **Freeze 3 hours**

10oz tin guava halves in syrup (285gm)
A little lemon juice
4 tbls water

3 tbls caster sugar
Orange-blossom water

RASPBERRY SAUCE
(see page 162)

Blend the guava halves, syrup, lemon juice and orange blossom water until smooth. Sieve the purée and remove any pips. Make a syrup with the water and sugar and stir it into the guava pulp. Freeze until 'mushy', then beat with a fork for a few minutes so that the sorbet is smooth and return it to the freezer. Serve with a raspberry sauce.

HALVA ICE CREAM   Micki Hildebrand

Serves 6–8   **Preparation 10 mins.**   **Freeze 3 hours**

1 pt double cream (560ml)
6 eggs, separated

⅔ cup of caster sugar
8oz halva (225gm)

DECORATION: nuts or flaked chocolate

Beat egg yolks and sugar until fluffy. Whip cream and when stiff fold in yolks. Beat whites until stiff and fold in, followed by flaked halva. Pour mixture into slightly oiled mould and leave in freezer until set. Decorate with flakes of halva, nuts or chocolate flakes if desired.

KIWI FRUIT SORBET   Lynne Goldwyn

Serves 6   Preparation 10 mins.   Freeze 3 hours

2 oz caster sugar (55 gm)   2 egg whites
6 kiwi fruit   1–2 tbls Cointreau or orange liqueur

Dissolve sugar with $\frac{1}{4}$ pt (140 ml) water in a pan. Bring to boil and boil for 1 to 2 minutes. Cool. Halve fruit, remove skins and purée flesh. Blend with sugar and water syrup. Whisk egg whites and fold into kiwi mixture. Pour into container, cover and freeze until firm. Serve with liqueur poured over.

FROZEN LEMON DESSERT   Angela Harding

Serves 6–8   Preparation 10 mins.   Freeze 4 hours

1 cup biscuit crumbs   3 eggs
  (Nice type or coconut flavoured) $\frac{1}{2}$ pt thick cream (280 ml)
$\frac{1}{4}$ cup lemon juice $\frac{1}{2}$ cup caster sugar
2 tsp lemon rind, grated

Whip the cream and reserve. Beat the egg yolks until thick and then add the sugar. Beat well. Add the lemon juice and rind, and fold in the cream. Finally fold in the stiffly beaten egg whites. Line a loaf tin with half the crumbed biscuits. Add the lemon mixture carefully. Sprinkle on the remaining crumbs. Freeze, until 5–10 minutes before serving, then unmould dessert and slice to serve.

 LEMON YOGHURT ICE CREAM   Elaine Knobil

Serves 4   Preparation 10 mins   Freeze 3 hours

3 cups plain yoghurt $4\frac{1}{2}$ tbls lemon juice
3 tsp lemon rind, grated   Artificial sweetener (to equal 6 tbls) sugar

Combine all ingredients and mix well. Freeze ice cream. When mixture begins to freeze remove from freezer and beat well. Return to freezer. Repeat procedure once more during freezing process to ensure a smooth texture.

Variation: for orange flavoured ice cream use 3 cups orange juice instead of lemon rind and juice.

**ICED LIME AND KIWI
FRUIT TERRINE** Anna Cohen

Serves 8 **Preparation 30 mins.** **Freeze 2 hours**

2 limes
½oz powdered gelatine (15gm)
8oz strained Greek yoghurt (225gm)
8oz fromage frais (225gm)

2 kiwi fruits
2 egg whites
1lb loaf tin (450gm)

Line loaf tin with greasproof paper. Grate the zest from the limes into a bowl and squeeze the juice into a saucepan. Sprinkle on the gelatine and stir over a low heat until dissolved. Remove from the heat and allow to cool. Mix the yoghurt and fromage frais together with the lime zest. Peel the kiwi fruit and cut in half lengthways. Whisk the egg whites until stiff. Fold the cooled gelatine into the cheese mixture and when on the point of setting fold in the whisked egg whites. Pour half the mixture into the prepared tin and place the four kiwi halves, cut sides down, on top. Pour over the remaining lime mousse and place in the refrigerator to set and chill. To remove from the tin, place a flat plate over the tin and invert gently. Carefully peel off the paper as you cut slices for serving, laying each slice flat on a dessert dish.

 LYCHEE SORBET Gloria Goldberg

Serves 6 **Preparation 10 mins.** **Freeze 3 hours**

15oz tin lychees in syrup (425gm)
A little lemon juice

4 tbls water
3 tbls caster sugar

Liquidise the lychees in their syrup, with the lemon juice. Make a syrup by boiling the sugar and water and stir it into the lychee purée. Freeze until mushy then blend in the food processor until very soft and smooth. Return it to the freezer. Serve with raspberry or blackcurrant sauce (see Sauce section page 162).

  EASY MANGO SORBET Maureen Marks

Serves 8 **Preparation 20 mins.** **Freeze 6 hours**

3 large egg whites
8oz granulated sugar (225gm)
¼pt water (140ml)

2 ripe mangos
Juice of 2 small lemons

Whisk egg whites until they form soft peaks. Dissolve the sugar in the water over a low heat then boil fast without stirring for 3 minutes. Pour the syrup immediately in a thin stream onto the egg whites, whisking all the time at high speed until the mixture forms stiff peaks. Blend the mangos with the lemon juice in a food processor or blender. Whisk this purée into the egg mixture. Pour into serving bowl or container and freeze.

ORANGE ICE CREAM
Joy Bayes

Serves 10–12   Preparation 10 mins.   Freeze 3 hours

10 fl oz parev whip (285 ml)   12 fl oz frozen Jaffa juice (340 ml)
3 size 3 egg yolks   2 tbls golden syrup
                Chocolate chips (optional)

Whisk the parev whip until stiff then beat in the syrup and egg yolks and juice. Continue whisking until the volume has increased considerably. Pour into containers and freeze. This makes a delicious soft ice cream to which chocolate chips can be added.

 ## PEACH SHERBET
Lynne Goldwyn

Serves 6   Preparation 20 mins.   Freeze 3 hours

$2\frac{1}{4}$ lb ripe peaches, peeled (1 k 42 gm)   Juice of 1 orange
Juice of 1 lemon   6 oz caster sugar (170 gm)

Remove stones from peaches and then process the flesh. Add the lemon and orange juices to the peach purée as well as the sugar, and stir until the sugar has dissolved. Place the mixture in a plastic container and freeze until it is a stiff slush. Then put the sherbet into a chilled bowl and whisk vigorously. Return the mixture to the plastic container and re-freeze until firm.

PISTACHIO ICE CREAM

Serves 8   Preparation 30 mins.   Freeze 3 hours

4 oz unsalted and unshelled pistachio   2 eggs
  nuts (115 gm)   2 tbls clear honey
$\frac{1}{2}$ pt skimmed milk (280 ml)   8 oz strained Greek yoghurt (225 gm)
$\frac{1}{2}$ vanilla pod

Shell the nuts and roughly chop half, then grind the other half to a fine powder. Place the milk in a saucepan with the vanilla pod, which can be cut in half lengthways so it releases more of its flavour. Place over the heat and gradually bring to the boil. As soon as the milk boils remove from the heat. Cover and leave to infuse for 15 minutes, then remove the vanilla pod. Whisk together 1 egg, plus one egg yolk and honey and whisk in the milk. Sieve and return to a clean saucepan and stir over a moderate heat until the custard thickens enough to coat the back of a spoon. Do not boil or the mixture will curdle. Remove from the heat and allow to cool. Meanwhile whisk the reserved egg white. When cold, fold in the yoghurt, the whisked egg white and nuts then place in a container and freeze.

135 calories per serving.

PRALINE ICE CREAM Mirelle Dessau

Serves 4–6 Preparation 30 mins. Freeze 3 hours

4 oz caster sugar (115 gm)
4 egg yolks
½ pt milk, hot (280 ml)
½ pt double cream (280 ml)
1½ tsp vanilla essence

PRALINE

1 cup sugar
½ cup slivered almonds

Praline: Slowly dissolve 1 cup sugar until it turns brown. Place ½ cup slivered almonds in oven Gas No.3, 320°F, 180°C until brown. Mix together and pour onto oiled baking sheet. When cold pulverise in food processor.

Beat yolks and sugar, add hot milk, cook in double saucepan over hot water until it forms custard, stirring frequently. Add vanilla. When cold add cream. Put ice cream in Gelato Chef for 12 minutes, then add three quarters of praline and put machine on for further 10 minutes. Reserve the last praline to sprinkle over ice cream when you serve it. If not using an ice cream machine freeze until mixture is frozen ½" (1.25 cm) around edges then beat again and add three quarters praline. Freeze until firm and decorate with the rest of the praline.

PRUNE AND ARMAGNAC
ICE CREAM
Gillian Burr

Serves 10 Preparation 20 mins. Freeze 3 hours

8 oz prunes (225 gm)
½ pt strained Greek yoghurt (280 ml)
3 tbls Armagnac

2 egg whites
¼ pt soured cream (140 ml)

Cook the prunes in water until soft and, when cool enough to handle, remove the stones. Place the stoned prunes in a liquidiser with the yoghurt and Armagnac and blend to a purée. Whisk the egg whites until stiff. Mix the soured cream into the prune mixture then fold in the whisked egg whites, pour into a container and freeze. Just before it is completely frozen remove and break up with a fork, mash well and return to the freezer in a container that is deep enough to allow scoops to be taken. Remove the ice cream from the freezer 20 minutes before serving to allow it to soften.

105 calories per serving.

REDCURRANT ICE CREAM   Lynne Goldwyn

Serves 4   Preparation 15 mins.   Freeze 3 hours

1 lb redcurrants (450 gm) $\frac{1}{2}$ pt double cream, whipped (280 ml)
5 oz caster sugar (140 gm)   Squeeze lemon juice
$\frac{1}{4}$ pt water (140 ml)

Purée redcurrants and sieve well. Dissolve sugar in a saucepan with the water. Bring to the boil for 3 minutes, then stir this syrup into purée and cool. Fold purée mixture into cream, and add lemon juice to taste. Pour into a plastic container and freeze until firm, beating once during the freezing process when it becomes firm at the edges.

 ## TANGERINE ICE CREAM   Lynne Goldwyn

Serves 4   Preparation 30 mins   Freeze 3 hours

12 tangerines   1 pt double cream (570 gm)
4 oz caster sugar (115 gm)

Finely grate zest from 6 of the tangerines. Mix with the sugar and half the cream in a pan. Heat gently to dissolve sugar and then cool. Squeeze juice from all the tangerines and add to the cream and sugar mixture. Whip the remaining cream until it stands in soft peaks and fold in. Pour into a container and freeze.

 ## VANILLA AND LEMON
ICE CREAM   Marion Cohen

Serves 4–6   Preparation 10 mins.   Freeze 3 hours

$\frac{1}{4}$ pt milk (140 ml) $\frac{1}{2}$ tsp vanilla essence
2 oz caster sugar (55 gm) $\frac{1}{4}$ pt double cream (140 ml)
2 eggs yolks, beaten   1 tsp fresh lemon verbena leaves,
                                        chopped

Partially beat the cream. Make a custard by heating the milk and sugar and then pouring it onto the egg yolks stirring it constantly. Return mixture to the saucepan and heat very gently, stirring until the mixture becomes very thick. Strain and add the vanilla essence. Allow to cool then fold in the verbena and the cream. Pour into a container and freeze.

Puddings and Pies

(Decadent again)

Please let it be like his mother used to make.

ANGEL CHEEKS

Serves 8   **Preparation 10 mins.**   **Cook 20 mins.**   **Gas No.4, 350°F, 180°C**

2 egg whites
6 egg yolks
1 tsp baking powder
2 tsp flour

2 oz butter (55 gm)
1 lb caster sugar (450 gm)
16 fl oz water (455 ml)
1 tsp vanilla essence

Beat the egg whites, add the yolks one by one, beating all the while. Add the baking powder and flour and beat until the mixture becomes a firm cream. Butter round cup cake moulds. Fill them three quarters full with the mixture. Bake until a light golden colour. Remove from the moulds and place in a deep bowl. Make a syrup by heating the sugar and water until all the sugar is dissolved. Add vanilla essence and pour the mixture over the angel cheeks. Let the syrup soak into the cakes, then turn them over.

186

APFELTORTE

Barbara Tobias

Serves 6–8 Preparation 15 mins. Cook 1 hour Gas No.5, 375°F, 190°C Advance

$4\frac{1}{2}$oz soft margarine (130gm)
$5\frac{1}{4}$oz sugar (155gm)
1 egg, lightly beaten
Pinch of salt
2–3 drops vanilla essence
$\frac{1}{2}$ tsp cinnamon
2 lbs Granny Smith apples, peeled and
    sliced (900gm)

Icing sugar
Grated rind of $\frac{1}{2}$ lemon
Juice of 1 lemon
7 oz flour (200gm)
2 tsp baking powder
1 tbls brown sugar

7″ loose bottom cake tin, greased
    (18cm)

Stew the apples, lemon juice, brown sugar and cinnamon with 1 tablespoon of water gently until soft but not mushy. Reserve. Cream sugar and margarine, add eggs, salt, vanilla essence, grated lemon rind, flour and baking powder. Mix to a firm paste-like dough. Line the tin with two thirds of the dough and bake for 25 minutes until lightly browned. Strain the apples and spread them on the pastry in the tin, leaving a margin around the edge. Roughly spread remaining dough on top (it will spread evenly in cooking). Return to oven and bake until top is golden (about 20 minutes). Cool slightly and remove from tin. Sprinkle with icing sugar when tepid. Serve warm or cold.

APPLE AND GINGER LATTICE
FLAN

Anne Moss

Serves 6 Preparation 15 mins. Cook 25 mins. Gas No.5, 375°F, 190°C Advance

8 oz plain flour (225gm)
2 tsp ground ginger
5 oz butter or margarine (140gm)
$1\frac{1}{2}$lb cooking apples, peeled and
    cored (675gm)

2 tbls cold water
$\frac{1}{2}$ lemon, rind and juice
2 oz caster sugar (55gm)
Egg or milk to glaze
8″ flan ring (20cm)

Sieve the flour and ground ginger together and rub in the fat. Add water and make it into a dough. Roll out and line the flan ring. Reserve the trimmings for the lattice. Bake blind for about 20 minutes. Toss the apples in lemon juice, grated rind and sugar and arrange them in the flan case. Roll out the rest of the pastry and cut into $\frac{1}{4}$″ (6mm) strips and arrange them in a lattice pattern on top of the flan. Glaze with beaten egg or milk and bake until pastry is golden brown and apples are soft.

APPLE AND NUTMEG
BATTER PUDDING
Naomi Greenwood

Serves 4   Preparation 10 mins.   Cook 1 hour   Gas No.4, 350°F, 180°C

1 lb Bramley cooking apples, peeled
   and thickly sliced (450 gm)
4 oz plain flour (115 gm)
2 oz butter or margarine (55 gm)
2 oz soft brown sugar (55 gm)

Whole nutmeg
$\frac{1}{2}$ pt milk (280 ml)
2 eggs separated
Icing sugar for dredging
1$\frac{3}{4}$ pt oven proof dish (1 litre)

Make a smooth batter with the flour, egg yolks and milk. Lay half the apple slices on bottom of the greased dish. Cream the butter and sugar with a pinch of nutmeg and spread this over the apples. Cover with the remainder of the sliced apple. Whisk egg whites until stiff and fold into the batter. Pour the batter over the apples and bake for about 1 hour until golden brown.

To serve: Dredge heavily with icing sugar and cut into wedges.

BAKLAVA
Gillian Burr

Serves 6–8   Preparation 20 mins.   Cook 30–40 mins.   Gas No.5, 375°F, 190°C
Advance   Freezable

8 oz filo pastry (225 gm)
6 oz unsalted butter (175 gm)
3 oz blanched almonds, chopped (85 gm)
3 oz walnuts, chopped (85 gm)
Good pinch of cinnamon
Orange-flower water
Rose-water
3 tbls caster sugar

SYRUP

8 oz granulated sugar (225 gm)
$\frac{1}{4}$ pt water (140 ml)
$\frac{1}{2}$ lemon
Orange-flower water
Rose-water
Deep baking tin 10 x 12″ (25 x 30 cm)

Syrup: Melt the sugar in the water over low heat, simmer for about 10 minutes until syrupy, then add the lemon juice and a few drops of orange-flower water and rose-water until it is lightly perfumed. Chill really well before baklava comes out of oven.

Melt the butter gently in a saucepan. Combine the nuts with the caster sugar, cinnamon and enough orange-flower water and rose-water to taste and stir until the mixture just clings together. Brush the baking tin lavishly with melted butter. Place a layer of filo pastry in the tin, turning in the edges to fit. Brush with more butter and continue with layers of pastry and butter until about one third of the pastry has been used. Cover any unused pastry or it will dry up very quickly and crumble to pieces. Spread the nut filling all over the pastry and continue layering pastry and butter until all is used, but do not use all the white sediment of the butter. With a sharp knife cut the baklava into lengthways strips about 1$\frac{1}{2}$″ (4 cm) wide then cut diagonally to form diamonds. Bake until cooked and a good brown. As it comes out of the oven pour the cold syrup all over the baklava; using well chilled syrup on the hot pastry keeps the whole thing crisp. Serve cold. Baklava will keep 2–3 days in fridge or larder.

BLACKCURRANT TART
Estelle Laurier

Serves 6   Preparation 40 mins.   Cook 20 mins.   Gas No.6, 400°F, 200°C

FILLING

1 lb frozen blackcurrants (450 gm)
1 slice lemon
A little cold water
Sugar to taste
1–2 tsp arrowroot

8½" pie dish (22 cm)

PASTRY

4½ oz unsalted butter/margarine (130 gm)
8 oz flour (225 gm)
1 egg, size 2, separated
1 tsp vinegar
2 tbls cold water
1 tbls caster sugar

This quantity makes enough pastry for 2 tarts

Pastry: Mix fat and flour until they resemble fine breadcrumbs. Add sugar. Beat yolk lightly with vinegar and water and add to mixture. Knead until pastry is formed. Wrap and leave in fridge for 30 minutes. Roll out half the pastry and use it to line the dish. Break the egg white up a little with a fork and paint the inside of the pastry with it. Bake the pastry blind until golden brown.

Filling: Stew the blackcurrants in a pan with a little cold water, sugar and lemon, and allow to cool. Strain the juice into a saucepan and heat gently until it bubbles. Mix the arrowroot with a little water to form a paste and stir into the liquid. Simmer until the juice thickens and allow to cool, stirring occasionally. Fill the tart case with the blackcurrants and spoon the thickened juice evenly over them.

BREAD PUDDING
Pat Julius

Serves 6 Preparation 10 mins. Cook 50 mins. Gas No.3, 325°F, 175°C Freezable

1 stale cholla
2 eggs, beaten
4 oz margarine (115 gm)
6 oz mixed dried fruit (170 gm)

1 tsp cinnamon
1 tsp mixed spice
½ lemon, juice and rind

Place the margarine in the container you are going to bake the pudding in, and heat in the oven until melted. Meanwhile remove the inside of the loaf and put into a colander. Pour over boiling water and squeeze out all the liquid. Transfer it to mixing bowl and add eggs and then the rest of the ingredients. Take the melted margarine out of the oven and pour into the mixture, beating well. Put back into the container and bake for 50 minutes.

BREAD AND BUTTER
PUDDING
Rennie Mendelssohn

Serves 4   Preparation 40 mins.   Cook 3 hours   Gas No.2, 300°F, 150°C   Advance

2½ slices stale white bread, buttered	2 eggs
4 oz sultanas (115 gm)	1 dsp sugar
16 fl oz milk (455 ml)	Ovenproof bowl 6½″ diameter (16 cm)

Grease the bowl well. Cut the sliced bread into strips. Scatter some sultanas in the bottom of the bowl and cover with strips of buttered bread. Continue to alternate layers of sultanas and bread, until used up. Dissolve the sugar in the milk, over a very low heat; do not let the milk get hot. Beat the eggs in a bowl and add the milk. Pour this over the bread and sultanas and let stand for 30 minutes. Stand the bowl in a baking tin with enough water to come half way up the bowl. Cook near the bottom of the oven for about 3 hours.

SPICED BREAD PUDDING   Michelle Davidson

Serves 9   Preparation 15 mins.   Cook 1–1½ hours   Gas No.3, 325°F, 160°C
Advance   Freezable

¾ pt boiling water (425 ml)	12 oz crustless wholemeal bread (340 gm)
10 oz mixed dried fruit (285 gm)	3 tbls sunflower oil
2 oz chopped peel (55 gm)	3 tbls marmalade (preferably sugar free)
2 tbls mixed spice	Square 7″ baking tin (18 cm)

Pour water over bread and leave to soak until pulpy. Squeeze out excess water then beat in all remaining ingredients until smooth. Pour into tin and bake until firm to the touch.

CHEESE PEROGEN   Elizabeth Swift

Serves 6–8   Preparation 30 mins.

DOUGH	FILLING
3 eggs, lightly beaten	½ oz vanilla sugar (15 gm)
½ tsp salt	3 tsp sugar
2 cups flour	½ lb cottage cheese (225 gm)
1 tsp oil	1 egg
1 tsp water	

Dough: Combine ingredients in order given. Mix dough with hands until it comes away from the sides of the bowl. Roll out on floured board until thin. Cut into 3″ (7.5 cm) circles with edge of glass dipped in flour.

Place 1 tsp of cheese filling on each circle, close securely, making sure that filling does not penetrate closing. Press edges together tightly using floured fingers to seal. Drop into salted boiling water for 20 minutes. They can then be fried in butter for reheating. Serve with sour cream. An alternative filling is potato (fry onion and mash into potato with margarine or butter and salt).

190

CHERRY STRUDEL
Naomi Greenwood

Serves 12 Preparation 30 mins. Cook 40 mins. Gas No.4, 350°F, 180°C Freezable

4–5 sheets filo pastry
4oz butter, melted (115gm)
2 eating apples, peeled and chopped
12oz cherries, halved (340gm)
2oz toasted hazelnuts, roughly
  chopped (55gm)

3oz demerara sugar (85gm)
2oz sultanas (55gm)
2 tsp cinnamon
Icing sugar for dusting
Flat, oiled baking tray

Brush each sheet of filo pastry with melted butter and place one on top of the other on a damp cloth. Fry the apple in the remaining butter until softened, about 5–10 minutes. Stir in the cherries, hazelnuts, sugar and cinnamon and mix well together. Spread the cherry mixture evenly over the filo pastry. Using the edges of the cloth to help, roll up the pastry from the wide side. Place on tray and bake until golden.

To serve: Dust with icing sugar and slice diagonally. Serve with whipped cream.

CHOCOLATE FLAN
Ann Millett

Serves 6–8 Preparation 10 mins. Cook 30 mins. Gas No.4, 350°F, 185°C Advance

FLAN BASE
6oz ground almonds (170gm)
2oz caster sugar (55gm)
1 egg white

FILLING
8oz plain bitter chocolate (225gm)
$\frac{1}{2}$ pt single cream (280ml)

DECORATION: flaked almonds

Pastry: Mix together flan ingredients and knead into a loose bottomed greased flan tin lined with bakewell paper. Bake. Cool

Filling: Melt chocolate and cream together to scalding point. Pour into cooled base. Decorate with almonds. Leave in refrigerater to set.

CHOCOLATE SILK PIE
Betty Lipman

Serves 6–8   Preparation 20 mins.   Refrigerate 2 hours minimum

5oz soft butter/margarine (142gm)
5oz icing sugar (142gm)
2oz unsweetened chocolate (55gm)
1 large egg
1 tsp vanilla essence

DECORATION: 5floz whipped double
cream (142ml)
Flaked almonds
8" pastry case, cooked (20cm)

Beat butter or margarine in large mixing bowl at low speed until very smooth and creamy. Melt chocolate. Beat in sieved icing sugar and melted chocolate gradually until fluffy. Beat in egg and beat very well. Spoon mixture into pastry shell and chill. Top with whipped cream and nuts if desired. Refrigerate for at least 2 hours.

191

FRUIT TZIMMAS   Dorice Smith

Serves 10–12   Preparation 20 mins.   Cook 50 mins.   Gas   No.4, 350°F, 180°C
Advance

4 oz cornflake crumbs (115 gm)
1 lb cooking apples, cooked and
    puréed (450 gm)
4 oz tin peaches (115 gm)
4 oz tin apricots (115 gm)
14 oz tin pineapple chunks (400 gm)
14 oz tin cherry pie filling (400 gm)
Grated rind of 1 lemon

1 lb box pitted prunes (450 gm)
½ lb dried apricots (225 gm)
2 tbls honey
2 tbls soft brown sugar
4 fl oz lemon juice (115 ml)
¼ cup Cointreau or dark rum
    (optional)

Spread half the cornflakes on the bottom of a large shallow dish. Cook dried prunes and apricots in water for 20 minutes and drain. Mix with remaining well drained tins of fruit. Add cherry pie filling. Spread half the apple purée on cornflake crumbs. Top with fruit mixture. Sprinkle with lemon peel, honey and sugar. Then pour Cointreau over. Add remainder of the apple sauce, then lemon juice, then second half cornflake crumbs. Bake for 30 minutes.

Microwave instructions

After adding the second half of cornflake crumbs place a piece of kitchen paper gently on top. Cook in microwave oven on full power for 5–6 minutes.

GAINSBOROUGH TART   Gillian Burr

Serves 6–8 Preparation 5 mins. Cook 30 mins. Gas No.5, 375°F, 190°C Advance
Freezable

8 oz shortcrust pastry (225 gm)
1 oz butter or margarine (30 gm)
A little jam
¼ tsp baking powder

2 oz caster sugar (55 gm)
1 egg
4 oz dessicated coconut (115 gm)
8″ pie dish (20 cm)

Line a greased pie dish with the shortcrust pastry. Spread some jam over the pastry. Melt the fat, stir in the beaten egg, sugar, coconut and baking powder. Pour the mixture into the pastry case, place on a hot baking tray and bake for 30 minutes.

GRAND MARNIER SOUFFLE
Cynthia Clore

Serves 4   Preparation 15 mins.   Cook 35 mins.   Gas No.8, 450°F, 230°C

2oz butter (55gm)
½oz flour (15gm)
8 floz single cream (225ml)
6 egg whites
5 egg yolks

2oz sugar (55gm)
3 floz Grand Marnier (85ml)
8 sponge fingers
Additional Grand Marnier to soak

Melt the butter in a saucepan; add the flour and cook for a short time stirring slowly until mixture colours. Heat cream to boiling point and then add to butter and flour mixture. Cook for 5 minutes, stirring constantly. Beat egg yolks and sugar and stir into the mixture. Add the Grand Marnier, fold in the stiffly beaten egg whites. In a well-buttered and sugared soufflé dish, pour in half the mixture. Soak the sponge fingers in the additional Grand Marnier and spread them out on top of the mixture. Cover with remaining half of the soufflé mixture. Bake for 10–12 minutes then lower the heat and bake for a further 20 minutes on Gas No.4, 350°F, 180°C.

LEMON DAINTY
Vivienne Simon

Serves 4   Preparation 5 mins.   Cook 40 mins.   Gas No.5, 375°F, 190°C

6oz granulated sugar (170gm)
1 rounded tbls plain flour
½oz butter (15gm)

2 eggs, separated
1 large lemon, grated rind and juice
8 floz milk (225ml)

Mix 4oz (115gm) sugar with the flour. Beat yolks until thick, then add lemon rind and juice, the melted butter and milk and whisk well. Stir in sugar and flour and beat until smooth. Beat the egg whites until stiff then gradually add the remaining sugar. Fold egg whites and sugar into the first mixture. Pour into an oven-proof casserole dish set in a large pan of very hot water (to prevent curdling). Bake for about 35–40 minutes until firm and golden brown on top. The sponge floats to the top while at the bottom it remains a lemon custard/curd. Serve luke warm or cold.

LEMON FLAN
Janet Williams

Serves 4 Preparation 15 mins. Cook 8 mins. Gas No.2, 310°F, 160°C Advance

BASE

4 oz digestive or ginger biscuits (115 gm)
2 oz butter (55 gm)
1 level tbls caster sugar

TOPPING

2 oz double cream, lightly whipped (55 gm)
Lemon slices

FILLING

¼ pt double cream (140 ml)
6 fl oz tin sweetened condensed
  milk (170 ml)
2 large lemons, juice and grated
  rind
7″ flan dish (18 cm)

Crush biscuits. Melt butter then add sugar. Blend in biscuit crumbs. Press mixture into the base and sides of the flan dish. Bake for 8 minutes. Leave in the dish. Mix together cream, condensed milk and finely grated lemon rind. Slowly beat in the lemon juice. Pour mixture into flan and chill until firm. Decorate with cream and lemon slices.

SPICY LOCKSHEN PUDDING
Rennie Mendelssohn

**Serves 6 Preparation 10 mins. Cook 2½ hours Gas No.2, 300°F, 160°C Advance
Freezable**

1 pt jug of cooked lockshen (500 ml)
1 oz split blanched almonds (30 gm)
4 oz raisins (115 gm)
4 oz sultanas (115 gm)
3 oz soft dark brown sugar (85 gm)
3 oz butter or margarine (85 gm)
Pinch of salt

2 tsp cinnamon
2 tsp mixed spice
Rind of ½ lemon
1 cooking apple, finely diced
1 tbls golden syrup
1 large (or 2 small) eggs, beaten

Place lockshen in a large bowl, mix in the ingredients one at a time, stirring well after each addition. Turn into a greased ovenproof dish and bake near the bottom of the oven.

MANGO CREAM PUFFS
Maureen Marks

Serves 4   Preparation 30 mins.   Cook 25 mins.   Gas No.6, 400°F, 200°C
Advance puffs only

PUFFS
1½oz butter (45gm)
7 floz cold water (200ml)
4oz plain flour (115gm)
3 small eggs, beaten
Pinch of salt

FILLING
½ pt double cream, whipped (280ml)
1 large ripe mango, puréed
Caster sugar to taste

DECORATION: icing sugar
mango slices

Put the butter and water into a large saucepan and melt slowly. Sift the flour with the salt. When the butter has melted bring to the boil and pour on the flour. Beat well until it forms a soft ball. Allow to cool for 10 minutes and gradually beat in the eggs until the mixture will just drop from the spoon. Spoon the mixture in plum sized pieces onto a greased baking sheet and bake for about 20 minutes. Split the puffs and scoop out any uncooked paste. Return to the oven for a further 5 minutes. Cool on a wire rack.

Filling: Mix half the mango purée into the whipped cream, sweetened if liked, and spoon the cream into the puff bases and top with the remaining mango purée. Place lids on top and dust tops with icing sugar. Serve with slices of mango.

MANGO AND KIWI TARTLETS
Gloria Cohen

Serves 6   Preparation 20 mins.   Cook 10 mins.   Refrigerate

14oz shortcrust pastry (400gm)
ORANGE CREAM
¼ pt double cream, whipped (140ml)
Finely grated zest of 1 orange
Juice of ¼ orange, strained
1 dsp icing sugar, sifted

FRUIT FILLING
1 large ripe mango, peeled
3 ripe kiwi fruit

GLAZE
3 tbls apricot or guava jam
2 tbls kirsch

Roll out the pastry and line 12 tartlet tins. Bake the pastry blind, until crisp and golden. Cool on a wire rack. Cut the mango flesh into neat little slices and peel and slice the kiwi fruit. Make the orange cream by mixing all the ingredients together and fill each tartlet with the cream. Arrange the fruit over the cream. Warm the jam and the kirsch together in a small saucepan, cool slightly, and glaze each tartlet. Chill before serving.

ORANGES WITH SWEET CROUTONS
AND KIWI
Jane Finestone

Serves 10   **Preparation 30 mins.**   **Cook 5 mins.**

10 oranges
2 tbls sugar
8 slices white bread

$4\frac{1}{2}$oz butter (125gm)
$\frac{1}{2}$ tsp cinnamon
5 kiwi fruit, peeled and sliced

Grate the rinds of 3 of the oranges, then peel all the oranges and cut between the membranes to make clean segments. Remove the crusts from bread and cut into cubes. Melt butter in pan, toss in cubed bread and fry until golden and crisp, add cinnamon, orange rind and sugar. Toss for 1 further minute. Lay out orange segments on flat dessert plates and decorate with sliced kiwi, then spoon croûtons (warm or cold) alongside fruit.

PEAR AND FRANGIPANE TART   Gillian Burr

Serves 6 Preparation 20 mins. Cook 35 mins. Gas No.5, 375°F, 190°C Advance

PASTRY

8oz plain flour (225gm)
4oz unsalted butter (115gm)
1oz caster sugar (30gm)
1 egg

FRANGIPANE

1 egg
2oz butter (55gm)
2oz caster sugar (55gm)
$\frac{1}{2}$oz flour (15gm)

2oz ground almonds (55gm)
1 drop almond essence
1 tbls kirsch
1 tbls blackcurrant jam
2 large firm pears, peeled and cored
Apricot glaze, as needed

Pastry: Sift the plain flour onto a work surface, make a well in the centre, and put in the butter, cut into small pieces, and the sugar. Knead together well. Add 1 egg and mix. Gradually work in the flour until it becomes a firm dough. Roll out and line an 8″ flan ring (20cm). Chill, then bake blind for about 15 minutes.

Frangipane: Cream the butter and caster sugar together until soft; add the egg, work in quickly, then add flour, ground almonds, almond essence and Kirsch. Line the bottom of the cooked flan pastry with a thin layer of jam, then the frangipane, filling half the flan case. Put a rough layer of one pear over the frangipane, then place a second layer of thinly sliced pear on top. Bake at same oven tempreature for 20 minutes or until the frangipane is firm and a golden colour. Leave on the flan ring whilst cooking to avoid pastry turning too brown. When cool, brush lightly with apricot glaze and lift onto serving plate.

PEARS WARSAW
Marion Cohen

Serves 10   **Preparation 15 mins.**   **Standing time 1–2 hours**

10 pieces sponge cake
10 tinned pear halves
5 oz blanched almonds, grated
   (140 gm)

APRICOT SAUCE

1 lb tin apricots, drained (450 gm)
4 oz caster sugar (115 gm)
1 tbls lemon juice
4 fl oz Madeira wine (115 ml)

PUNCH
8 fl oz boiling water (225 ml)
7 oz sugar (200 gm)
1 tbls grated lemon peel
1 tbls grated orange peel
4 fl oz vodka (115 ml)
4 fl oz cognac (115 ml)
1 tbls rum

Punch: Bring water to boil, add all ingredients and mix. Set aside and cool for 1–2 hours.

Apricot sauce: Rub tinned apricots through sieve with a spoon. Add sugar, lemon juice and Madeira. Set aside.

Soak each portion of sponge cake in the punch, then put in a flat glass bowl and place a pear half on each piece of cake. Cover with apricot sauce and sprinkle with grated almonds.

PECAN PIE
Jennifer Davis

Serves 6–8 Preparation 10 mins. Cook 20 mins. Gas No.4, 350°F, 185°C Advance

8 oz shortcrust pastry (225 gm)
4 oz soft brown sugar (115 gm)
4 oz unsalted butter (115 gm)
3 eggs
Pinch of salt

6 oz golden syrup (170 gm)
8 oz pecan nuts, shelled (225 gm)
1 lemon, rind and juice
$8\frac{1}{2}$–$9\frac{1}{2}''$ flan tin (21–24 cm)

Line the flan tin with pastry and bake blind for 10 minutes. Cream together the sugar and butter until light and smooth. Beat in the eggs one at a time. Warm syrup very slightly until runny and stir into the creamed mixture. Add the pecan nuts, lemon juice, rind and salt and turn into pastry case. Bake until filling has risen and turned light brown. Serve warm or cold.

PINEAPPLE BETTY
Gillian Burr

Serves 6   Preparation 15 mins.   Cook 40 mins.   Gas No.3, 325°F, 170°C

1 lb tin of crushed pineapple (450 gm)
3 cups soft breadcrumbs
1½ oz melted margarine (45 gm)

2 level tbls brown sugar
1 orange, juice and grated rind
8″ soufflé dish, greased (20 cm)

Drain juice from pineapple and add 1 tablespoon to orange juice and reserve the rest for the sauce. Place layer of breadcrumbs in bottom of dish, cover with some pineapple, sugar and grated orange rind, pineapple and orange juice mixture, and a little of the margarine. Continue in this way finishing with a layer of breadcrumbs. Bake. Serve with the heated pineapple juice.

PLUM AND SOURED CREAM FLAN
Lynne Goldwyn

Serves 8 Preparation 20 mins. Cook 20 mins. Gas No.6, 400°F, 200°C Advance

6 oz shortcrust pastry (170 gm)
1 lb dessert plums (450 gm)
½ pt soured cream (280 ml)
1 oz caster sugar (30 gm)
10″ fluted flan dish, greased (25 cm)

½ tsp mixed spice
2 oz demerara sugar (55 gm)
1 tsp ground cinnamon
3 egg yolks

Line the flan tin then halve the plums and remove the stones. Beat the soured cream together with the caster sugar and egg yolks and mixed spice, then pour this into the flan case and arrange the plums over the top (flat side up). Place the flan on a baking sheet and bake for 20 minutes. Mix cinnamon with the sugar and sprinkle it evenly over the top. Turn the heat up to Gas No.8, 450°F, 230°C for the last 5 minutes so that the top browns nicely. Serve warm or cold.

SUGAR PLUM BEIGNETS   Naomi Greenwood

Serves 6–8   Preparation 20 mins.   Standing time 20 mins.   Cook 20 mins.

BEIGNETS

5 oz flour, sifted (140 gm)
4 fl oz white wine (115 ml)
2 eggs, separated
2 eggs whites
1 oz caster sugar (30 gm)
Pinch of salt
Pinch of cinnamon
1¾ pt grapeseed oil (1 litre)

8 ripe plums, stoned and halved

SAUCE

2 tbls Grand Marnier
14 oz tin of stoned plums in syrup
  (400 gm)

DECORATION: icing sugar

Purée the tinned plums and juice and reserve. Place the flour in a bowl and whisk in the egg yolks, wine, salt, cinnamon and half the sugar, until smooth. Leave to stand for 15–20 minutes. Beat the egg whites until stiff, add the remaining sugar and fold the mixture into the batter. Heat the oil in a deep fat fryer or pan to 375°F, 190°C. Using a spoon, dip the fresh plums into the batter and drop immediately into the hot oil. Fry for 5 minutes until golden and puffed up. Drain on kitchen paper. Heat the plum purée and Grand Marnier gently. Dust the plum beignets with icing sugar and serve with the plum sauce.

SYRUP TART   Maureen Marks

Serves 4–6   Preparation 20 mins.   Refrigerate 2 hrs.   Cook 40 mins.   Gas No.6,
                                              400°F, 200°C Advance Freezable

PASTRY

6 oz flour (170 gm)
4 oz firm butter (115 gm)
2 oz icing sugar (55 gm)
2–3 drops vanilla essence
2 egg yolks

9″ loose bottomed flan tin (24 cm)

FILLING

8 tbls golden syrup
2 oz butter (55 gm)
3 tbls cream or milk
6 tbls fresh white breadcrumbs
1 lemon, grated rind and juice
1–2 eating apples, peeled and grated

Pastry: Sift the flour and sugar into a bowl or food processor with a metal blade and add the butter in hazelnut-sized pieces. Rub in or process to the breadcrumb stage, then bind with the yolks. Form into a flat disc and rest the pastry in the fridge for 2 hours. Roll out and line flan tin. Prick, line with tinfoil and dried beans, and bake blind for 8–10 minutes until the pastry is set. Remove the foil and outer ring and cook for 2–3 minutes more until just beginning to colour. Fill with filling and finish baking until golden brown in a moderately hot oven Gas No.5, 375°F, 190°C for 20–30 minutes.

Filling: Gently melt the butter, and heat together with the syrup and cream. Remove from the heat and add the lemon juice and rind, the grated apple and enough breadcrumbs to make a soft dropping consistency.

TARTE AUX FRAISES
Marion Cohen

Serves 4–6 Preparation 20 mins. Refrigerate 2 hours. Cook 40 mins. Gas No.6, 400°F, 200°C

PASTRY

8oz flour (225gm)
2oz icing sugar (55gm)
5oz firm butter (140gm)
2 egg yolks
½ tsp vanilla essence
Pinch of salt

FILLING

1lb fresh strawberries (450gm)
⅓ pt double cream (200ml)
1 egg white
Vanilla sugar to taste
Loose bottomed 9″ flan tin (24cm)

Pastry: Sift the flour, icing sugar and salt into a bowl or the food processor, add the butter cut into small pieces and rub in with the fingertips or process until it resembles breadcrumbs. Add the vanilla and yolks and work up to a paste. Turn the pastry on to a board and knead with the heel of your hand. Knead into a flat disc and chill for 2 hours. Roll out the pastry and line the flan tin, prick, line with tinfoil and bake on Gas No.6, 400°F, 200°C for 8–10 minutes. When the pastry has set remove the tinfoil and outer ring and continue to bake in a moderate oven Gas No.4, 350°F, 180°C for about 20 minutes until cooked through and very lightly browned. Cool on a rack.

Filling: Whip the cream and lightly sweeten with the vanilla sugar. Whip the egg white until just holding a peak and fold into the cream. Hull the strawberries and halve or quarter them if large. Just before serving fold together the cream and most of the strawberries, pile into the pastry shell and decorate with the remaining fruit.

TARTE TATIN
Monica Levinson

Serves 6–8 Preparation 25 mins. Cool 40 mins. Cook 25 mins. Gas No.4, 350°F, 180°C Advance

8 crisp apples, peeled and sliced
5oz unsalted butter (140gm)
6oz caster sugar (170gm)
2 tbls water
Cinnamon to taste
8–9″ tart tin (20–23cm), greased

PASTRY

3oz butter (85gm)
5oz flour (140gm)
1oz ground almonds (30gm)
1 egg yolk
1 tbls water

Pastry: Sift flour and rub butter well into the flour. Mix to a stiff dough with remaining ingredients, form into a ball and leave in a cool place wrapped in foil for 1 hour.

Melt the butter in a large pan, add sugar and water and stir over a high flame for two minutes, without letting the mixture caramelise. Quickly add the apple slices and turn them in the syrup for 6–8 minutes until soft. Take the pan off the heat and transfer apples to flan dish, leaving the syrup in the pan. Dust the apples with cinnamon. Return the pan to the heat and boil until the syrup caramelises. Pour this over the apples and leave to cool for at least 40 minutes. Roll the pastry into a circle slightly larger than the dish and lay it over the apples. Trim and push edge of pastry well down. Make a slit in the top and bake for 25 minutes approx. Cool for 10 minutes and then invert onto a serving dish with apples uppermost. Best served slightly warm.

TREACLE TART
Carole Chesterman

Serves 6–8 Preparation 10 mins. Cook 30 mins. Gas No.5, 375°F, 190°C Advance

8oz shortcrust pastry (225gm)
2oz breadcrumbs (55gm)
9″ diameter ovenproof plate (24cm)

8oz golden syrup (225gm)
A little lemon juice to taste

Roll out the pastry a little larger than the plate, cut off the extra strip and place half the strip around the dampened edge of the plate. Damp this and line the plate with the round of pastry. Sprinkle a layer of crumbs on this, pour on the golden syrup, sprinkle with lemon juice and the remaining crumbs. Roll out the remaining strip thinly; cut into lengths the size of the plate and place in crossways strips across the plate. Serve hot or cold.

VANILLA SPONGE WITH FRESH FRUIT AND MOUSSE
Shirley Schlagman

Serves 8–10 Preparation 45 mins. Cook 5 mins. Gas No.8, 450°F, 230°C Advance
Refrigerate

8oz raspberry jam (225gm)
1lb assorted fresh fruit (450gm)
$\frac{1}{2}$ vanilla pod, split
$\frac{1}{2}$oz gelatine (15gm)
$\frac{3}{4}$ pt whipping cream (430ml)

VANILLA SPONGE CAKE

4oz caster sugar (115gm)
4oz SR flour (115gm)
4 eggs
Swiss roll tin, lined

APRICOT GLAZE

8oz apricot jam (225gm)
2oz granulated sugar (55gm)
$\frac{1}{4}$ pt tinned apricots, liquidised (140ml)
$\frac{1}{4}$ pt apricot syrup from apricot tin (140ml)

SUGAR SYRUP

$\frac{1}{2}$ pt water (280ml)
8oz sugar (225gm)
9″ round loose bottomed tin, $1\frac{3}{4}$″ deep (24 x 4cm)

Vanilla sponge cake: Whisk together the sugar and eggs in a bowl over hot water until the mixture forms ribbons. Remove bowl from heat and fold in flour. Pour mixture onto lined Swiss roll tin and spread thinly. Bake for 5 minutes approx. and cool.

Sugar syrup: Boil water and sugar together. Leave in a cool place.

Apricot glaze: Bring all the ingredients very gently to the boil and then put them through a fine sieve.

Assembly: Cut a 9″ (24cm) circle of sponge and reserve. From the remaining sponge, sandwich four rectangular strips of sponge with the raspberry jam and press well. Slice these into strips $\frac{1}{4}$″ thick and line sides of cake tin with the vertical strips. Line bottom of the tin with silicone paper. Inside the tin put a layer of fresh fruit slices.

Mousse: Bring 7 fl oz (200ml) sugar syrup and vanilla pod to boil and add the soaked gelatine. Pass the hot syrup through a sieve and cool. Whip the cream and as the mixture begins to set, fold in the cream. Spread a layer of mousse on top of the fresh fruit in the tin and continue spreading alternate layers of fresh fruit and mousse ending with a layer of mousse. Place the circle of sponge (taken from sponge sheet) on top of flan. Chill well in the fridge. When this flan is chilled turn it over and remove from tin. Brush the top and sides with apricot glaze.

Cakes

You forgot the other 'P'

HINTS

To brighten the appearance of a meringue cake, cover it with lightly whipped cream and sprinkle with coconut.

Add 1 teaspoon instant coffee dissolved in a little Kiddush wine, plus 1 teaspoon brown almonds to a butter cream mixture to make it richer.

If 1 teaspoon of marmalade is added to an uncooked cake mixture, it will ensure that it remains moist in storage.

Always preheat oven at least 5 minutes before putting the cake in, regardless of the type of oven.

Small Cakes

To hell with the angel cake – try the devil's food

APPLE AND GINGER PUFFS   Gillian Burr

Serves 6   Preparation 20 mins.   Cook 15 mins.   Gas No.7, 425°F, 220°C

12 oz cooking apples, peeled and
   chopped (340gm)
$\frac{1}{2}$ oz crystallised ginger, chopped (15gm)
3 tbls caster sugar

$7\frac{1}{2}$ oz frozen puff pastry (215gm)
$\frac{1}{4}$ pt carton double cream (140ml)

DECORATE: icing sugar

Place apples and ginger in a bowl with 1 tablespoon caster sugar; mix well. Roll out pastry on a floured surface to about $\frac{1}{8}''$ (0.3cm) thickness. Cut out 6 rounds, 5″ (12.5cm) in diameter. Gently roll the rounds across centre to form an oval shape. Place 1 tablespoon of apple mixture in centre of each round. Dampen edges of pastry with water. Fold over to form semi-circular shapes, enclosing the apple mixture, seal edges. Brush with a little water and sprinkle with caster sugar. Cook for 15 minutes on a dampened baking sheet until golden brown. Cool on wire rack. Whip cream; place in piping bag with a large star nozzle. Carefully split each puff along the join and pipe in cream. Sprinkle with icing sugar.

CREAMY APPLE SLICES
Sara Raiher

Makes 12 squares Preparation 15 mins. Cook 1 hour Gas No.3, 325°F, 160°C

PASTRY
5oz plain flour (142gm)
3oz butter (85gm)
1 tbls caster sugar
½ egg yolk
½ tbls water
Swiss roll tin 8 x 12" (20 x 30cm)

FILLING
3½oz caster sugar (100gm)
2 tbls plain flour, sifted
2 tsp lemon rind, finely grated
5 floz double cream (142ml)
7oz curd cheese (200gm)
1 tbls chunky marmalade
1½oz sultanas (42gm)
Pinch of salt
2–3 dessert apples, thinly sliced

Pastry: Mix flour into butter until it resembles fine breadcrumbs, then add sugar. Mix in enough egg yolk and water to make firm dough. Leave in fridge for 30 minutes. Roll out and line tin.

Filling: Beat eggs and sugar until pale and thick. Fold in flour, lemon rind, cream, cheese, marmalade, sultanas and salt. Place the apples neatly over the pastry, then pour over the creamy mixture. Bake and leave until cold. Turn out onto rack and then turn over again on to platter so that the pastry is at the bottom. Cut into squares.

TUROS BELES
(Cheese Squares)
Eva Schwarcz

Makes 48 Preparation 20 mins Cook 30–35 mins. Gas No.2, 300°F, 160°C

PASTRY
4 cups flour
3oz soft margarine (85gm)
2 egg yolks
2 heaped tbls caster sugar
1oz dry yeast (30gm)
¾ cup of tepid water
Tin 13 x 9" (33 x 22cm)

FILLING
11oz curd cheese (750gm)
5 floz carton sour cream (140ml)
10 dsp vanilla flavoured sugar (approx)
Grated rind of 1 lemon
3 egg yolks
(mixed together)

Dissolve the yeast in 2 teaspoons of the water and 1 teaspoon of the sugar and leave in a warm place for about 5 minutes until it bubbles. Put the flour, margarine, egg yolks, sugar and yeast in food processor and mix, adding the tepid water until the pastry has a good texture. Roll out half the pastry. Place in greased tin. Spread with the filling. Cover with the second half of pastry. Brush top with slightly beaten egg white. Prick with fork.

GINGER MARMALADE SLICE   Esther Nathan

Preparation 10 mins. Chill 2 hours Cook 30–40 mins. Gas No. 4, 350°F, 180°C
Advance

PASTRY

8oz SR flour (225gm)
6oz butter or Tomor margarine (170gm)
2oz ground almonds (55gm)
1 egg, beaten

FILLING

1lb ginger marmalade (450gm)

TOPPING

Flaked almonds
Swiss roll tin 8 x 12″ (20 x 30cm)

Mix fat, flour, sugar, ground almonds and most of beaten egg (reserving a little for glaze). Knead mixture and chill for 2 hours. Roll out half the pastry and line swiss roll tin. Spread with most of marmalade then cover with rest of pastry. Glaze with remaining egg and sprinkle with flaked almonds. Bake until golden brown. Allow to cool and cut into squares.

HONEY BUNS   Marion Cohen

Makes 12 Preparation 15 mins. Cook 20 mins. Gas No.5, 375°F, 190°C Advance

6 floz sunflower oil (170ml)
3oz raw brown sugar (85gm)
$\frac{1}{4}$ pt orange juice (140ml)
1lb 100% wholemeal flour (450gm)
2 tsp baking powder
Grated rind of 2 lemons
2oz shelled walnuts, chopped (55gm)

SYRUP

4 floz clear honey (114ml)
4 floz water (114ml)
4oz raw brown sugar (115gm)

Place all ingredients except walnuts into mixing bowl and mix until they form a soft dough. Sprinkle the walnuts onto a dish. Form the dough into 12 ovals and press onto the walnuts. Place the oval shapes on a greased baking sheet so that the walnuts are on the top. Bake until golden and just firm.

Syrup: Place the syrup ingredients in a saucepan and heat, gently stirring until the sugar dissolves then bring to the boil for 5 minutes. Spoon the syrup over the buns whilst still on the baking sheet and leave to soak in for 15 minutes. Cool on a wire rack over a baking tray.

MERINGUE KISSES Ruth Bernstein

Makes 48 Preparation 10 mins. Cook 40 mins. Gas No.2, 300°F, 160°C Advance
Freezable

3 egg whites
¾ cup sugar

½ tsp vanilla essence

DECORATE: chocolate chips

Beat whites until stiff. Add sugar slowly beating all the time. Line baking sheets with
Bakewell paper. Drop teaspoonfuls of meringue onto baking tray. Press a chocolate
chip in centre of each meringue before baking. After 30 minutes turn off oven,
leaving the meringues inside for a while, depending on how crunchy you like them.

 NUT AND APPLE SLICES David Burr

Preparation 10 mins.   Cook 45 mins.   Gas No.4, 350°F, 180°C   Advance

8 oz thick apple purée, unsweetened
   (225 gm)
4 tbls clear honey
2 oz soft margarine (55 gm)
4 oz wholemeal flour (115 gm)
1½ tsp baking powder
1 lb loaf tin (450 gm)

¼ tsp ground cloves
½ tsp ground nutmeg
2 oz sunflower seeds, lightly toasted
   (55 gm)
2 oz hazelnuts, chopped and lightly
   toasted (55 gm)

Cream the honey and the margarine thoroughly. Sift the flour, baking powder and
spices together and mix into the creamed honey and margarine. Stir in the nuts,
sunflower seeds and then the apple mixture. Pour into a greased loaf tin. Bake. When
cool, cut into bars.

NUTTY CHOCOLATE RINGS Bondi Zimmerman

Preparation 20 mins. Cook 22 mins. Gas No.6, 400°F, 200°C Advance Freezable

Choux pastry (see page 232)
1 oz flaked almonds (30 gm)
1 greased baking sheet

FILLING

4 oz plain chocolate (115 gm)
2 eggs, separated
¼ pt double cream, whipped (140 ml)
Icing sugar

Pastry: Use method on page   . Put pastry in icing bag with a plain nozzle and pipe
3″ (7.5 cm) rings onto greased baking sheet. Sprinkle with the almonds and bake. Cut
a slit in each to release steam and cook a further 2 minutes. Cool.

Filling: Melt chocolate. Cool slightly then beat into the egg yolks. Whisk egg whites
until stiff and fold them into chocolate mixture. Chill until almost set then fold in the
whipped cream.

Split the choux rings and sandwich with the filling. Sprinkle lightly with icing sugar.

206

NUT AND POPPYSEED SQUARES   Eva Schwarcz
(Flodny)

Preparation 30 mins.   Cook 30 mins.   Gas No.5, 375°F, 190°C   Advance

PASTRY

1 lb 5 oz flour (600 gm)
1½ oz yeast (45 gm)
4 oz soft margarine (115 gm)
4 egg yolks
4 oz sugar (115 gm)
½ glass white wine
A little tepid water

FILLINGS

(1) 7 oz ground poppyseeds (200 gm)
1 cup caster sugar
⅓ tsp mixed spice
(make into a paste with water)

(2) 7 oz ground walnuts (200 gm)
1 tsp cinnamon
1 cup vanilla sugar
(make into a paste with a little white wine)

(3) ½ jar Povidle (Hungarian plum jam)
or a good plum preserve

Dissolve yeast in tepid water with a little sugar and leave in a warm place until bubbling. Then mix well with all the other pastry ingredients. Divide pastry into 3. Roll out and place the first piece into a greased tin. Spread with Povidle and then the poppyseed filling. Place second pastry layer over the top and spread this with the Povidle and then the nut filling. Cover with third piece of pastry and brush with water. Prick with a fork and bake.

PEAR AND ALMOND SLICE   Michelle Davidson

Preparation 15 mins.   Cook 20–25 mins.   Gas No.6, 400°F, 200°C

6 oz soft margarine (170 gm)
6 oz caster sugar (170 gm)
1 tsp baking powder
6 oz SR flour (170 gm)
Icing sugar

2 eggs, size 3
½ tsp almond essence
4 pears
1 oz flaked almonds (30 gm)
9 x 13″ (23 x 33 cm) tin

Mix fat, sugar, flour, baking powder, eggs and almond essence until smooth. Spread evenly into tin. Wash and dry pears. DO NOT PEEL. Cut them in halves and core. Slice each half lengthwise into 5 slices. Lay evenly over cake mixture and sprinkle with flaked almonds. Bake. Whilst still warm sift icing sugar on top. Cut into slices.

Large Cakes

APPLE CAKE
Fay Trup

Serves 6–8   Preparation 15 mins.   Cook 1 hour   Gas No.4, 350°F, 185°C

* 7oz SR flour (200gm)
* ½ tsp baking powder
(* sieved together)
3oz caster sugar (85gm) plus 1 tbls for apples
5oz margarine (140gm)
1 large egg

5oz apricot jam (140gm)
1lb cooking apples, sliced
(450gm)
8″ (20cm) loose-bottom cake
tin, greased and floured

Cream the margarine and sugar, beat in the egg, then fold in the flour and baking powder. Put three quarters of the mixture into the tin, cover with the apples and a tablespoons of sugar. Alternate spoonfuls of the remaining mixture and the apricot jam in blobs over the apples. Bake.

AUVERGNE CHERRY CAKE
Sally Samuels

Preparation 5–10 mins.   Cook 30–45 mins.   Gas No.7, 425°F, 220°C   Freezable

3 eggs
4 tbls caster sugar
4oz SR flour (115gm)
1 tsp dried yeast

1lb fresh cherries (450gm), if
unavailable use bottled or tinned
1 tbls milk (approx.)

Beat sugar and eggs together. Slowly add flour, then yeast. Mix well. Add enough milk to make a smooth batter, not too thin. Butter a flan dish and pour in the batter. Arrange the cherries on top. Bake. Dust with sugar and serve hot or cold.

BANANA AND APRICOT CAKE   Lynne Goldwyn

Serves 10   Preparation 20 mins.   Cook 65 mins.   Gas No.5, 375°F, 190°C
Refrigerate 1½ hours

14 oz tin apricot halves, drained (400 gm)
2 oz walnuts, chopped (55 gm)
2 ripe bananas
2 carrots, peeled and grated
6 oz light muscovado sugar (170 gm)
3 eggs
10 oz plain flour (285 gm)
Pinch of salt   *(sifted*
1 tsp bicarbonate of soda   *together)*
2 tsp baking powder
6 fl oz corn oil (170 ml)

ICING

3 oz soft butter (85 gm)
3 oz cream cheese (85 gm)
7 oz icing sugar (200 gm)
½ tsp vanilla essence

DECORATION: 2 reserved apricot
halves
sliced banana

2 lb loaf tin (900 gm) greased and lined

Mash 4–5 oz (114–142 gm) apricots and blend together with walnuts, 2 mashed bananas, carrots, sugar and eggs in a bowl. Add the flour mixture. Pour in oil and mix all ingredients together. Place in tin and bake until spongy to the touch. Leave to cool in tin. Turn out onto a wire rack. Cut cake in half through the middle. Place icing ingredients in a bowl and blend to a cream. Sandwich halves together with the cream and spread remainder over the top. Decorate with remaining sliced apricot halves and sliced banana. Serve chilled.

CARROT CAKE   Jennifer Davis

Preparation 25 mins.   Cook 40 mins.   Gas No.2, 325°F, 160°C   Advance

6 oz soft brown sugar (170 gm)
2 medium eggs, beaten
8 oz plain flour (225 gm)
1 tsp bicarbonate of soda
1 tsp cinnamon
6 oz carrots, coarsely grated (170 gm)
4 oz walnuts, chopped (115 gm)

7 fl oz groundnut oil (200 gm)

TOPPING

4 oz full fat soft cheese (115 gm)
2 oz unsalted butter (55 gm)
2 oz sieved icing sugar (55 gm)
11 x 7 x 2″ (28 x 18 x 4 cm) baking tin,
lined with oiled greaseproof paper

Sieve together the plain flour and bicarbonate of soda. In a large mixing bowl beat oil and sugar together and then beat in the other ingredients one after another in order. Spread mixture in prepared tin and bake in centre of preheated oven for 40 minutes or until cake is nicely risen and firm to the touch and beginning to shrink away from sides of the tin. Leave to cool in tin and when only just warm turn out on to wire rack.

Topping: When cake is completely cold beat all topping ingredients together and spread over the cake and leave in cool place to firm up.

OLD FASHIONED CHEESECAKE   Sally Bloom

Preparation 20 mins.   Chill 30 mins.   Cook 25 mins.   Gas No.4, 350°F, 185°C

PASTRY

8oz SR flour (225gm) *or*
1 tbls less and 1 tbls custard
4oz butter (115gm)
3oz sugar (85gm)
1 large egg
8″ (20cm) diameter sandwich tin

CAKE

1lb cooking cheese (450gm)
2 small eggs
2 tbls double cream
3½ tbls caster sugar
2oz soft butter (55gm)
Sultanas may be added

Pastry: Place flour in a bowl, add butter cut into small pieces and mix until it resembles fine breadcrumbs. Add sugar. Mix in the egg until it become a ball. Wrap in greaseproof paper and refrigerate for 30 minutes. Roll out and bake in tin lined with greaseproof paper. Bake until golden brown. Cool.

Cake: Beat cheese slowly. Add softened butter and beat again. Add sugar and eggs and beat. Mix in cream. Pour into prepared case. Decorate with egg yolk and bake.

SUPER CHEESECAKE   Jay Lewis

Preparation 10 mins.   Cook 15–20 mins.   Gas No.5, 375°F, 190°C   Advance

1lb curd cheese (450gm)
3 large eggs (separated)
1 level tbls flour
Vanilla essence

1 cup caster sugar
2oz soft butter (55gm)
5 floz sour cream (140ml)

DECORATION: whipped cream and fruit

Beat all ingredients together very well except egg whites; then fold in the stiffly beaten egg whites. Bake for 15–20 minutes until just set. Turn off oven and leave to cool in oven with door open. When cool decorate.

TOFU CHEESECAKE   Janine Waterman

Preparation 10 mins.   **Cook 15 mins.**   **Gas No.4, 350°F, 180°C**
                              Refrigerate overnight   Advance

BASE   TOPPING

4oz margarine (115gm)   10½ packet silken tofu (290gm)
8oz porridge oats (225gm)   4oz curd cheese (115gm)
1–2 tbls honey   2 ripe bananas
1 tbls unrefined granulated sugar   2 tbls honey
8" (20cm) greased spring sided   Juice and rind of 1 orange or lemon
   cake tin
                              DECORATION: whipped cream
                                          almonds/hazelnuts, toasted

Base: Melt ingredients and stir in porridge oats. Bake until golden.

Topping: Blend all ingredients until smooth. Pour over base and chill overnight.

Decorate by piping whipped cream around outer edge of cake. Sprinkle with nuts.

TARTE AU FROMAGE BLANC   Helen Meller
(White cheese cake)

Preparation 30 mins.   **Cook 45– 50 mins.**   **Gas No.7, 425°F, 220°C for 20 mins.**
                          Refrigerate pastry 1 hour   Advance   Freezable

PASTRY   FILLING

9oz plain flour (255gm)   1¼lb drained fromage blanc or cottage cheese (600gm)
4½oz butter (128gm)   4½oz double cream (125ml)
2½ floz water (70ml)   2 eggs plus
1 tsp salt   2 egg yolks
                              6oz caster sugar (175gm)
10" flan tin (25cm)   1 tbls plain flour
                              Pinch of salt
                              ¼oz vanilla sugar (7½gm) or grated rind of 1 lemon

Mix flour with butter until it resembles breadcrumbs. Add water and salt, mix until
pastry forms into a ball. Refrigerate for 1 hour. Sieve the cheese then whip into cream
until smooth. Mix in whole eggs one by one, followed by the extra yolks, then add the
sugar and flour which have been mixed together with the salt and either vanilla or
lemon flavouring. Grease and dust the flan tin with flour. Roll pastry to a thickness of
$\frac{1}{6}$" (4mm) and line the tin with it. Prick base all over and pour in the cheese mixture.
Bake at temperature above for 20 minutes, then reduce to Gas No.4, 350°F, 185°C for
25 minutes. Serve hot or cold sprinkled with icing sugar.

CHESTNUT GATEAU

Anne Moss

Preparation 10 mins.   **Cook 1–1½ hours**   **Gas No.3, 325°F, 180°C**

¾ of 15 oz tin chestnut purée
  (unsweetened) ((425 gm)
6 egg yolks
2 oz grated hazelnuts (55 gm)
6 egg whites

9" (23 cm) cake tin or 3 x 5" (12.5 cm)
  sandwich tins

11 oz sugar (312 gm)
A little vanilla essence
½ pt whipped cream (280 ml)

DECORATION

Marron glacé and pistachio nuts

Whisk yolks and sugar until light and fluffy. Then add chestnut purée, grated hazelnuts and vanilla essence. Whisk whites until stiff and fold into mixture. Transfer to one large cake tin, or three small ones, greased and lined with bakewell paper. Bake. When cool sandwich together with whipped cream. Decorate top and sides with marron glacé and nuts.

CHOCOLATE CAKE A LA VALERIE

Valerie Colton

Preparation 15 mins.   **Cook 45 mins. approx.**   **Gas No.4, 350°F, 185°C**

CAKE

6 oz butter (170 gm)
4 oz plain chocolate, melted in 3 tbls
  boiling water (115 gm)
4 eggs, separated
5 oz SR flour (140 gm)
6 oz soft brown sugar (170 gm)
½ tsp vanilla essence
1 oz cocoa (30 gm)

ICING

3 oz icing sugar (85 gm)
1 oz cocoa (30 gm)
3 dsp water
2 dsp caster sugar
2 drops vanilla essence
1½ oz butter (45 gm)

Cake: Melt chocolate in boiling water. Sift flour and cocoa together. Whisk egg whites to soft peak stage. Cream butter and sugar, add essence. Beat in the melted chocolate, then the yolks one at a time. Fold in the flour and cocoa and lastly the egg whites. Bake.

Icing: Sift icing sugar and cocoa together – reserve. Melt butter, water, caster sugar and vanilla essence over hot water. When this mixture is hot pour it over the icing sugar and cocoa. Beat well. Use a spatula dipped in hot water to smooth over cake.

212

CHOCOLATE MERINGUE
CAKE
Lynne Goldwyn

Preparation 30 mins. Cook for 1 hour approx. Gas No.½, 275°F, 140°C Advance

MERINGUE

5 egg whites
9 oz caster sugar (255 gm)
Bakewell paper

FILLING

2 tbls instant coffee
9 oz bitter chocolate (255 gm)
3 tbls water
¾ lb unsalted butter (730 gm)
5 egg whites
14 oz icing sugar (400 gm)

Meringue: Beat egg whites until stiff, fold in half the sugar and whisk until the mixture
is stiff again. Fold in the remaining sugar and beat again. Spread 5 thin layers of meringue on baking paper 4 x 8″ (10 x 20 cm) and cook them in a very slow oven until dried out.

Filling: Slowly melt the chocolate, coffee powder and water until smooth. Cream the butter and add the chocolate mixture. Over boiling water whisk the egg whites and sugar until thick. Cool and combine with the chocolate mixture.

Layer the meringue sheets with the chocolate filling and cover the top and sides also with the filling. Chill and serve in slices.

CHOCOLATE MOUSSE
CAKE
Michelle Davidson

Preparation 35 mins.   Cook 7–10 mins.   Gas No.7, 425°F, 220°C
Chill 12 hours   Advance

CAKE

2 oz caster sugar (55 gm)
2 eggs, size 2
1 oz cornflour (30 gm)
1 oz cocoa (30 gm)
9″ springform tin (23 cm) greased and
  lined with non-stick paper

MOUSSE

2 oz caster sugar (55 gm)
2 fl oz boiling water (56 ml)
2 fl oz rum (56 ml)
15 oz plain chocolate (425 gm)
1 pt whipping cream (570 ml)

DECORATION: icing sugar or cocoa

Cake: Whisk sugar and eggs over hot water until mixture leaves a trail for 5 seconds. Add cornflour and cocoa then pour into tin. Bake. Allow to cool. Dissolve caster sugar in boiling water, add rum and brush over sponge.

Mousse: Break chocolate into pieces and melt. Whip cream until it forms peaks and fold in the chocolate. Pour over cake in tin. Sift icing sugar or cocoa over top and refrigerate.

FRUIT CAKE

Fay Trup

Preparation 20 mins.   **Cook 1¼ hours**   **Gas No.4, 350°F, 185°C**   Freezable

¾lb mixed fruit (340gm)
Cup of caster sugar
Cup of wine or water
1 tsp of bicarbonate of soda

6oz margarine (170gm)
2 large eggs
½lb SR flour (225gm)

8″ (20cm) loose-bottom cake tin,
greased and floured

Boil fruit, sugar, margarine, wine or water and bicarbonate of soda for 10 minutes. Use non-stick saucepan and wooden spoon and stir whilst boiling to prevent sticking. Cool for about 30 minutes. Stir in eggs and flour still using wooden spoon. Pour mixture into tin. Bake. When cool, ice or sprinkle with icing sugar.

FRUIT LOAF

Susie Barnett

Preparation 10 mins.   **Soak overnight**   **Cook 1 hour**   **Gas No.4, 350°F, 185°C**

Advance

¾ pt milk (425ml)
10oz dark brown sugar (285gm)
10oz SR flour (285gm)

8oz sultanas or mixed fruit (225gm)
3 weetabix
2 eggs

2 x 1lb loaf tins (450gm)

Place milk in a large bowl and add sugar, fruit and weetabix, leave overnight. Next day, beat 2 eggs and add to mixture; gradually stir in flour. Pour into greased loaf tins. Bake.

WHITE CHOCOLATE MERINGUE
CAKE

Gillian Burr

Preparation 15 mins.   **Cook 4 hours**   **Gas No.½, 250°, 120°C**

6 egg whites
14oz sugar (400gm)
3oz icing sugar (85gm)
10oz white chocolate (285gm)

2 tbls rum
16 floz whipping cream (455ml)
White chocolate shavings for decoration

Baking tray covered with Bakewell paper

Meringue: Beat egg whites until stiff. Add sugar a few ounces at a time and mix well. Spread mixture on baking trays in two circles and bake 4 hours or until thoroughly dry. Leave oven door slightly open.

Filling: Melt chocolate on a low heat. Add sugar and rum. Whip cream and fold into the chocolate mixture.

To assemble the cake, place some chocolate cream mixture between the layers of meringue. Cover the cake with the remaining cream and decorate.

GRAND MARNIER AND ORANGE
CAKE
Anne Moss

Preparation 15 mins.   **Cook 30–35 mins.**   **Gas No.5, 375°F, 190°C**

CAKE

6 oz butter (170 gm)
6 oz caster sugar (170 gm)
3 eggs
6 oz SR flour (170 gm)
2–3 tbls Grand Marnier

2 x 7" sandwich tins (17 cm), greased
  and floured

DECORATION

$\frac{1}{2}$ pt double cream (280 ml)
1 orange rind, grated
1–2 tbls orange juice
$\frac{1}{2}$ tsp sugar
2 tbls walnuts, chopped
5 oz sifted icing sugar (140 gm)
Candied orange slices

Cream fat and sugar and beat in eggs one at a time. Fold in the flour and divide into the two sandwich tins. Bake. When slightly cooled, sprinkle with the Grand Marnier.

Decoration: Whip the double cream and sugar, add the orange rind and use half of it to sandwich the cakes together. Spread some more of the cream around the sides of the cake and press on the chopped walnuts to decorate. Add sufficient orange juice to the icing sugar to make icing. Spread it on the top of the cake. Pipe the remaining whipped cream into twirls on top of the cake and decorate with candied orange slices.

LOUISE'S CAKE
Sheila Rosen

Preparation 15 mins.   **Cook 30 mins.**   **Gas No.6, 400°F, 200°C**

8 oz margarine or butter (225 gm)
8 oz caster sugar (225 gm)
10 oz SR flour (285 gm)
3 eggs
2 tbls milk, approx.
1 tsp vanilla essence

OPTIONAL EXTRA

2 handfuls of dried fruit or mix half of
  the mixture with some cocoa powder
  to make a marble cake.

10" (25 cm) spring form cake tin, greased
  and floured

Cream fat and sugar together. Add lightly beaten eggs a little at a time. Fold in flour, add essence and a little milk until mixture drops off spoon easily. At this stage the fruit or cocoa powder can be added. Bake.

MARBLE CAKE
Hilda Gilbey

Preparation 20 mins. Cook 45 mins. Gas No.3, 325°F, 180°C Advance Freezable

8oz flour (225gm)	5oz butter (140gm)
Pinch of salt	5oz caster sugar (140gm)
1½ tsp baking powder	2 small eggs, beaten
½oz cocoa (15gm)	2½ floz milk (80ml)
¼ tsp vanilla essence	1lb loaf tin (450gm)

(The first four ingredients bracketed:) sifted together

Grease and flour the tin. Place sugar and flour in a bowl, add the softened butter and blend the ingredients together, then add the milk and eggs and mix well. Place half of the mixture into another bowl and stir in the cocoa and vanilla essence. Drop alternate tablespoons of the white and chocolate mixtures into the prepared tin. When the bottom of the tin is covered, put in a second layer of the mixtures covering a brown square with a white one and vice versa. Bake.

MARMALADE FRUIT CAKE
Rita Stitcher

Preparation 20 mins.   Cook 1½–1¾ hours   Gas No.4, 350°F, 180°C   Advance Freezable

6oz softened butter (170gm)	5 tbls orange marmalade
6oz granulated sugar (170gm)	½ tsp almond essence
2 eggs	4–5 tbls milk
8oz SR flour (225gm)	1½oz flaked almonds (42gm)
8oz mixed dried fruit (225gm)	8″ (20cm) round cake tin, lined with buttered greaseproof paper

Put all ingredients except flaked almonds into a large bowl and beat well with a wooden spoon until well mixed. If using an electric mixer run for only about 1 minute. Batter should be of dropping consistancy. Pour into prepared tin and smooth top with back of spoon. Cover thickly with flaked almonds. Half way through the baking time cover top of the tin with foil to prevent almonds from burning. When cooked, allow the cake to cool in the tin for about 5 minutes. Turn onto a wire rack and peel off the lining paper. Then turn right side up.

FRESH RASPBERRY SPONGE
FLAN
Estelle Laurier

Preparation 10 mins.   Cook 35–40 mins.   Gas No.5, 375°F, 185°C

4oz butter (115gm)
4oz caster sugar (115gm)
4oz SR flour (115gm)
2 eggs, size 2
A few drops vanilla essence or
　lemon juice

1lb fresh raspberries (450gm)
Lemon juice
2 tsp sugar
1–2 tsp arrowroot
9" (22cm) flan dish, greased and
　floured

Cream butter and sugar together. Add flavouring and gradually beat in eggs. Fold in flour. Bake. When cooked, turn out and allow to cool. Wash raspberries by soaking in cold salt water for a few minutes. Rinse thoroughly in a colander. Return fruit to bowl and sprinkle with sugar and lemon juice. Leave until they have made a quantity of juice. Strain the juice through a plastic colander into a saucepan and reserve the raspberries. Heat the juice gently until bubbling. Mix the arrowroot into a paste with a little cold water and stir into the juice. Heat until thickened stirring all the time. Allow to cool stirring occasionally. Place fruit in flan case and spread juice evenly over it. Other fruit may be substituted.

Optional: Make crème patissière. Spread over baked pastry before placing fruit in flan case.

RHUBARB CRUMBLE CAKE
Maureen Marks

Preparation 20 mins.   Cook 1 hour   Gas No.4, 350°F, 180°C

1lb rhubarb (450gm)
6oz SR flour (170gm)
Pinch salt
4oz butter (225gm)
$\frac{1}{2}$ tsp vanilla essence
1–2 tbls milk
4oz caster sugar (115gm)
2 eggs

TOPPING

4oz SR flour, sifted (225gm)
3oz butter, cut in pieces (85gm)
3oz caster sugar (85gm)

DECORATION: icing sugar

9" (22.5cm) spring-clip cake tin,
　greased and floured

Topping: Mix butter and flour together until the mixture resembles coarse crumbs then add the sugar. Reserve.

Cake: Sift the flour and salt for the cake onto a plate. Cream the butter and sugar until soft and light. Lightly mix the eggs and essence and add to the creamed mixture a little at a time beating well after each addition, adding a little flour to the last addition. Gently fold half the flour into the mixture. Add the remaining flour and milk and blend well. Spoon mixture into the greased tin and spread evenly. Cover with the rhubarb cut into 1" (2.5cm) pieces and sprinkle the topping over them. Bake. Allow to cool in the tin and dust with icing sugar.

RUSSIAN COFFEE-TIME CAKE
Rosalind Berenbaum

Preparation 15 mins. Cook 50 mins. Gas No.4, 350°F, 180°C Advance Freezable

4oz butter (115gm)
6oz caster sugar (170gm)
2 eggs
8oz soured cream (225ml)
6oz self raising flour (170gm)
Pinch salt
4oz walnuts, roughly chopped
   (115gm)
2lb loaf tin, greased (900gm)

1 tsp baking powder
1 tsp bicarbonate of soda
1 tsp vanilla essence
1 tsp lemon juice

TOPPING

2oz caster sugar (55gm)
2 tsp cinnamon

Cream butter and sugar then add eggs, flour, soured cream and all other ingredients except for nuts and mix thoroughly. Lastly fold in nuts. Place half the quantity of mixture in greased loaf tin. Mix topping ingredients together and cover mixture with half the topping. Add rest of cake mixture and finish with rest of topping. Bake.

FATLESS SPONGE CAKE
Helen Meller

Serves 8   Preparation 15 mins.   Cook 20–30 mins.   Gas No.5, 375°F, 190°C
Freezable

6 eggs, separated
8oz caster sugar (225gm)
2 tbls water or lemon juice
Grated rind of $\frac{1}{2}$ lemon

3oz plain flour (85gm)
$\frac{1}{2}$oz cornflour (15gm)
Pinch of salt
2 sandwich tins 8½" (20cm)
   diameter, greased and floured

Beat egg yolks, sugar, lemon juice or water, lemon rind and salt until nearly white and the whisk leaves a trail. Sift flour and cornflour and mix little by little into mixture. Whisk egg whites until very stiff but not dry and fold into mixture carefully. Divide into the tins and bake. Sandwich together with jam, cream or fruit as desired. This cake is beautifully light but does not keep.

YOGHURT CAKE
Fay Trup

Preparation 5 mins. Cook 1¼ hours Gas No.4, 350°F. 180°C Advance Freezable

5 floz carton plain or hazelnut
   yoghurt (140ml)
1 carton oil
2 cartons sugar

3 cartons SR flour
3 eggs
Dried fruit, optional
8" (20cm) loose-bottom cake tin,
   greased and floured

Mix all ingredients well with a wooden spoon and pour into tin. Bake.

218

Bread, Biscuits, Pastry

HINTS

Plain flour should be used for shortcrust pastry if you want to achieve a crisp finish. SR flour tends to make the pastry soft and cakey.

Choux and flaky pastry rise better if made with a strong flour.

Milk gives pastry a softer texture.

There is less fat in 4 oz (115 gm) of filo pastry, even when brushed with oil, than in 4 oz (115 gm) of any other pastry (shortcrust, puff or flaky).

Always keep remaining filo pastry in a sealed bag or under a damp cloth to prevent it drying out.

For bread making: 10 minutes before cooking bread put a tin half full of water into the oven, this will make the oven steamy, so helping the bread to rise well. Remove water as you put bread in the oven.

David Burr's Popcorn: Heat 1 tbls sunflower oil until very hot; add $\frac{1}{2}$ tbls caster sugar with 1 tbls popping corn. Cover immediately with well fitting lid. Cook on high heat and as soon as 'popping' is heard, shake pan vigorously until noises stop. Remove from heat immediately. Transfer to bowl and sprinkle with another $\frac{1}{2}$ tbls sugar.

Ready-to-hand vanilla sugar: keep some icing sugar or caster sugar with a vanilla pod in it.

Breads

 BETTY SHEPHERD'S BREAD   Betty Shepherd

Makes 2 loaves   Preparation 15 mins.   Rising time 15–30 mins.   Cook 20 mins.
Gas No.8, 450°F, 230°C

1 lb stoneground wholemeal flour (450 gm)
4 oz strong white flour (115 gm)
1 oz fresh yeast (30 gm) *or*
½ oz dried yeast (15 gm)
Warm water

Small tsp salt
2 tsp molasses
2 fl oz milk (55 ml)

2 × 1 lb loaf tins (450 gm)

Mix milk with warm water to make up to 1 pint (570 ml). Dissolve yeast in a little of the liquid together with the molasses and leave until well risen and fluffy. Oil tins and put on top of stove to warm. Mix all ingredients in a warm bowl and mix well together, then punch firmly until a spongy ball is formed, adding more flour if too sticky. Divide into chosen tins and put in a warm place to rise, covered, until doubled in size then bake.

BRIOCHE LOAF   Gloria Goldberg

Preparation 15 mins. Rising time 2 hours Cook 40 mins. Gas No.5, 375°F, 190°C

8 oz strong white flour (225 gm)
½ oz fresh yeast (15 gm)
4 fl oz tepid milk (115 ml)
1 tbls white sugar

4 oz butter (115 gm)
2 eggs
½ tsp salt
1 lb loaf tin or brioche mould (450 gm)

Cream the sugar and yeast until runny and stir in the milk. Sieve the flour and salt into a bowl or food processor. Rub in the butter until it is of breadcrumb consistency, then add the yeast mixture and the eggs to make a very soft dough. Beat with your hand or a wooden spoon for 10 minutes (or 1 minute in the food processor). Scrape the mixture from the sides of the bowl, cover with a plastic bag or damp cloth and leave to rise for about 1 hour until double in size. Knead for a few moments or process for 10 seconds and turn into oiled tin. Cover with the plastic bag and leave to double in bulk and fill the mould, again for about 1 hour. Transfer carefully to oven and bake. Cover the top if it starts getting too brown. Turn out on to a wire rack and cool. If time is short turn the dough into the tin after kneading, allow to rise only once, and cook. Serve with rich patés.

HAZELNUT ROLLS

Valerie Halpern

Serves 6   Preparation 25 mins.   Cook 15 mins. approx.   Gas No.6, 400°F, 200°C
Advance Freezable

PASTRY

4 oz wholemeal flour (115 gm)
2 oz soft vegetable fat (55 gm)
Cold water to mix

FILLING

2 oz onion, finely chopped (55 gm)
1 tbls sunflower oil
Pepper

2 oz mushrooms, finely chopped (55 gm)
2 oz carrots, grated (55 gm)
2 oz ground hazelnuts (55 gm)
2 oz wholemeal breadcrumbs (55 gm)
1 tbls fresh parsley, chopped
$\frac{1}{2}$ tsp dried thyme
1 egg, beaten
Sesame seeds (optional)

Pastry: Make pastry in usual way and put in fridge.

Filling: Sauté onion in oil slowly over low heat for 10 minutes without browning. Add mushrooms until juice runs, add carrot, hazelnuts, breadcrumbs, parsley and thyme. Mix thoroughly and season with freshly ground pepper. Add egg, leaving a little to glaze, and mix. Divide mixture into two sausages, 8″ (20 cm) long. Roll out pastry into rectangle 8 x 6″ (20 x 15 cm). Cut in half lengthwise and put one sausage on each half. Roll each half into a strüdel and cut each of them into six pieces. Cut a slit in each one, brush with beaten egg and scatter sesame seed on top (optional). Bake.

NUTTY OLIVE BREAD

Jane Finestone

Serves 8–10   Preparation 20 mins.   Cook 50 mins.   Gas No.4, 350°F, 180°C
Advance   Freezable

3 oz melted butter (85 gm)
1 onion, chopped
$\frac{1}{2}$ cup pecan nuts, chopped
$\frac{1}{2}$ cup blanched almonds, chopped
$\frac{1}{2}$ cup stoned black olives
1$\frac{1}{2}$ cups buttermilk

2 eggs
1 cup SR flour
$\frac{1}{2}$ cup plain flour
1 cup wholemeal flour
1 tsp bicarbonate of soda
Loaf tin 4 x 6$\frac{1}{2}$″ (11 x 18 cm)

Sauté onion in butter until transparent. Add nuts, stir over low heat for 3 minutes then set aside. Mix olives and buttermilk with eggs and lightly fork over. Sift flours and soda into bowl, then add egg mixture and mix until very well combined. Put mixture into loaf tin. Bake.

HERBY SCONES
Jane Finestone

Makes 18   Preparation 15 mins.   Cook 15–20 mins.   Gas No.6, 400°F, 200°C
Freezable

2 cups SR flour
1 tsp sugar
1 oz butter (30 gm)
$\frac{1}{4}$ cup chives, chopped
$\frac{1}{4}$ cup fresh dill, chopped

$\frac{1}{4}$ cup parsley, chopped
$\frac{1}{2}$ cup milk
$\frac{1}{3}$ cup water
Pinch fresh ground black pepper

Rub butter into sifted flour and sugar. Stir in all herbs. Pour in milk and some water to form a sticky dough. Turn onto floured board and knead until smooth. Roll out to about $\frac{3}{4}''$ (2 cm) thick. Cut into small rounds using egg cup or similar and place on greased flat tin. Brush tops with milk and bake until golden brown.

LAKELAND SCONES
Lisa Rose

Makes 12   Preparation 10 mins.   Cook 10 mins.   Gas No.6, 400°F, 200°C

1 lb SR flour (450 gm)
6 oz very soft butter, cut into 6 pieces
  (170 gm)
Generous pinch salt

3 tbls caster sugar, sieved
Sultanas, to taste
2 eggs, lightly beaten
Milk/sour cream/yoghurt, to mix

Sieve flour into plastic bowl and gently work in the butter until the mixture resembles breadcrumbs. Add salt and sugar and combine with the sultanas. Very gently work in the eggs and add either the milk, sour cream or yoghurt, a little at a time, until the mixture forms a firm holding dough. Turn out onto a work surface and roll out. Using a palette knife cut into diamond shapes and transfer to a baking tray. Bake.

WALNUT CRANBERRY BREAD
Kate Bennett

Preparation 20 mins.   Cook 1–$1\frac{1}{4}$ hours   Gas No.3, 325°F, 170°C   Advance

2 tbls butter
1 cup caster sugar
1 egg, lightly beaten
Grated rind of 2 oranges
$\frac{3}{4}$ cup orange juice
$\frac{3}{4}$ cup walnuts, chopped

2 cups flour
$\frac{1}{2}$ tsp salt
$\frac{1}{2}$ tsp baking soda
$1\frac{1}{2}$ tsp baking powder
1 cup whole cranberries
Loaf tin

Cream the butter and sugar, add the beaten egg, the orange rind and juice. Sift the dry ingredients together. Dust the cranberries and nuts with one extra tablespoon of flour. Blend the sugar/orange mixture with the sifted dry ingredients. Stir in the nuts and cranberries. Pour batter into greased and floured loaf tin. Bake. When cooked, allow to cool and then store in an air tight container.

WHOLEMEAL BREAD
Gillian Burr

Makes 4 loaves   Preparation 25 mins.   Rising time 2 hours   Cook 40 mins.
Gas No.7, 425°F, 220°C   Advance   Freezable

1¼lb strong white flour (675gm)
1½lb wholemeal or granary flour (675gm)
1oz fresh yeast (30gm)
1½oz sea salt (45gm)

1 tsp sugar
1½ pt water approx (850ml)
A few drops oil

Cream yeast and sugar together until runny, add ½ pint (280ml) tepid water and pour into a well in the flour. Flick flour over the liquid and leave in a warm place for 10 minutes or until cracks appear in the flour and the yeast is beginning to froth. Stir into the flour and add about 1 pint (570ml) tepid water until you have a medium soft dough. Knead for 10–15 minutes, or process in 4 batches in a food processor for ¾–1 minute until pliable and elastic, then form into a ball. Put a few drops of oil in the bottom of your bowl, turn the ball of dough so that it is coated all over then cover the bowl with a damp tea towel or greased cling film, leave in a warm draught free place. When the dough has doubled in size, knock it down and knead for a few moments only, then divide into 4 equal pieces, press them out flat and roll up carefully to form free standing loaves. Make 3 cuts in the top of each loaf. Place the loaves on a greased and floured baking tray and cover with a plastic bag. Leave until risen to double the size. Remove bag and cook for 20 minutes. Turn the oven down to Gas No.5, 375°F, 190°C for a further 20 minutes. The loaves are cooked when they sound hollow when tapped on the bottom. Cool on a rack.

 # WHOLEMEAL FRUIT SCONES
Gillian Burr

Makes 8   Preparation 10 mins.   Cook 10–15 mins.   Gas No.6, 400°F, 200°C

8oz SR wholemeal flour (225gm)
Pinch salt
3oz butter or margarine, cut into
  small pieces (85gm)

1oz raw brown sugar (30gm)
3oz raisins (85gm)
4floz milk (115ml)

Sift flour and salt into a bowl, rub in the fat until mixture resembles fine breadcrumbs, stir in sugar and raisins and add sufficient milk to give a soft manageable dough. Knead gently on a lightly floured board and roll out to ¾" (2cm) thickness. Cut into 3" (7.5cm) circles. Place fairly close together on a lightly greased baking sheet and bake until golden. Cool on a wire tray.

223

ZUCCHINI BREAD
Barbara Davidson

Preparation 15 mins.   Cook 1 hour   Gas No.4, 350°F, 185°C   Advance

3 large eggs
2 cups caster sugar
1 cup corn oil
2 cups peeled courgettes, grated
3 cups SR flour
$\frac{1}{4}$ tsp baking powder
2 x 1lb loaf tins (450gm) greased

3 tsp vanilla essence
1 tsp bicarbonate of soda
3 tsp cinnamon
1 cup almonds or walnuts, chopped
    coarsely
1 tsp salt

Beat eggs until light and foamy, add the sugar, oil, courgettes and vanilla essence. Mix lightly but well. Combine the flour with the salt, bicarbonate of soda, baking powder and cinnamon, then add to the courgette mixture and stir until well blended, lastly add the cup of walnuts or almonds. Line the loaf tins with foil and two thirds fill them with the mixture. Bake until cooked then invert over a wire rack and remove tins and foil so that steam may escape.

RICH SESAME OR POPPY
SEED ROLLS

Makes 24   Preparation 30 mins.   Rising time $2\frac{1}{2}$ hours   Cook 15 mins.
Gas No.7, 425°F, 220°C   Advance   Freezable

1lb strong white flour (450gm)
1 tsp salt
1oz fresh yeast (30gm)
1 tsp sugar

4oz butter (115gm)
12 floz mixed tepid milk and water (340ml)
A few drops oil
A little egg wash or white of egg
Sesame or poppy seeds

Sift the flour and salt into a large bowl and warm a little. Cream the sugar and yeast until runny, then add half the liquid. Pour into a well in the flour and flick flour over to cover the liquid. Leave for 10 minutes or so until the flour cracks and the yeast bubbles. Melt the butter and, when tepid, combine it and the remaining liquid and add to the flour to make a soft dough. Knead for 10 minutes or process in a food processor in two batches for $\frac{3}{4}$–1 minute until the dough is smooth, elastic and no longer sticking to everything. Put a few drops of oil in the bowl and turn the ball of dough into it. Turn over leaving the greased side upwards, and cover with a plastic bag or damp cloth. Leave to rise in a warm draught-free room for 1–$1\frac{1}{2}$ hours or until doubled in bulk. Turn out onto a floured surface, knead briefly and cut into 24 equal pieces. Form each into a flattish round bun or roll and space out on a greased and floured baking sheet. Brush with egg and scatter with sesame or poppy seeds. Cover with a plastic bag and leave to rise for about $\frac{3}{4}$–1 hour until well risen and doubled in bulk. Bake until brown and cool on a rack. Cover with a cloth if you want a soft crust. Best kept in a freezer so that they stay fresh. They only take a few minutes to thaw, then warm in the oven or under a low grill.

Biscuits

BUTTER BISCUITS
Esther Nathan

Preparation 15 mins.

Chill pastry 2 hours
Gas No.5, 375°F, 190°C

Cook 10–15 mins.

Advance   Freezable

12oz SR flour (340gm)
8oz butter (225gm)
1 egg, beaten
6oz caster sugar (170gm)

DECORATION
Glacé cherries
Almonds or walnuts
Chocolate drops

GLAZE: milk or beaten egg

Cream butter and sugar together. Add the egg, then flour and mix thoroughly. Wrap in greaseproof paper and refrigerate for several hours. Roll out and cut into shapes. Decorate as required and glaze with a little milk or beaten egg.

CHERRY NUT BISCUITS
Bondi Zimmerman

Makes 30   Preparation 10 mins.   Cook 15–20 mins.   Gas No.4, 360°F, 185°C

4oz butter (115gm)
$\frac{1}{4}$ cup caster sugar
1 egg
1 tsp vanilla essence

1 cup SR flour, sifted
4oz mixed nuts, chopped (115gm)
Glacé cherries

Cream butter and sugar, add egg and vanilla and beat well. Mix in flour to make a soft dough. Add the nuts. Roll into balls, press down placing a cherry on each biscuit. Allow room for spreading when placing on greased tray. Bake until golden. Cool before removing from tray.

CHOCOLATE WHEATIES   Miki Hildebrand

Makes 35 approx.   Preparation 10 mins.   Cook 15–20 mins.   Gas No.4, 350°F, 185°C Advance Freezable

3 oz butter (85 gm)
¼ cup brown sugar
1 egg
¼ cup coconut

¼ cup wheatgerm
¾ cup wholemeal flour
½ cup SR flour
3 oz dark chocolate (85 gm)

Cream butter and sugar, add egg and beat well. Stir in coconut, wheatgerm and sifted flours (return husks to bowl). Roll mixture into balls and place on lightly greased baking trays. Flatten slightly with fork before baking. When cooked cool on a wire tray. Melt chocolate and dip half of each biscuit in it. Allow to set on wire rack in refrigerator.

COFFEE NUT CRESCENTS   Rosanna Burr

Makes 35   Preparation 10 mins.   Refrigerate 30 mins.   Cook 12 mins   Gas No.4, 350°F, 185°C Advance Freezable

1¼ cups flour, sifted
4 oz butter (115 gm)
2 tbls caster sugar
2 oz walnut pieces, ground (55 gm)

1 egg yolk
2 tsp instant coffee powder
2 tsp hot water
Caster sugar to dredge

Place the flour in a mixing bowl and add sugar. Mix in butter until the mixture resembles breadcrumbs. Add ground walnuts and mix. Dissolve coffee powder in water and add to walnut mixture with the egg yolk. Stir until all ingredients are combined. Wrap dough in greaseproof paper and refrigerate for 30 minutes. Take 2 tsp at a time of the dough and roll into crescents 2″ (5 cm) long. Bake on a greased baking tray. Remove crescents while still warm, cool on a wire rack and dredge with caster sugar.

DATE CRUNCHIES   Susie Barnett

Makes 12   Preparation 10 mins.   Cook 10 mins.   Advance   Freezable

8 oz stoned dates, cut into pieces (225 gm)
1 tbls dessicated coconut
8 oz petit beurre biscuits (225 gm)

8 oz margarine (225 gm)
3 tbls caster or brown sugar
1 egg, beaten

Melt sugar and margarine and cool slightly. Slowly add the beaten egg and mix. Add the dates and bring to the boil, stirring constantly until the mixture forms a smooth paste. Remove from heat and add broken biscuits. Stir well so that all the biscuits are covered. Place in a greased oblong tin and flatten to ½″ (13 mm) thick. Sprinkle the coconut over the mixture and refrigerate. Cut into squares.

GRANDMA'S BISCUITS   Sally Samuels

Preparation 10 mins. Cook 35 mins. Gas No.6, 400°F, 200°C Advance Freezable

¼lb butter (115gm)
3oz caster sugar (85gm)
1 egg

10oz SR flour (285gm)
Jam

Cream butter and sugar. Beat in egg. Add sufficient flour to make a soft pliable dough, depending on size of egg. Divide into 2 pieces. Roll out thinly, spread with jam and roll up. Bake for 25 minutes approx. until light brown, cut into slices and put back in oven for 6–7 minutes.

GINGERNUTS   Lynne Goldwyn

Makes 40 approx. Preparation 10 mins. Cook 15 mins. Gas No.4, 350°F, 180°C
Advance Freezable

2 cups flour
1 cup caster sugar
½ tsp bicarbonate of soda
1 tsp cinnamon
Pinch of salt

2 tsp ground ginger
4oz butter (115gm)
1 small egg
1 tsp golden syrup

Place flour, sugar, bicarbonate of soda, cinnamon, salt and ginger in a bowl. Rub in butter to make fine breadcrumbs. Beat egg with golden syrup and add to dry ingredients making it into a dough. Roll mixture into small balls. Flatten slightly on lightly greased baking trays 2″ (5cm) apart. Bake.

 ## LEMON DELIGHTS   Miki Hildebrand

Makes 30 Preparation 10 mins. Cook 15 mins. Gas No.4, 350°F, 180°C Advance
Freezable

1oz raw cane sugar (30gm)
3oz polyunsaturated margarine (85gm)
5oz wholemeal flour (140gm)

Juice of a lemon
Grated rind of ½ lemon
2oz honey (55gm)

Mix honey, sugar and margarine until creamy. Work in flour, lemon juice and rind. Form dough into small balls and place on greased baking tray. Flatten slightly. Bake.

MALTESE BON-BONS
Barbara Jane Scott

Preparation 10 mins. Cook 10 mins. Refrigerate 30 mins. Advance Freezable

14 oz smooth peanut butter (400 gm)
2¾ oz butter (80 gm)
7 oz dark chocolate (200 gm)

2½ cups icing sugar
3 cups Rice Krispies

Melt peanut butter and butter gently in a saucepan. Combine icing sugar and Rice Krispies in a large bowl. Pour melted butter mixture over Krispies slowly and mix thoroughly. Roll into balls and place in fridge to chill for 30 minutes. Melt chocolate in a double boiler and coat top of balls with chocolate. Chill again. Can be kept in fridge or freezer. They are very addictive.

MELTING MOMENTS
Barbara Green

Makes 12–14 Preparation 10 mins. Cook 15–20 mins. Gas No.4, 350°F, 180°C

5 oz butter or margarine (140 gm)
3 oz raw brown sugar (85 gm)
4 oz 100% wholemeal SR flour (115 gm)
1 oz porridge oats, rolled (30 gm)

1 tbls beaten egg
½ tsp vanilla essence
Extra porridge oats to coat

Cream the butter and sugar until light and fluffy. Beat in the egg and vanilla essence. Work in the flour and rolled oats. Form the mixture into balls the size of a walnut, and coat with rolled oats. Place well apart on a greased baking sheet and flatten slightly. Bake in the oven until golden. Cool slightly before transferring to a wire tray.

OATMEAL NUT COOKIES
Debby Winter

Preparation 10 mins.   Cook 15 mins.   Gas No.5, 375°F, 190°C   Advance

2 cups cooking oatmeal
1½ cups flour
1 cup margarine
1 cup brown sugar
1 cup caster sugar

2 eggs
½ tsp salt
1 tsp baking soda
1 tsp vanilla essence
1 cup walnuts, chopped

Place all ingredients in bowl, mix thoroughly and roll into balls. Place on greased baking trays and bake.

ORANGE COOKIES

Debby Winter

Preparation 10 mins. **Cook 20–25 mins.** **Gas No.4, 350°F, 180°C** **Advance**

8 eggs
2½ cups sugar
2 packets vanilla sugar
2½ tsp baking powder

¾lb butter or margarine (340gm)
2 oranges, juice and rind
2½lb flour (1.3k)

Mix together all ingredients. Knead until smooth. Roll out on floured board to ¼″ (8mm) thickness. Cut into desired shapes. Place on greased cookie sheet. Bake.

PASSION FRUIT CREAM BISCUITS

Gillian Burr

Makes 30 **Preparation 10 mins.** **Chill 30 mins.** **Cook 10 mins.**
Gas No.4, 350°F, 180°C **Advance** **Freezable**

4oz butter (115gm)
⅓ cup caster sugar
1 tsp lemon rind, grated
2 tbls golden syrup
1 cup SR flour
⅔ cup plain flour
2 passion fruit
1 tbls lemon juice

½ tsp ground ginger
Pinch of salt
1oz glacé ginger (30gm)

PASSION FRUIT CREAM

2oz butter (55gm)
¾ cup icing sugar
1 passion fruit
2 tsp brandy

Cream butter, add sugar and rind and beat until creamy. Add golden syrup and mix well. Add dry ingredients, finely chopped ginger, passion fruit pulp and juice. Turn onto lightly floured board and knead until smooth. Refrigerate 30 minutes. Roll out between 2 sheets of greaseproof paper and cut into biscuits. Place on a greased baking sheet and bake until golden (10 minutes). When cold sandwich 2 biscuits with the cream.

Passion fruit cream: Cream soft butter and sifted icing sugar until fluffy. Add passion fruit pulp gradually, mixing well to avoid curdling. Add brandy and mix again.

229

TAIGLECH – PURIM CONFECTION

Marion Finestein

Preparation 10 mins. **Cook 30 mins.** **Advance**

2 eggs, well beaten
7oz SR flour (200gm)
Pinch of salt
1 tbls oil

DECORATION: dessicated coconut

SYRUP
1lb honey/golden syrup (450gm)
5oz caster sugar (140gm)
2 tsp ground ginger
$\frac{1}{8}$ cup water

Mix oil and eggs together. Sieve together the flour and salt and add to the mixture. Knead by hand adding more flour if necessary and combine. Break off pieces of dough and roll into $\frac{1}{2}$″ (12mm) thick sausages. Cut them into $\frac{1}{2}$″ (12mm) pieces. In a large saucepan combine honey/syrup, sugar and ginger and bring to the boil once sugar has dissolved. Carefully drop the pieces of dough into the syrup mixture one at a time. DO NOT COVER PAN. Reduce the heat slightly and then cook the pieces for 25–30 minutes stirring occasionally being careful not to break them. Check that they are cooked through. Lastly add the water to prevent the syrup from caramelising. Drop the taiglech onto a flat baking tray covered with Bakewell paper which has been liberally sprinkled with coconut. Allow to cool and dry. Store in airtight tin, if they last that long.

VANILLA BISCUITS

Sally Bloom

Preparation 10 mins. **Cook 12–15 mins.** **Gas No.3$\frac{1}{2}$, 355°F, 182°C**

6$\frac{1}{2}$oz flour (185gm)
5oz butter (140gm)
Vanilla flavoured icing sugar, sifted

3oz caster sugar (85gm)
3oz ground almonds (85gm)

Mix flour and butter until the mixture resembles breadcrumbs then knead into a dough with the sugar and ground almonds. Form the dough by hand into crescent shapes and bake until a light golden brown. Before serving dust with vanilla flavoured icing sugar.

VIENNESE ORANGE KISSES   Rosanna Burr

Makes 30 Preparation 25 mins. Cook 15 mins. Gas No.4, 350°F, 180°C Advance
Freezable

14oz butter (400gm)
1 cup icing sugar, sifted
2 tbls cornflour
4 tbls orange rind, grated
* 2 cups plain flour
* 1 cup SR flour

(sifted together)*

ORANGE CREAM
4oz butter (115gm)
2 cups icing sugar, sifted
4 tbls orange juice

DECORATION: icing sugar

Biscuits: Cream butter, icing sugar and orange rind. Add the cornflour, then the flours gradually beating until smooth. Pipe the mixture into 1″ (2.5cm) star shapes. Bake until pale golden brown and cool on a wire rack.

Orange cream: Beat butter and icing sugar until smooth. Gradually beat in orange juice. Use to sandwich two biscuits together, then sprinkle with icing sugar.

 ## WHOLEMEAL BRAN BISCUITS Miki Hildebrand

Makes 36 approx. Preparation 5 mins. Cook 15 mins. Gas No.4, 350°F, 180°C
Advance   Freezable

2 cups unprocessed bran
1 cup wholemeal plain flour
2 tbls brown sugar

4oz butter (115gm)
2 eggs

Combine bran, flour, sugar and butter in food processor. Add eggs and mix. Place on floured board, divide in two and press each half evenly over a lightly greased 12 x 10″ (30 x 15cm) Swiss roll tin. With a knife, mark out 18 biscuits in each tin. Prick each biscuit with a fork and bake for 15 minutes until lightly browned. Cut through biscuits while hot. Cool on a wire tray.

Pastry

CHOUX PASTRY
Lynne Goldwyn

Preparation 15 mins.   **Cook 20 mins.**   **Gas No.6, 400°F, 200°C**

3 oz flour (85 gm)   2 oz butter (55 gm)
Pinch of salt   2 eggs, beaten
$\frac{1}{4}$ pt water (140 ml)

Sift flour and salt into a bowl. Cut the butter into small pieces and place in saucepan with the water. Heat until butter has melted then bring to the boil. Remove saucepan from heat and immediately pour in all the flour and beat vigorously with a wooden spoon. Allow to cool slightly, then gradually beat in the eggs until the mixture is shiny. Pipe into desired shapes and bake until golden. Cut a slit in pastry to allow steam to escape. Cook for a further 2 minutes then leave to cool. See Small Cake Section for filling suggestions.

SWEET EGGLESS SHORTCRUST PASTRY
Fay Trup

Preparation 10 mins.   **Refrigerate 30 mins.**   **Advance**   **Freezable**

8 oz SR flour (225 gm)   4 oz caster sugar (115 gm)
4 oz margarine, cut into pieces (115 gm) $\frac{1}{2}$ cup cold water

Place flour and margarine in a bowl and rub lightly until the mixture resembles fine breadcrumbs. Add the sugar. Mixing with a knife, add the water and form into a ball of pastry. Refrigerate.

WHOLEMEAL SHORTCRUST PASTRY
Gillian Burr

Preparation 10 mins.   **Advance**   **Freezable**

7 oz wholemeal flour (200 gm) $1\frac{3}{4}$ oz butter/margarine (50 gm)
2 tsp baking powder $1\frac{3}{4}$ oz white fat (50 gm)
3 tbls water

Place flour and baking powder in food processor. Add the fats and process until the mixture resembles fine breadcrumbs. Add sufficient water to give a soft but manageable dough. Wrap in greaseproof paper and refrigerate.

GOOD-NATURED PASTRY FOR BISCUITS
AND FRUIT PIES
Betty Korn

Preparation 5 mins. Cook 15 mins. Gas No.5, 375°F, 190°C Advance Freezable

8 oz firm margarine (225 gm)
2 oz white fat (55 gm)
1 lb SR flour (450 gm)

1 large egg
4 oz caster sugar (115 gm)
2 tbls peanut butter (optional)

Place all ingredients in food processor and mix for 30 seconds. Wrap in cling film and either refrigerate or freeze. For biscuits either roll out or form into balls and press flat with a fork. Decorate. Bake.

Variations: Substitute 2 oz (55 gm) ground almonds and a few drops almond essence for 2 oz (55 gm) of the flour or you may add 2 tablespoons of peanut butter to the original recipe.

STRUDEL PASTRY
Ruth Smilg

Preparation 15 mins.   Standing time 30 mins.

8 oz flour (225 gm)
1 tsp oil
1 tsp vinegar
A little melted margarine

A little salt
1 egg
4 tbls tepid water

Knead all ingredients together on a floured board or in a large bowl until a smooth dough is obtained, brush over a little oil, cover and leave for at least 30 minutes in a warm draught free place. Sprinkle flour over a tablecloth, roll the dough once lenthways and then, palms uppermost pull the pastry out from underneath in all directions until it is paper thin and covers the cloth. Cut off the thick edge surround. Place the filling in a thick strip about a third of the way along the pastry. Fold over the short end, grip the tablecloth with both hands and roll up the strudel. Place carefully onto a greased baking tray, brush with a little melted margarine and bake for $\frac{3}{4}$–1 hour in medium hot oven.

VERSATILE PASTRY
Eileen Brecker

Preparation 5 mins.   Advance   Freezable

6 oz flour (170 gm)
3 fl oz vegetable/corn oil (85 ml)

2 tbls cold water
Pinch of salt (optional)

Mix all ingredients together and knead into a roll or ball. Wrap in greaseproof paper and refrigerate until required. May be mixed in food processor.

Kitchen Know How

THE STORE CUPBOARD

FLOURS

100% Wholemeal Wheat Flour	Nature's most complete form of flour contains all the valuable vitamins and minerals as well as protein and starch. Organically grown, stone-ground wholemeal flour is the purest.
85% Wholemeal Wheat Flour	This is wholemeal flour with most of the bran removed. Finer and paler than 100% wholemeal, it is therefore lighter in texture but still nutritionally more valuable than white flour.
Barley Flour	Made from milled barley grains. It is pale and fine and normally used in conjunction with wheat flour.
Maize Flour or Cornmeal	Used as a thickening agent, or in breads or puddings.
Rice Flour	Made from milled brown rice, it can be fine, medium or coarse in texture.
Buckwheat Flour	A fine dark speckled flour which is particularly good for batters.
Soya Flour	A rich source of protein, it can be added to normal bread dough to give additional food value.
Rye Flour	It has a low gluten content and is rich in vitamins and minerals. Most suitable for bread.

BEANS AND PULSES

N.B. All beans and pulses should be soaked in cold water for at least 4 hours unless otherwise stated. Certain beans must be boiled for at least 10 minutes to eliminate toxins.

Beans

Aduki beans	They have a slightly sweet, nutty taste and are delicious cooked in vegetable stews and risottos. Rich in protein, calcium, iron and B vitamins.
Black-eyed beans	They have a soft flaky texture and slightly savoury taste. Used in soups, casseroles and savoury bakes. High in calcium and iron.
Borlotti beans	These have a mild, slightly sweet taste and can be used in salads, soups, dips and purées.
Broad beans	The tough skin is best removed before serving. They are good in vegetable dishes, soups and poultry dishes. High in protein and fibre.
Butter beans	Excellent in soups and bean-bake dishes. Good source of protein and potassium.
Haricot beans	They have a delicate flavour and stay whole even when tender. Used for baked beans and in casseroles and vegetable bakes. High in protein, iron, calcium and B vitamins.
Lima beans	These are a good substitute for butter beans. Used in casseroles or hot bean loaf. High in potassium and also valuable for calcium, iron and B vitamins.
Mung beans	Originating in India and China, they can be sprouted (in which case they do not need soaking), and served in salads, sandwiches and stir-fry recipes. Highly nutritious, they are an important source of iron, protein, calcium and B vitamins.
Pinto beans	A variety of the haricot bean, they are excellent in salads and vegetable dishes.
Red kidney beans (Mexican or Chilli beans)	They have a good flavour and a floury texture. They are excellent for serving with rich sauces or salads. High in protein, phosphorus, potassium and iron.
Soya beans	The most nutritious of all, they have a bland flavour and fleshy texture. Used in salads or to enrich vegetable casseroles or soups. They have a higher fat content than most beans but they are high in calcium, phosphorus, potassium, iron, magnesium and of course as a source of protein.

Lentils

All lentils help lower blood fat levels and prevent hardening of the arteries, they are a good source of protein, iron and vitamins A and B. They are used in soups, casseroles, rissoles and salads.

Red/Orange lentils	Do not need to be soaked before cooking.
Indian Brown lentils	These are red lentils with the seed coat on. They are used in spicy cooking and purées.
Green lentils	They are used throughout the Middle East and Eastern Europe in soups and stews. They can be eaten cold with a spicy vinaigrette.
Puy lentils	These are considered the best of all. Used in casseroles or in a savoury vegetable dish, or salad.

Peas

Chick peas	They have a nutty flavour and crunchy texture. Used in salads, soups, stews and curries and are the basis of hummous. Chick peas contain three times as much iron as red meat, as well as calcium and vitamins. They are an excellent source of protein.
Dried peas	They have a floury texture useful in soups and purées. They are a rich natural source of protein, low in cholesterol and high in potassium and iron.
Split peas	They are used in soups, stews, casseroles, rissoles, and spicy vegetable stews. They are a good source of protein, iron and vitamins A and B.

OILS

Corn or Maize oil	Mainly used for frying and the manufacture of margarine. Not good in salad dressings or mayonnaise. An excellent source of phosphorus and vitamins A, D and E. Composition: 15% saturated fat 35% mono-unsaturated fat 50% polyunsaturated fat.
Grape-seed oil	A delicate flavoured oil excellent in salads and mayonnaise. Rich in vitamin E and high in polyunsaturated fats.
Hazelnut oil	A light oil, suitable for salad dressings. It has a slightly sweet taste and should be used sparingly.
Olive oil	Excellent in salad dressings and mayonnaise and for light, but not deep frying. Virgin and Extra Virgin olive oil are the top grades made by cold-pressing fresh olives. Because heat is not involved, the quality is very high and the taste excellent. Composition: 15% saturated fat 75% mono-unsaturated fat 10% polyunsaturated fat.
Palm oil	Used commercially in margarine and confectionery manufacturing. Not as healthy as most vegetable oils. Composition: 40% saturated fat 40% mono-unsaturated fat 10% polyunsaturated fat 10% others
Groundnut or Peanut oil	Mainly used for deep frying as it can be heated to high temperatures without deteriorating. Composition: 20% saturated fat 50% mono-unsaturated fat 30% polyunsaturated fat.
Safflower oil	Not to be confused with sunflower oil, this is a very delicate oil suitable for dressings, mayonnaise and shallow frying. It is a good source of vitamin E. Composition: 10% saturated fat 75% polyunsaturated fat 15% others
Sesame seed oil	Pungent and strong-tasting with a good nutty flavour. Used very sparingly in salad-dressings and stir-frying.

236

Soya oil	This is a good quality oil and can be used in all forms of cooking, including deep-frying.
	Composition: 10% saturated fat
	25% mono-unsaturated fat
	55% polyunsaturated fat
	10% others
Sunflower oil	May be used for frying, salad-dressings, mayonnaise, and most general cooking. Very low in saturated fats and rich in vitamins D and E.
Walnut oil	This has a delicious nutty flavour, and is excellent in salad dressings (with lemon juice rather than vinegar). Do not use in cooking, as it deteriorates when heated.

SUGARS

White Sugars

Caster sugar	A white, refined, free-flowing, fine sugar with many uses: cakes, pies, puddings and meringues. Because of the size of the grains, it dissolves quickly and is useful for sprinkling on fruits and over cakes for decoration.
Granulated sugar	This has a coarser grain but is still a crystalline, refined sugar. Used in jams, chutneys etc. and for sweetening pie-fillings and desserts.
Icing sugar	A finely powdered sugar made by grinding the sugar crystals. It dissolves rapidly and is mainly used in cake icings and decoration.
Jam sugar	This sugar with pectin is specially produced for jams, jellies and preserves.
Lump sugar	Refined sugar compressed into small cubes.
Preserving sugar	A coarse larger-grained variety of granulated sugar, ideal for making jams and chutneys etc.

Brown Sugars

N.B. Not all brown sugars are unrefined and thus 'healthy'. Real unrefined cane sugar does not have added flavourings and colour and is always labelled as such.

Demerara	Large, clear crystals and a crunchy, sticky texture. It has a rich aroma from the natural molasses it contains.
Muscovado	Sometimes called Barbados sugar, this is a soft, sticky, fine-grained, dark brown sugar, rich in natural molasses.
Molasses sugar	Also known as Black Barbados, it is stronger in flavour then Muscovado. Sticky and almost black, it is very rich in minerals and trace elements.

PASTAS

Anelli	Small rings of pasta, either plain or wholewheat, for use in clear soups, with a cheese or tomato sauce, or in salads.
Bucatini	Small wholewheat macaroni. Used with a cheese or tomato sauce.
Cannelloni	Large tube-shaped pasta. Filled with a meat or vegetable mixture and baked in a rich sauce.
Farfalle	Small bow-tie shapes. Served with a delicate creamy sauce, or with mushrooms.

Fettuccine	Thin ribbon pasta, available plain or egg-enriched. Often sold curled round in a 'nest' which unravels on cooking. Served with butter and fresh herbs in a creamy sauce.
Fiochetti	Pasta bows, available plain or 'verdi'. Served with rich well-flavoured sauces.
Fusilli	Corkscrew shapes. Served with meat sauces and with salads.
Gnocchi	Small dumplings, available plain or wholewheat. Served with simple sauces.
Lasagne	Broad strips of pasta, available plain, egg-enriched, wholewheat or verdi. Also available is lasagne which needs no pre-cooking. The strips are layered with sauce and baked in the oven.
Penne	Quill shaped pasta, available plain or wholewheat, in small and large sizes. Served with simple sauces – tomato, creamy cheese or meat.
Rigatoni	Large ribbed tubes which can be served with any type of sauce.
Spaghetti	Long strips of pasta available plain, wholewheat, red or verdi. Served with simple sauces such as tomato, or with herbs, garlic or butter, or with rich tomato and meat sauces.
Tagliatelle	Ribbon noodles available plain, egg enriched or verdi. Used with almost any sauce, but especially poultry, or a simple butter and cream or cheese sauce.
Vermicelli	The thinnest, most delicate pasta, available plain or egg-enriched. Served with very simple light sauces or used in clear soup.

RICE

Basmati rice	Known as the prince of rice, the slender, slightly curved white grains have a specially delicate flavour and aroma, perfect for curries and pilaffs. Cook until firm about 20 minutes.
Brown Basmati rice	This has all the flavour of white basmati rice plus the extra goodness of brown rice.
Brown rice	A highly nutritious grain with a delicious, nutty flavour and chewy texture. Brown rice contains 80% more vitamin B1, 40% more vitamin B2, and 60% more vitamin B3 than white rice, as well as more minerals and protein. Brown rice takes longer than white rice to cook, about 30–40 minutes, and needs more cooking liquid.
Easy-cook rice	Easy cook or parboiled rice has been subjected to a steam-pressure process which helps it retain much of its natural vitamin and mineral content. Available white or brown. Cooking time 10–15 minutes.
Patna or Long Grain rice	The cheapest and most versatile rice. Ideal for most savoury dishes. The husk and bran of the grain have been removed. The grains tend to separate on cooking and don't stick together. Cooking time 15 minutes.
Pudding rice	A short round grain from Italy. With gentle cooking, the rice absorbs the liquid it is cooked in (usually milk) and forms a thick creamy pudding. Cooking time up to an hour.
Wild rice	Not a true rice at all, but a form of grass. Most wild rice is grown in North America and has long, slim dark brown grains. Can be mixed with long grain rice. Cooking time 45 minutes.

COFFEES

Brazilian	A good quality coffee with plenty of flavour and no bitterness.
Colombian	A strong well-flavoured coffee with just a trace of bitterness.
Decaffeinated	Coffee grounds from which most of the caffeine has been extracted. The taste varies — some decaffeinated coffees are insipid while others are indistinguishable from normal coffee.
Jamaican or Blue Mountain	A blend of coffee with a rich mellow flavour and no bitterness.
Kenyan	When lightly roasted this has a full-bodied flavour. When fully roasted is deliciously bitter.
Mocha or Arabian	A full-flavoured coffee with a rich almost chocolaty taste. Turkish coffee is usually made from powdered mocha coffee beans.
Viennese	A mixture of ground coffee and ground dried figs. It has a mild, fragrant taste.

TEAS

Assam	A full-bodied tea, with a reddish colour and a rich malty flavour. Ideal for breakfast.
Ceylon	A refreshing tea with a golden colour and a full taste. Excellent with lemon.
Darjeeling	A fine rich tea with an aroma of muscatel. It is often called the champagne of teas.
Earl Gray	A blend of black China and Darjeeling teas which have been treated with oil of Bergamot which gives a scented aroma and taste. It makes an excellent afternoon drink and is best served without milk or sugar.
English Breakfast	A robust, full-bodied tea, ideal for early morning and usually served with milk.
Keemun	A fine quality China tea with a fragrant clear, light colour, and a slightly nutty and sweet flavour. Drink with or without milk.
Kenya	A coppery coloured tea with a fine rounded flavour. Usually served with milk.
Lapsang Souchong	A large leaf, black China tea with a smoky flavour. Best served with a slice of lemon, it makes a very refreshing drink on a hot day.
Orange Pekoe	A fine quality highly-scented Indian tea. It is excellent blended with Jasmine tea.
Gunpowder Green	A delicate, straw-coloured liquid, with a low caffeine content. Served without milk.
Jasmine	The classic Chinese tea. It is scented due to the addition of jasmine flowers. Better without milk.

SPICES, HERBS AND FLAVOURINGS

Allspice	A dried berry of the pimento tree grown in the West Indies. The flavour resembles a blend of cinnamon, nutmeg and cloves. Use the whole berry in pickling and for spicing meat, fish and gravy. Use ground allspice for cakes, biscuits and puddings.

Anchovy	A small herring-like fish. It is used in the preparation of anchovy essence and can be bought preserved in brine or oil. Use the essence to flavour sauces and the fish as a flavouring and garnish in hors d'oeuvres and savouries.
Angelica	The tender tubular stems of a plant of the parsley family preserved in sugar. Used for decorating and flavouring sweet dishes.
Balm	An aromatic herb with a marked lemon flavour. Use whole leaves to flavour wine and fruit cups; chopped, they can be added to salads, soups and stews.
Basil	An aromatic herb with a suggestion of sweet cloves. Use in soups and sauces, with grilled and baked fish and tomato dishes. A few chopped leaves can be added to salads. Use sparingly.
Bay leaf	Dried aromatic leaf of a species of laurel. Use particularly in cooking meat and pickling herrings, and also in vegetable and meat soups and sauces. Originally infused in milk to perfume blancmange, custard and rice pudding.
Borage	The leaves of an aromatic plant with a cucumber flavour. Use in salads and fruit cups.
Bouquet Garni	A small bunch of herbs tied together or in muslin. It usually consists of parsley, thyme and bay leaf or marjoram. Use to give additional flavour to stock, soups, sauces, meat and fish dishes.
Burnet	The leaves of a herb with a flavour suggesting cucumber. Use in soups, salads and omelettes.
Candied peel	The sugared and candied skins of lemons, oranges, limes and citrons. Use to add flavouring to puddings, cakes, mincemeat, etc.
Capers	The flower buds of the caper bush, dried and preserved in brine and vinegar (nasturtium seeds may be used to make mock capers). Use to flavour sauces and, finely chopped, in savouries, sandwich fillings, salads and hors d'oeuvres.
Carraway seeds	The deep brown spicy seeds of an aromatic herb. Use principally in cake and biscuit making but also to season boiled cabbage, boiled potatoes, sauerkraut and goulash.
Cayenne	A pungent, hot, red pepper. Use sparingly in savouries, meat, fish, egg and cheese dishes.
Celery salt	Ground celery seeds combined with table salt. Use to flavour cheese and tomato dishes, tomato soup and potato salad.
Chervil	A herb with feathery leaves with a mild flavour of parsley. Use fresh or dried in salads, soups and omelettes. Use as a garnish in place of parsley, but it withers quickly.
Chillies	Very hot dried pods of a tropical red pepper. Use to flavour meat, pickles, savoury rice and macaroni, and savoury sauces.
Chilli powder	Ground chilli pods blended with other spices. Use in cocktail sauces, gravies and stews.
Chives	A small green perennial onion. The leaves are used to impart a delicate onion flavour. Use to flavour soups, stews, salads, open sandwiches, stuffings, omelettes, mashed potatoes, etc. Particularly good with cream cheese.

Cinnamon	The dried aromatic bark of the cinnamon tree. Use stick cinnamon in pickling and preserving and with stewed fruits and hot spiced drinks. Use ground in cakes, biscuits, puddings, mincemeat and savoury dishes other than cheese ones.
Cloves	The dried nail-shaped flower buds of the clove tree. Use whole to flavour roast ham and stewed fruit and in pickling, preserving, spiced syrups and drinks. Use the traditional 'onion stuck with cloves' to flavour stews, sauces and soup. Use ground in cakes and puddings.
Coralline Pepper	A red pepper less pungent than cayenne. Use for decorating savoury dishes.
Coriander	Both the leaves and seeds of this plant can be used. They have a pleasant flavour slightly suggesting sage. Powdered coriander is one of the ingredients of curry powder. Use the leaves in salads, soups and curry sauce. Use the seeds to flavour biscuits, cakes, etc., in much the same way as carraway seeds.
Curry powder	A blend of spices originating in the Orient. Use to flavour curry of meat, egg or fish and to give additional flavour to soups, stews and savoury fillings.
Dill	An annual herb. Use the leaves in soups and sauces (particularly those seved with boiled mutton or beef) and with any cucumber dish. Use the seeds to flavour dill vinegar for pickling and in cakes as a substitute for carraway seeds.
Fennel	An aromatic herb especially suitable for fish dishes. Use the leaves in fish sauces and put a sprig inside fish before it is grilled or baked. Add chopped leaves to fish salad.
Fine Herbs	A mixture of chervil, chives and tarragon, chopped or powdered. Use in omelettes.
Garlic	A root resembling an onion. The white-skinned bulb is divided into 10 or 12 sections called cloves. It has a very pungent flavour and smell. Use to flavour salads by rubbing it round the salad bowl, or stews by rubbing it round the casserole. Use very small amounts to flavour soups, sauces and meat and fish dishes.
Ginger	The root of a plant grown in some tropical countries. Use root ginger in pickling and with marrow in jam making. Use small quantities to flavour stock, meat and fish dishes, removing it before serving. Use ground ginger in cakes, puddings, biscuits and stewed fruit. Add a little to whipped cream. Use crystallised ginger in ice creams, sauces and cakes.
Horse-radish	A root with a particularly hot flavour. Use horse-radish sauce as an accompaniment to reast beef. Small quantities, grated, often improve sauces, stuffings and stews. Use young tender leaves in salads.
Lemon	The fruit of the lemon tree; excellent for bringing out flavours. Use the juice when a milder flavour is required in mayoannaise or mint sauce. Use also in lemon icing. Use grated lemon rind in pastry dishes, cakes, biscuits and puddings. Use strips of lemon rind to flavour stewed fruit and drinks. Infuse it in milk for flavouring sauces and puddings. Use slices or wedges of lemon as a garnish or to serve with fish, particularly fried fish. Use the whole fruit for marmalade and in making hot and cold fruit drinks.

Mace	That part of the nutmeg between the shell and the outer husk; the flavour resembles nutmeg. Use a blade of mace in pickling, preserving, fish sauces, etc. Use ground mace in puddings, cakes and biscuits. Small amounts can be added to marinades, bread sauce, and sauces or stuffings to serve with chicken. A small pinch of mace improves many chocolate dishes.
Marjoram	A very pungent herb of the mint family. Use fresh or dried. Use with any savoury dish, particularly lamb and poultry. Add to soups, forcemeats, stuffings, stews and salads.
Marigold	A garden flower. Use the well-chopped petals in salads and soups.
Mint	A herb much used in this country. Use chopped in mint sauce as an accompaniment to roast lamb and mutton. Cook a sprig of mint with new potatoes, peas and carrots or sprinkle chopped mint on the cooked vegetables. Add chopped leaves to both green and fruit salads or mix with dried fruit in pasties and pies. Float mint leaves on fruit drinks, iced tea, etc.
Mustard	The powdered seeds of the mustard plant. Use as a condiment mixed to a smooth thick paste with water, milk or spiced vinegar. Use sparingly to bring out the flavour of cheese and meat dishes. Use more generously to give a hot flavour to devilled dishes and small savouries. Mustard sauce is excellent with herrings.
Nasturtium	A garden plant. Use the chopped leaves in salad and pickle the seeds to use instead of capers.
Nutmeg	The nut kernel of a tropical tree. It is sold whole or ground. Use sparingly in soups, meat dishes, cakes, biscuits and puddings. Sprinkle on milk puddings, custards and egg-nog.
Onion	It is often served as a vegetable but small quantities combine well with practically all vegetables, meat and fish and with some fruits, e.g., apples and oranges.
Orange	The fruit of the orange tree. Use the juice in orange icing, fruit drinks, etc. Use the grated rind to flavour apple pies, in butter cream, fruit salads, cakes, biscuits, puddings, etc. Use the whole orange (bitter oranges are best) in making marmalade.
Paprika	A Hungarian red pepper with a mild flavour. Use as an essential ingredient of goulash. It will add colour and a mild pepper flavour to many savoury dishes. Use to decorate and colour meat, fish, egg and cheese dishes, sandwiches, small savouries, salads and soups.
Parsley	The most commonly-used herb. The roots and stems contain more flavour than the leaves. Use chopped parsley lavishly for sprinkling on and garnishing soups, stews, meat and fish dishes, salads and vegetables. Add to white sauce and mashed potatoes. Use small sprigs to garnish cooked dishes.
Pepper (Black and White)	The small round berry of a climbing vine. Black pepper is the immature berry and white pepper the mature berry with the covering removed. More flavour is obtained if a pepper mill is used and the berries ground as required. Use whole in pickling or tied in muslin to flavour meat stews, sauces and soups. Use ground in most meat, fish, vegetable, egg dishes, etc.
Poppy seeds	The tiny seeds of the poppy plant. Use as a topping for breads, rolls and biscuits.

Rosemary	A fragrant herb. Use with all meat dishes. A sprig placed inside a chicken or tucked near the bone of lamb gives an unusual flavour. Add also to mushroom soup.
Saffron	The dried stigmas of a species of yellow crocus. Use mainly to impart an interesting yellow colour to risotto, rice, fruit cakes, etc.
Sage	A garden herb used fresh or dried. Use to season stuffing for poultry and meat. Often combined with onions; it also goes well with sausages. Use sparingly or its flavour will be overpowering.
Salt	An essential kitchen condiment used to bring out the flavour of other foods.
Savory	A herb of the mint family used fresh or dried. There are both summer and winter savories. Used, often combined with other herbs, to flavour meat and egg dishes, salads and soups. Use summer savory especially with broad beans and peas.
Shallot	A bulb of the onion family. Use instead of onion when a milder flavour is required. Cook with green peas, use raw in salads, and grate before adding to cream cheese.
Sorrel	A herb with a tart flavour. Use in salads, soups and sauces.
Tarragon	A herb related to wormwood. Its leaves have a slightly bitter aromatic flavour. Use the leaves, finely chopped, in soups, stews, salads and omelettes. They make an unusual addition to tomato soup, boiled chicken. Use also to flavour vinegar.
Thyme	An aromatic herb. Lemon thyme has a characteristic lemon flavour. Use sparingly in stuffings, stews, salads and sauces. Use lemon thyme with veal, chicken or fish.
Turmeric	The root of a plant of the ginger family. An ingredient of curry powder. Use, with mustard, to give flavour and a yellow colour to piccalilli.
Vanilla	The fruit of a fragrant plant. Sold as an essence or as vanilla pods which can be washed after use, dried and used over and over again. Use the essence to flavour cakes, biscuits, puddings, etc. Store the pods in sugar to flavour it or boil in milk for blancmanges, custard, etc., to impart a vanilla flavour.

Glossary of Kitchen Terms

Al Dente	Applied to vegetables and pastas which are slightly undercooked so that they are just biteable.
Bain Marie	To cook at a temperature just below boiling point in a saucepan which stands in a larger pan of simmering water.
Bake blind	To cover a pastry case or flan with paper and dried beans or rice, during baking, to retain the shape of the pastry. The paper etc. is removed for the last 10 minutes of baking.
Baste	To spoon hot fat on to poultry or fish to prevent dryness during roasting or grilling. The fat from the tin or grill-pan is usually used for this.
Batter	A smooth mixture of flour, eggs, milk and water used to coat foods before frying.
Bind	To moisten a mixture with egg, milk, cream, melted fat, water or stock so that it will hold together.
Blanch	To cover with boiling water for 1–5 minutes and then plunge into cold water (for the purpose of removing skins from peaches, tomatoes, almonds etc.).
Boil	To cook in water, stock, or other liquid at boiling point, i.e. when bubbles rise continuously and break on the surface.
Bouquet Garni	A mixture of parsley stalks, bay leaf, peppercorns and thyme wrapped with celeriac and carrots tied together. A white bouquet garni (used for white stocks) consists only of onion, white of leek, celeriac and herbs.
Braise	To cook by a combination of stewing and roasting, or frying and stewing.
Broil	Another name for grilling.
Caramel	Sugar and water cooked together until the sugar turns brown; used for colouring and flavour.

244

Clarify	To render cloudy liquids clear by straining through a fine muslin.
Coulis	A liquid purée of fruit or vegetables, made without flour.
Cream	To beat together fat and sugar until the mixture is soft and very pale, resembling cream.
Croûtons	Thin slices of bread cut into shapes and fried.
Dariole mould	A small cup-shaped mould.
Decant	To pour off clear liquid carefully so that any sediment is left behind.
Dice	To cut into small cubes.
Dredge	To sprinkle or coat with flour, seasoning or sugar.
Feuilletes	Puff pastry cases cut into different shapes.
Fleurons	Small cuts of puff pastry usually half-moon shape.
Fold	To mix together two mixtures, one light and containing air. Use a metal spoon and bring some of the mixture from the bottom of the bowl and fold it over the other mixture. Continue until the two are blended.
Fritters	Food coated in batter, or in egg and breadcrumbs, and fried in deep fat.
Fry	To cook food in pan containing hot fat or oil.
Frying temperatures	When deep-fat frying is in progress, the following temperatures (°F) will be found a useful guide:
	350°–375° for uncooked food such as doughnuts, fritters and fish (faintly smoking);
	375°–385° for cooked food such as croquettes;
	385°–395°–400° for chipped potatoes.
Garnish	To decorate.
Gelatine	A manufactured product used for setting liquids.
Gratin	Applied to dishes covered with breadcrumbs or grated cheese and browned in the oven or under the grill.
Grill	To cook under or over direct heat.
Infuse	To steep in hot liquid without boiling in order to extract flavour.
Julienne	Vegetables, or other foods, cut into fine strips (supposedly not longer than the width of a soupspoon!).
Liaison	A mixture of egg yolks and cream used for thickening and enriching white soups and sauces.
Marinade	A liquid containing oil, vinegar, wine, herbs etc., in which fish or meat is soaked before cooking to tenderise and give additional flavour.
Mask	To cover completely using a mayonnaise or rich thick sauce.
Mirepoix	The foundation of vegetables etc. on which a braise is cooked.
Panada	A thick binding sauce used for croquettes etc., and as a foundation for soufflés.
Parboil	To boil only partly, not until cooked.
Papillote	The wrapping of fish or meat in tinfoil or greaseproof paper in which it is then cooked.
Pare	To remove the outer peel of citrus fruit in a thin strip.
Paupiettes	Stuffed and rolled fillets of fish or slices of meat.
Pectin	A substance extracted from some fruits during boiling for the preparation of jams, jellies, etc. It combines with sugar to set the preserve. Gooseberries, apples, blackcurrants and lemons are especially rich in pectin.
Pickle	To preserve meat, fish, vegetables, fruit etc. in brine or vinegar.
Pipe	To decorate cakes, etc. with icing or to decorate meat or fish with mashed potatoes; the paste is forced through small pipes to form a pattern.
Piquant	Sharply flavoured and stimulating.
Poach	To cook in water just below boiling point.
Purée	Cooked food rubbed through a sieve or reduced to a pulp.
Quenelles	Dumplings of fish or poultry made by finely mincing the flesh, adding seasoning and mixing with cream and perhaps egg white. The quenelles are poached in salt water or a strong stock.

Reduce	To boil a liquid vigorously in an uncovered pan until it is reduced in quantity through evaporation.
Roux	A cooked mixture of fat and flour; it is the foundation of sauces, stews and some soups.
Sauté	A cooking process in which foods are browned quickly in a little fat.
Scald	(a) To pour boiling water over food and leave it to stand for a few minutes. (b) To bring milk nearly to boiling point.
Score	To make incisions on the surface of fish, vegetables and meat.
Season	To add salt, pepper, herbs, spices etc. to food to make it more appetising.
Shortening	An edible fat which, when added to flour or dough and cooked, makes it richer and more tender.
Shred	To slice anything so finely that the edges curl.
Simmer	To cook in liquid just below boiling point.
Sippets	Small shapes of bread, fried or toasted and used to decorate savoury dishes.
Spice	Aromatic vegetable condiments, whole, ground, or in paste or liquid form, used to give additional flavour to food.
Spiced vinegar	Made by infusing various herbs in vinegar.
Steam	To cook food in the steam from boiling water.
Stew	To cook food in liquid at a low temperature for a long period in a tightly-closed vessel.
Sweat	To sauté food gently without browning, usually in a covered pan.
Tammy	To strain soup or sauce through a fine-mesh cloth.
Thickening	The term applied to the process of rendering gravies and soups etc. richer by the addition of egg yolks, flour or cornflour etc.
Tronçon	A thick slice of a small fish, or a piece of the tail of a large fish.
Trim	To cut away ragged or unsightly portions to improve the appearance.
Truss	To tie a bird or joint into a good shape for roasting or boiling.
Vol-au-vent	A case of puff pastry usually filled with a well-flavoured savoury mixture.
Weights and measures	It must be emphasised that good results can only be expected when the correct amount of each ingredient is used. This is of special importance when making cakes, biscuits, etc., and can only be achieved by using reliable scales.

To measure spoonfuls of dry ingredients

One spoonful is heaped, with as much above the level of the spoon as below it.
Half-spoonful is a level spoonful.
Quarter-spoonful is half a level spoonful, the division being made the long way of the spoon.

To measure spoonfuls of liquids

The most accurate way of measuring spoonfuls of liquid is to dip the spoon into the liquid in a wide-mouthed utensil such as a basin. Pouring the liquid into the spoon is not so satisfactory.

To weigh syrup, treacle, honey, etc.

When weighing rather sticky semi-liquids such as syrup the easiest and cleanest way is as follows:

Remove the lid from the container and weigh the container and its contents. Subtract from this weight the amount required and then spoon out the contents into the utensil (pan or bowl) until the scales balance.

Whip	To beat up frothily, introducing air to lighten the mixture.
Zest	The grated peel of citrus fruits.

246

Index

HEALTHIER EATING

STARTERS

SOUPS

FISH

MEATLESS MAIN COURSES

VEGETABLES

SALADS

SAUCES

DESSERTS

BREADS, BISCUITS, PASTRY

KITCHEN KNOW HOW